W9-AXP-330

Nursing Perspectives on Humor

Edited by
Karyn Buxman, RN, MS
&
Anne LeMoine, PhD

Library of Congress Catalog Card Number: 95-069075

ISBN: 0-9627246-5-3

Printed in the United States of America

Cover Design & Book Production
Adam E. Blyn

Published by
POWER PUBLICATIONS
56 McArthur Avenue
Staten Island, New York 10312
1-800-331-6534

Karyn Buxman, RN, MS

As a nurse for over a dozen years, Karyn Buxman's experience includes surgery, intensive care, emergency department, obstetrics, home health, psychiatric nursing, teaching, air ambulance, and consulting as a clinical nurse specialist. She was voted "Nurse of the Year" by the Missouri Nurses' Association, 9th District, and "Young Business Woman, 1991" by the Business and Professional Woman. Karyn was recently named in "Who's Who in the Midwest," "Who's Who in American Women," and "Who's Who in Nursing," and "Who's Who Worldwide." She is currently working full time as a speaker, writer, and consultant in therapeutic humor and serves as contributing editor and vice-president for the humor magazine for nurses: Journal of Nursing Jocularity. She is a member of the International Society of Humor Studies and the American Association of Therapeutic Humor, as well as editor for Therapeutic Humor. Karyn presents numerous workshops to business and health professional lives. With her love of humor and her zest for nursing, Karyn's mission in life is to inform and inspire people in all walks of life to gain the benefits of laughter in their personal and professional lives.

Anne LeMoine, PhD

Anne LeMoine, Editor-Writer for Medical Sciences, holds a quadruple doctorate in linguistics (French, English, Dutch, German) and a triple doctorate in politicoeconomics (obtained in Europe, 1945-48). In 1948, she entered the French Diplomatic Corps as an International Economics Researcher (she speaks seven languages). After moving to the United States in 1970, she obtained two medical diplomas (laboratory techniques and medical terminology). In New York City (1970-79) and then in Tampa, Florida, (1979-86), she was the President of American of American International Manuscript Services - AIMS. Her client list ranges from Time/Life Encyclopedias (Associate Producer, 24 volume series) and the major publishers, to celebrity authors, hospitals, and universities. She now lives in Atlanta and works mainly with the medical community of that city. She now views the basic function of editing as infinitely more than correcting grammar, syntax or presentation: "The essence of rewriting — and editing — is to landscape the text and remove the weeds, so that the reader is free to think beyond the written word."

III

DEDICATION

To Vera, Fairy Godmother of Humor, may I carry your "wand" to continue your message; to Laura, who wouldn't accept no for an answer; to Anne, who polished the diamond in the rough; and to all my friends in laughter who have inspired me. But especially to the "Buxman Boys" who continue to be the wind beneath my wings.

Karyn Buxman - 1995

LAUGHTER IS THE BEST MEDICINE

Every situation in life, even death, is subject to humor (Robinson, 1977). Humor tends to be spontaneous, making it difficult to document and study. Put too much inspection on the situation, and the humor disappears. Try to observe it, and it goes away. Humor draws on cognitive differences and past experiences. Individual differences in appreciation and comprehension are observed (Shaeffer & Hopkins, 1988).

CONTENTS

Unit 2:

Focus: Patients

INTRODUCTION

How The Book Came to Be

by Karyn Buxman, RN, MS

This book is a product of what has evolved over more than six years. It has been said that "coincidence is God's way of remaining anonymous." It is no coincidence that this book came together now.

In 1989, while I was doing graduate work in nursing at the University of Missouri, one of my friends mentioned casually (coincidence?) that a couple of our advisors had recently attended a conference on the therapeutic benefits of laughter and play. This intrigued me and began to gnaw at my thoughts. Therapeutic benefits of laughter? Mmmm.... Where could I find out more about this?

Going into graduate school I had assumed that my research would revolve around "eating disorders and locus of control." But my thoughts became consumed with this absurd idea that professionals were taking laughter seriously. I had to know more.

Literature searches turned up a few articles, most of them written by people outside the nursing profession. A nurse researcher named Vera M. Robinson had written a book in 1977 entitled Humor and the Health Professions that proved to be the most valuable piece, although I could only access it through interlibrary loan.

I went to my advisor, Virginia Bzdek, and shared with her that I wanted to do research on humor. She was one of the professors who attended the conference on laughter and play. Virginia agreed that this was a fascinating topic, but that it would be too difficult to approach as a research project. It was too broad, too vague.... She'd even thought of doing research on it herself when she was working on her dissertation. But the topic didn't lend itself to doing serious studies.

I couldn't accept "no" for an answer. Virginia said that I could look into it some more and try to figure out how I could narrow the topic down into a manageable product. I pored over the literature I'd been able to find, and came back the following week with a list of ideas that were specific applications of humor. She seemed a little surprised at my tremendous enthusiasm, and began to help me shape my ideas. She said, "If you are truly serious about this topic, then you must attend one of these conferences on laughter and play yourself." She gave me some literature she'd received on an upcoming conference in Florida.

My heart sank. A poverty-stricken graduate student taking off for a conference in Florida? How in the world would I manage that? But, again, there are no true

1

coincidences. The trip was meant to be, and things literally fell into place. I was headed to the Fifth Annual Laughter and Play Conference sponsored by the International Association of Human Behavior.

The three and a half days were an intense but thrilling experience. I was thrust in with 750 other extroverts-nurses, counselors, teachers, doctors, social workers, patients, volunteers-who were all there to validate what they knew in their hearts to be true: Humor and laughter are good for you. I learned about organizations, such as The American Association of Therapeutic Humor (AATH). I made contacts that would later turn out to be invaluable, such as Alison Crane, founder of AATH, and Leslie Gibson at the Morton Plant Hospital. I made friends that will last a lifetime, including Kathy Passanisi, friend, mentor, and past-president of AATH. I heard experts such as Joel Goodman, Annette Goodheart, Peter Alsop, Steve Allen, and his son Steve Allen, Jr., MD. My brain was in overload. I came back a changed person. I knew from that point on that sharing the benefits of humor and laughter was how I was meant to spend the rest of my life. It became my passion.

I returned home and completed my research project on "The Development and Implementation of a Humor Room by a Professional Nurse." In addition to Virginia Bzdek, I chose two other advisors who were perfect for the work I had chosen: Mary Mandarino and Sherry Mustapha. I began to discuss and share my findings with others. Friends and colleagues began to send me clippings and articles on my newfound passion.

One of these clippings was from a nurse in Arizona, Doug Fletcher, who was looking for nurses interested in humor and writing (coincidence?!). This seemed too good to be true. I wrote to Doug and shared some of my ideas. He called and shared with me his idea of starting a humor magazine for nurses, to include both wit and serious articles on the application of humor. That was the conception of The Journal of Nursing Jocularity. (Please refer to Chapter 9 to read more on that historical undertaking.)

Through Doug, I continued to meet people who have become key players in this book and in my life: Vera M. Robinson, Patty Wooten, Donna Strickland, Bob Quick, John Wise, Sandy Ritz, Colleen Gullickson. He connected me with David Norris and the National Nurses in Business Association (NNBA), where I later contacted and met Laura Gasparis Vonfrolio who encouraged me to write this book.

Soon after I began public speaking in my spare time, I realized that I loved being in front of an audience. I was amazed to discover that most people would rather have dental work done without anesthetic than speak in front of a group. Could this be considered a talent? Could a nurse make a living as a speaker? I looked for a mentor, someone who was doing what I wanted to do, and doing it successfully. The answer was obvious: Melodie Chenevert. But could I approach her for help? Mmmmm.

When she was visiting my area on a speaking engagement, I managed to have lunch with her and shared with her my hopes and aspirations. She was very receptive and encouraging. The next day I returned to where she was presenting and showed her samples of my work. Several weeks later, she called with a lead on a large speaking engagement in New Mexico. The group wanted a speaker on therapeutic humor. I will never be able to repay her for her input, her encouragement, her support. Her belief in me enabled me to believe in myself. And my life has been a joy ever since.

With each incremental step, I set my new goals a little higher. Now I not only wanted to be a national expert in this field but eventually an international expert. So I joined The International Society of Humor Studies (ISHS), a group that takes humor very seriously. The organization sent a call for abstracts at an upcoming conference in Paris, France. Because of the goals I'd set, I felt obligated to submit an abstract, realizing that it would be good practice, but not really believing that it would be accepted. You cannot imagine my surprise and elation when I received a letter confirming my acceptance to the ISHS conference in Paris.

At the conference, I met more key players in my life — Paul McGhee, William Fry, Waleed Salameh, Peter Derks, Larry Ventis, Karen Peterson, Mary Hardy, Andre Stein, Regina Barreca, Jeff Goldstein, Garrett Higbee, Gloria Kaufman-people who continue to influence me directly and indirectly on a daily basis. I was exposed to many cultures and a wealth of information. Again, I came home on overload. But as I processed the event while flying home, I was struck by the fact that I was the only nurse who presented at this conference. So where were the other experts who were making great strides in the arena of humor and nursing? I toyed with the idea of somehow bringing this vast group together to share their contributions.

A few weeks later, I was "visiting" with Colleen Gullickson on the phone. We discussed the ISHS conference and decided that nurses needed better representation. Colleen said she would call Don Nilsen, secretary of ISHS, and get his thoughts on a proposal for a nursing panel to present at a future conference. She called me back with his response: "He thought it was a good idea, but suggested we hook up with Bill Fry. What do you think?"

I was taken aback. Of course who wouldn't want to hook up with William Fry? He's recognized as one of the leading experts in the field today. But he's a physician. And the whole point of this was to share what the nursing profession had to contribute to this field. I hung up the phone, and began to mull the conversation over in my head. It seemed obvious that people outside the profession of nursing had no idea what we as nurses had to offer. For that matter, did those inside the profession know about this small but diligent group committed to the studies of humor?

I knew then that this book was not just a desire, but a necessity.

The Obstacles

First I listed all the nursing experts I knew personally that I could contact as potential authors. A wide variety of topics were represented, although several gaps were immediately obvious. Another literature search provided new possibilities on some of the topics that were lacking. I contacted my list of potential contributing authors and got favorable responses. I asked them to provide me with additional contacts that they thought might be helpful. The list grew. And grew.

The book's primary purpose was to inform, not to entertain. A wide variety of topics and styles was inevitable. There were no books to use as role models in the field of nursing, so I looked outside and found suitable role models in Humor and Aging (Nahemow, McCluskey-Fawcett, & McGhee, 1986) and the Handbook of Humor and Psychotherapy (Fry & Salameh, 1987). With high aspirations and great intentions, I sent vague guidelines to the authors who agreed to contribute.

That's when the learning experiences really began. In my naivete', I had believed that I could just "whip" this together by pulling together the work done by everyone else. I was soon to learn that it would have been mighty easier just to write the whole book by myself! Take Murphy's Law, then multiply it by 23 and you start to get the picture.

The biggest obstacle to be overcome by myself and several other authors was procrastination. The project now seemed so overwhelming that at times it was just too much to think about. It sat by my desk seeming to glare at me, constantly reminding me that my priorities needed some adjustment. Self-doubts continued. And grew. Who was I to be undertaking this project? There were many out there who were certainly more qualified than me to be handling this project. Well, perhaps. But they were obviously procrastinating too. I had too much else to do. As a nurse, speaker, teacher, writer, editor, consultant, wife, mother, daughter, sister, school-board member, and everything-to-everybody, how could I possibly commit the time it would take to get this project completed? But everyone else had too much to do, also. And I knew that this book must be done.

When I would finally pull my act together, someone else's would fall apart. It was absolutely incredible the number of obstacles to be overcome. Authors wrote and called to tell me about the crises each one faced. Problems ranged from minor obstacles- including difficult work schedules, school schedules, family schedules — escalating to new jobs, moving, muggings, accidents, marriages, pregnancies, and surgeries. And climaxing with deaths in the family, hurricanes, floods, and earthquakes. I truly believe that if humor had not been the expertise of these authors, this book would not have been written. Thank God we all maintained our sense of humor!

Just when I thought I saw the light at the end of the tunnel, I was run over by a train.

4

No kiddin'. The following is an excerpt from a newsletter that I wrote during that period.

A personal crisis and natural disaster on my own home front left me in a brief depression that was quite astonishing to me a depressed humorologist?! but that I was powerless to control. I couldn't sleep, yet was always tired. I looked at my work but couldn't bring myself to do anything. I dreaded opening my mail or returning phone calls. Work piled on my desk and pounds piled on my hips!

On a personal level, at first I questioned if there was really anything to all this humor therapy I'd been preaching for the last five years. However, my humor colleagues were quick to send mirth aids to lift my sagging spirits. Funny books, props, cartoons, tapes, and buttons began to shift my negative perspective. I donned my glasses with windshield wipers, turned on my CD of "water tunes," wound up my clacking-giggling teeth, sat on my picnic blanket, and laughed along with Dave Barry and Ashleigh Brilliant while I ate chocolate-covered macadamias from Hawaii! (We must not overlook the healing power of chocolate!)

No one likes discomfort, either physical or psychological. And yet it was necessary for me to undergo this discomfort to truly know firsthand that humor can be an effective coping mechanism. As an expert in mental health nursing, I had read much on depression. But it's one thing to read about it and another thing entirely to experience it, even briefly. I pray that none of you has to endure a disaster on either a personal or a community level. Yet disasters will occur in most of our lives.

Yes, there is a time to cry, and a time to laugh. And I can now truly assure you from the bottom of my heart that LAUGHTER IS THE BEST MEDICINE" (Buxman, 1993, p.3).

The Mississippi floodwaters receded, but I still felt like I was swimming against the current. After consulting with the publisher, she suggested that I seek additional help with the editing. After a long search, a colleague of mine agreed to take a look at the project and then agreed to help. I was delighted. At last we would be able to wrap up this monumental project.

Time passed. No word. More time. A promise of things to come. Several months later, the dreaded message was on my answering machine. The other editor was undergoing a severe personal crisis and would be unable to complete the project. My heart sank. It seemed that anyone who came in contact with this project met with some kind of predicament. Perhaps this project was somehow cursed! I felt I was at a dead end-again.

Then a phone call came from one of the contributing authors, Kathi Cannella. She was seeking the other editor's phone number for some input on her chapter. "Don't bother," I replied, "she's unable to complete the editing due to personal problems." That's when Kathi turned this project around. "I have the name of someone who may be able to help you." Enter Anne LeMoine. While she had no background in therapeutic humor, the woman is a genius when it comes to editing. After agreeing to tackle this project, she managed to pull things together in a phenomenally short time. And she broke the curse — no more disasters!

At last, our dream was to become reality.

The Product

This book contains a sampling of the work being done today. The book has been designed to include the applications of therapeutic humor for the patient and the applications of therapeutic humor for the nurse. Because of the vast amount of new work being generated in this field, this book is by no means complete. Indeed, there is every indication that a second volume is in order.

I believe I can speak for the contributing authors as well as myself when I say it is with much excitement that we present this book to you. We hope to not only make an impact within our own profession, but demonstrate what we have to offer to those in other professions. We are proud to play a part in creating validity for the work being done in such a worthy profession. We recognize that laughter is an essential tool in the growing repertoire of nursing skills. The following beliefs are the underpinnings of this book:
1. It is imperative for nursing to recognize the validity of humor use by nurses for others.
2. It is crucial for nursing to also recognize the use of humor for nurses: We must be able to take our profession seriously but ourselves lightly.
3. As Vera Robinson points out in Chapter I, it is vital that we be able to laugh at our profession.
   This book helps demonstrate that we have matured as a profession in that we can laugh at ourselves. So read, learn, laugh. Then re-read and capture what you may have missed the first time. And look for more to come. Until then, I remain. . .
   Yours in laughter!

6

Bibliography

Buxman, K. (1993). Editor's note. *Laugh It Up*, 7 (4), p. 3.

Fry, W. F., & Salameh, W. A. (Eds.) (1987). *Handbook of humor and psychotherapy: Advances in the clinical use of humor.* Sarasota, FL: Professional Resource Exchange.

Nahemow, L., McCluskey- Fawcett, K. A., & McGhee, P. E. (Eds.). (1986). *Humor and aging.* Orlando, FL: Academic Press.

Robinson, V. (1977). *Humor and the health professions.* Thorofare, NJ:Slack.

Unit 1:
Focus: Nurses

CHAPTER I

HUMOR IN NURSING: A HYSTERICAL PERSPECTIVE

by Vera M. Robinson, RN, EdD

The vermin might, if they had but unity of purpose, carry off the four miles of beds on their backs and march them into the War Office.
Florence Nightingale in a letter from Scutari, Crimea, to the Secretary of War, circa 1858 (Kelly, 1981).

Florence Nightingale's reaction to the filth, horrors, and stresses of a Crimean War hospital may have been the first time anyone used gallows humor in nursing.

There is little recorded humor from the early years of nursing, but we know it has always been there. The humor has been about nursing, by nurses and patients, and in reaction to the stresses and reality shocks of illness, hospitalization, and health care. Humor and laughter are natural cognitive and biological phenomena used by all humans. The world of literature is full of comedy. Since the beginning of recorded history, people have used humor in their communications, and it is logical to assume that the humor carried over into the health care arena. However, it is only in the past few decades that the humor has been reported, researched, and recognized for its therapeutic value.

Nightingale was described as "fun-loving" in her social life, and she seemed to carry this over into her serious missionary zeal. At Scutari during the Crimean War, she was "adored" by her patients, who wrote "what a comfort it was to see her pass. She would speak to all and nod and smile . . . she was all full of life and fun when she talked to us, especially if a man was a bit downhearted" (Kelly, 1981, pp. 29-30). In her Notes on Nursing (1860), Nightingale acknowledged that "these painful expressions were better dismissed by a real laugh" (p. 60).

In establishing the first Training School for Nurses in 1860, Nightingale included in her "Duties of Probationer" the requirement to be patient, cheerful, and kindly. In reaction to the "Sairy Gamp" image of the loose alcoholic woman caregiver, she required that the student must also be sober, honest, trustworthy, clean, and chaste, so that "to utter even an immodest jest in her presence" (p. 60) should seem impossible. These professional standards seemed to set the tone for the restrained use of humor and humorous

9

interactions for decades to follow.

The use and style of humor in nursing has fluctuated over time with the changing role of the nurse. Driven by changes in society, medical and technological advances, and the changes in nursing practice, nurses have moved from the comfort-giving mothering role to post-World War II technology and the introduction of interpersonal relationships, communications, psychosocial nursing, holistic health, advanced nursing practice, and theory/research based nursing.

The use of humor reflects the changing status and image of nursing. Most of the early humor was about nursing and the caregiving, stress-related activities. The use of humor in interactions with patients was minimal; rather, humor reflected the patients' perceptions of nurses and the care they received. Historically, the nurse has been portrayed humorously in four major images: the nurturer, the servant/handmaiden, the sex-object, and the old battle-axe. This is how the public sees us, as a reflection of their own fears, anxieties, misconceptions, and stereotypes about being sick, anger at illness and hospitalization, and concerns about both the care they will receive and the competency of the health professionals (Muff, 1982).

In jokes, cartoons, film, and television, the nurse has been portrayed both positively and negatively (Kalish & Kalish, 1982a,b; Muff, 1982). As the nurturer, she has been the angel of mercy, the gentle sister. She has also been viewed negatively, as "Nurse Nightingone," the absent-from-the-bedside nurturer! The nurse is also the servant, the physician's handmaiden, who takes and carries out orders and bedpans, and who is maid and housekeeper for the unit. The nurse, whether male and female, is also the sex-object, the person who touches our bodies in the most intimate and invasive procedures. And yet, she is seen as the "old battle-axe" who tortures with needles and medications and procedures, who appears insensitive and uncaring, who is more concerned with rules and regulations and keeping order, such as Nurse Ratched of the movie and book, "One Flew Over the Cuckoo's Nest."

Of course, the nurse plays complex and diverse roles. We are the nurturer, caring but not smothering. We provide a service to society, not as servants but as highly skilled professionals. We are professionals, but not sex objects. And we are leaders, managers, and decision-makers-not old battle-axes. But, in humor, these roles are always an exaggeration of the image or stereotype.

As nursing has changed, so has the humor about nurses from patients and from nursing itself. There is acceptance of this humor as a therapeutic force in nursing for the professional as well as the patient. One indication of any group's coming of age in a society is that it allows jokes to be told about it and is an entity worth joking about. A further sign of maturity is when a group can laugh at itself. The ability to make jokes about one's own profession, the stereotypes, the issues and errors, conveys one's own self-esteem and confidence (Boskin, 1979).

Just as Nightingale laughed at the situation in Scutari, the earliest recorded use of humor by nurses is in reaction to stresses and reality shocks, especially those experienced by new student nurses. Perennially Yours, Probie, a series of cartoons by Jo Brown (1958), first appeared in RN magazine in the early 1940s. The cartoons laughed at the trials and tribulations, errors and gaffes and stresses faced by the Probationer (the 6-month period of nurses' "training" prior to official acceptance into nursing school). There are the personal memories of the "dumb student" incidents, the joking, practical jokes, the gallows humor, humorous skits at school parties and cartoons in year books, which are still so vivid and were so therapeutic! Humorous interactions with patients are less vivid, since they were not encouraged. But they did occur. There was always the humor about the floppy gowns, the hospital food, bedpans, and "finishing the bath!" There were the humorous get-well cards. A 1950 "Fun and Games for the Convalescent" card included such jokes as:

Patient: *Nurse, this food isn't fit for a pig!*
Nurse: *I'm sorry, Sir. I'll take it back and bring you some that is.*

There were cartoons which appeared in Medical Economics and RN and the American Journal of Nursing in the 1950s and 1960s. Odds and Ends of Ward Wit by Thelma Canarecci (1976) was a compilatiton of her cartoons. Her Florence Nightingale Jones in Tender Loving Comedy (1986) reflected the comedy of nursing. During this era, the American Journal of Nursing included a "time off" page of "some of the lighter, sometimes funny, sometimes nostalgic material that comes across our editorial desks" (p. 240). There were jokes, cartoons, and humorous stories. One reader (Storlie, 1965) wrote,

With this page I relax. I laugh with other nurses to make it easier to laugh at myself. "Before I'm through I realize that, for every earthshaking problem in nursing, there is a humorous counterpart . . . . " (p. 240).

It was in the 1960s, with the advent of community mental health, psychosocial nursing, recognizing and meeting the emotional needs of patients, moving to a focus on health promotion rather than disease, and a humanistic approach to nursing, that we first began to take humor seriously. Catherine Norris (1961-62), in an article in Nursing Forum, looked at the messages communicated in get-well cards. Sister Mary Kevin in RN (1964) humorously addressed "How to recognize your patients' humours." Gayle Pearson reviewed "A child's humor" in 1965.

However, the first research into the concept of humor with application to nursing and nursing care began in 1965 with an NIMH grant to identify mental health content to be integrated into the nursing education curriculum, content that had not before been applied to nursing. Studies of such concepts as anxiety and grief had begun earlier, but the more

11

positive emotions and methods for coping with the stresses of illness needed to be investigated. As one of the "mental health integrators" at the 24 participating baccalaureate programs in the western United States, I chose the concept of humor to study and apply.

Why humor? My choice at that point was serendipitous. At the initial meeting of the group, we identified the concepts that we felt should be studied, with each of us becoming the major researcher for one concept. But, looking back at my choice, it was a natural evolution of my interest. As a psychiatric nurse and pioneer in the community mental health movement, having come through all the revolutions in psychiatry, I was a firm believer in the influence of the mind over the body and the concept of healing behaviors.

As a basic student I had participated in and benefited from humor. Even then, I collected humor. Ogden Nash and Dorothy Parker were my favorites. I had minored in English, studying human behavior in fiction, and loved the literature of comedy, especially Greek and French comedies. I was not a comedian. But, like most other nurses, I used humor to survive the rigors of nursing school, used gallows humor, saw the humor used by patients, played practical jokes, and used jocular talk in practice. As a teacher, I incorporated humor into my teaching. However, I had not given adequate credit to humor for its therapeutic power, especially in relation to patients, nor had I made a planned use of humor in nursing care. So, the time was ripe!

It seemed appropriate with the focus on nursing process to add humor to the intervention and communication skills of the nurse, along with such other concepts as trust, hope, and listening. Assessment and intervention related to grief, loss, body image, hostility, shame, stigma, denial, and privacy also added to this humanistic, holistic approach to nursing care. This three-year project culminated in a book, with the first edition published in 1970, including the first chapter ever in the nursing literature on humor in nursing (Robinson, 1978).

What was humor? What purpose did it serve? Why did it exist in health care? And, how could we apply it in our nursing care? Those were the questions addressed in the initial study. I drew on all the theories, research, and literature from the humanities and the behavioral and natural sciences. I did participant observations, collected anecdotes, and identified the major functions of humor in health care.

Continuing the research in my doctoral studies, I looked at the styles of humor; the variables to be considered (e.g., culture); its use in education; how to increase one's own humorous attitude; and provided some beginning guidelines for cultivating humor as a planned tool in communication, teaching, and intervention in nursing care. It resulted in a book published in 1977, which is now in its second edition (Robinson, 1991).

Despite that 1965 study and similar study groups in other parts of the country, while

12

there was a surge of integration of the other psychosocial concepts during the early 1970s, only a smattering of humor was integrated into the curricula. There were a few graduate students who chose to study humor, but for the most part it was still not considered a scholarly subject to investigate. One doctoral student was forced by her committee to change her topic after her initial proposal. My own speaking engagements were mainly as a luncheon or dinner speaker, to add some "lightness" or a few jokes to a meeting or conference.

This may have been a function of the paradoxical nature of humor itself. It is fun, it is not serious. Yet, it is this very quality which is the healing, therapeutic antidote for all the "heaviness" and seriousness of life. It provides a balance, a perspective. But to be serious about it might mean the loss of this wonderful therapy!

Those from other disciplines who had been doing research in this area-psychiatrists, psychologists, and sociologists-also experienced this phenomenon of not being taken seriously. In nursing, it also may have been a function of nursing's concern at this time in its history, on equal status within the health professions, on doctoral preparation, on nursing practice based on theory, on nursing models, nurse practitioner roles and raising nursing's image as a profession. As with early women comedians, humor was not well received.

It took the experience of a patient to catalyze the acceptance of humor as a therapeutic modality. Norman Cousins' planned use of humor through programmed sessions of laughter in his recovery from ankylosing spondilitis, a life-threatening disease, was first reported in 1977 (although it actually happened in 1964) and then discussed in his book, Anatomy of an Illness in 1979. It spurred research on the biochemical and physiological effects of all the positive emotions. The prior research and works of humor specialists in all the disciplines were suddenly recognized, and it stimulated further study and practice and publications. The humor movement was on!

The Workshop Library on World Humor was introduced in 1975, and the First International Conference on Humor in Wales was held in 1976. The Second International Conference on Humor in Los Angeles in 1979 was attended by several nurses.

In the 1980s, humor in nursing became a scholarly subject to investigate and teach. There were many studies by graduate and doctoral students. The 1980s also saw the incorporation of humor into practice, education, and management. Humor was integrated into health care with tools like humor rooms, humor carts, and closed circuit TV, as part of the healing process. There were workshops, conferences, courses, and staff development programs by nurses for nurses, as well as a proliferation of conferences and programs and workshops by other disciplines and groups.

Nurses For Laughter (NFL) (1982-86) was organized by some 50 nurses who attended one such interdisciplinary conference, for the purpose of "promoting the use of humor in nursing and health care." Its membership quickly rose to over one thousand, produced a newsletter, and disseminated information on research and practice. It stimulated smaller networking groups in regional areas like southern California, the Bay area in northern California, and in North Carolina. Upon the demise of NFL from sheer administrative overload, the American Association for Therapeutic Humor was organized, again by a nurse. It pursues similar goals and purposes, including presenting conferences and workshops. Humor has become the subject of many articles in nursing and other refereed journals and books and in nursing textbooks. Humor has been included in many national nursing conferences since the early 1980s, and not as the light topic luncheon speaker, but as keynote or seminar presentations.

In the spring of 1991, a humor magazine for nurses, the Journal of Nursing Jocularity, burst onto the scene. It was conceived, written, edited, illustrated, and published by nurses. It brought humor back full circle to the benefit of the professional, demonstrating that humor is as healing for the professional as it is for the patient. For nurses to be comfortable using and accepting humor with their patients, they must accept and be comfortable with their own laughter and comedy.

Humor is the "saving grace!" It is one of the most healthy coping strategies for all human beings. And, in that perspective, it retains the humanness in nursing.

Why Humor in Nursing?

Why does humor exist in the health care arena? What is it? What is its function and purpose in nursing and health care? How can we cultivate the use of humor in our communications, teaching, as well as in our interventions with clients and professional lives? Those were the questions raised in the original study of humor in nursing and subsequent research (Robinson, 1970/78, 1977/91, 1983).

Why has humor been a missing element in nursing care for so long? The "professional" demeanor first demanded by Nightingale socialized nurses not to laugh. Also, the kind of humor which exists and naturally erupts in health care is not sanctioned by the system. That kind is usually raunchy, sexual, scatological, hostile, and "gallows," i.e., gross, macabre, "sick," often referred to as the typical "medical humor." The nature of humor, however, is that it is always relevant to the situation, and we cope daily with the stress of illness, naked bodies, excrement, blood and guts, invasive procedures, trauma, disabilities, and death.

Another factor is the potential for abuse of this kind of humor, with patients and families feeling put down, rejected, or neglected. In the process, even milder forms of humor were rejected and suppressed: jocular talk and jokes about the little "hassles" related to daily activities, to management, to the "crazy world" of health care itself, in which so many ludicrous, spontaneous situations occur. Humor persists, however, because it serves a vital purpose. It is a human response to stress, for balance, equilibrium, perspective, and survival.

In health care, humor is used as an indirect form of communication; it has sociological and psychological functions and, although not researched in this original study, laughter produces physiological and biochemical effects which were observed in anecdotal accounts of a patient's recovery and in positive responses to the use of humor in therapeutic interactions. It is a major coping mechanism for patients and staff, and is a powerful tool in healing (Cousins, 1979; Moody, 1978; Robinson, 1991; Siegel, 1986, 1989).

As a form of communication, humor has been called the "oil of society." In health care, it facilitates all social relationships and manages all the "delicate" situations which can occur. Humor conveys messages instantly, but indirectly. The message may be one of comic relief; however, more often, a message is so emotionally tinged that it might be unacceptable if expressed directly. The message can be one of anxiety, fear, anger, frustration, embarrassment, apology or, more positively, it can be a sharing of a common concern, of love, warmth, support, and understanding. The beauty of humor is that it is in a "joke" framework. With that little joke, banter, teasing, witticism, or cartoon, we deliver our message without ever having to discuss it. And, when we laugh, we let go of the associated feelings.

Humor also has a face-saving quality. Even if the listener doesn't find it funny, one laughs "to be a good sport." And if the listener reacts negatively or doesn't get the message, we can back off with, "I was just joking!" Humor is used often as a "trial balloon" to open up to a serious discussion, a vehicle for easily moving in and out of the serious as the situation warrants. Humor strengthens bonds between people. By laughing together, we let each other know we share their views, we understand their feelings, without ever having to say so, especially about uncomfortable topics.

Both patients and staff bring this kind of communication into the health care arena with them. It provides a way to deal with all the external pressures imposed by society and the health care system, as well as helping the individual cope with all the intrapsychic pressures of disease, trauma, and illness. Two major functions of humor are evident in health care. Sociologically, humor establishes relationships, reduces the social conflicts inherent in health care, promotes group cohesion, provides for group control, facilitates change and survival in the system. Psychologically, humor is a major relief mechanism. It relieves anxiety, stress, and tension; it provides a healthy outlet for frustration and anger. It is a healthy denial of reality which lightens the heaviness related to crises, tragedy, trauma, disabilities, and death.

In any situation, these functions may overlap, although one might predominate.

15

Humor can range from pleasantries and witticisms to the gallows type. In areas of the greatest stress, humor will become more aggressive, hostile, sexual, and gallows. We need to laugh harder to reduce tension.

With tragedy, humor becomes a major source of coping for the caregiver and for the prevention of burnout. It is important to recognize that the aggressive, gallows humor, so therapeutic for staff at this time, may not be appreciated by patients, although the patients may be using their own. There is a fine line which humor does not cross. For the health professional, the key to the therapeutic use of humor is to be sensitive to whose needs are being met.

In using humor with clients, one must also be sensitive to the right time, the right place, and the right amount. Know your audiences. Assess their receptiveness. Listen to their joking. Consider the age, values, culture, level of anxiety, physical condition, organic change, medication, and level of pain. And, always, the humor must be used in the context of warmth and caring, a "laughing with," not a "laughing at."

This phenomenon of humor and laughter, with which we as humans have been endowed, is more than just fun and trivia. It is a healthy therapeutic tool we must recognize, cultivate, and use. It is healing for both clients and professionals.

Conclusion

We have come a long way in the use and acceptance of humor. There are still some who fear that humor will take the profession of nursing one step backward, and who still maintain that laughter has no place in nursing. However, there are increasing inroads into the health care arena. Humor carts, humor baskets, humor rooms are appearing; and humor therapy is being requested by patients and delivered by staff.

Nursing journals and hospital publications are devoting whole issues to the subject. Research in every clinical area, as well as education and management, is being conducted- as evidenced by the authors and chapters in this book. Healing arts networks and departments are being established in health care institutions offering humor therapy along with other alternative therapies as massage, therapeutic touch, music, art, and aroma therapy.

With the increased emphasis on and acceptance of holistic health practices and the expanding research in psycho-bio-neuro-endocrine-immunology and the mind-body connection (Cousins, 1989; Moyers, 1993), humor is here to stay. The use of humor will become an integral part of the communication and intervention patterns in nursing, recognized and accepted as one of the healing adjuncts to health care.

Bibliography

Boskin, J. (1979). *Humor and social change in twentieth-century America.* Boston: Trustees of the Public Library.

Brown, J. (1958). *Perennially yours, Probie.* New York: Springer.

Canarecci, T. (1976). *Odds and ends of ward wit.* Oradell, NJ: Medical Economics Co.

Canarecci, T., & Canarecci, L. (1986). *Florence Nightingale Jones in tender loving comedy.* Mishawaka, IN: TLC Books.

Cousins, N. (1979). *Anatomy of an illness.* New York: Norton.

Cousins, N. (1989). *Head first: The biology of hope.* New York: Dutton.

Kalisch, B. J., & Kalisch, P.A. (1982a). Nurses on prime-time television. *American Journal of Nursing,* 82(2), 264-270.

Kalisch, B. J., & Kalisch, P. A. (1982b). The image of the nurse in motion pictures. *American Journal of Nursing,* 82(4), 605-611.

Kevin, Sister M. (1964). How to recognize your patient's humors. *RN,* 64(12), 51-53.

Kelly, L. Y. (1981). *Dimensions of Professional Nursing,* 4th edition. New York: Macmillan.

Moody, R. A. (1978). *Laugh after laugh.* Jacksonville, FL: Headwaters Press.

Moyers, B. (1993). *Healing and the mind.* New York: Doubleday.

Muff, J., (1982). Handmaiden, battle-axe, whore: An exploration into the fantasies, myths, and stereotypes about nurses. In J. Muff (Ed.) *Socialization, sexism, and stereotyping: Women's issues in nursing* (pp. 113-156). St. Louis: Mosby.

Nightingale, F. (1860). *Notes on nursing: What it is and what it is not.* London: Harrison.

Norris, C. (1961-62). Greetings from a lonely crowd. *Nursing Forum,* 6(1), 73-78.

Pearson, G. (1965). A child's humor. *Nursing Science,* 3(4), 95-108.

Robinson, V. M. (1978). *Humor in Nursing. In C. Carlson & B. Blackwell (Eds.) Behavioral Concepts and Nursing Intervention* (pp. 191-210), 2nd edition. Philadelphia: Lippincott.

Robinson, V. M. (1983). Humor and Health. In P. E. McGhee & J. H. Goldstein (Eds.). *Handbook of Humor Research,* vol. II, Applied Studies (pp. 109-128). New York: Springer.

Robinson, V. M. (1991). *Humor and the health professions,* 2nd edition. Thorofare, NJ: Slack.

Siegel, B. S. (1986). *Love, medicine, and miracles.* New York: Harper & Row.

Siegel, B. S. (1989). *Peace, love, and healing.* New York: Harper & Row.

Storlie, F. (1965). Time off. *American Journal of Nursing,* 65(9), p. 240.

17

CHAPTER II

LISTENING BEYOND THE LAUGHTER: COMMUNICATING THROUGH THE USE OF HUMOR

by Colleen Gullickson, RN, PhD

When ten nurses were asked, "Can you tell me a story about a patient that you'll never forget because it taught you what it means to be able to laugh with your patient?," the stories they shared each demonstrated a different understanding of the power of laughing. For patients, using humor becomes a way to speak the unspeakable and ask the unspoken questions. The language of laughter connects in a very intimate way, and in some instances more deeply than words convey. Nurses in this article discuss how they listen beyond the laughter.

As members of the health care team, nurses have more opportunities and more frequent encounters with patients and family members than any other health care provider. The continuity this provides is essential to the development of a unique relationship or understanding between the patient and the nurse, an understanding that goes beyond the mundane conversations of dietary preferences, bowel programs, and activity tolerance. Laughter is one form of conversation that "connects" nurses and patients on a very personal plane and involves sharing fears, insecurities, and joyful moments.

The segments of conversation presented in this chapter represent portions of audiotaped interviews with ten practicing nurses. These nurses were asked to share their stories about patients or events that stood out in their minds because it demonstrated to them what it meant to be able to laugh with their patients. The stories they shared show a different understanding of the power of laughing, as well as how laughter can communicate more deeply than words alone.

"I can remember one night in the middle of the night getting a patient ready for a kidney transplant and this is a young man who I have since become very good friends with and he is a delight, but he was very light-hearted and very, very kind of jovial and kind of laughing about all this stuff and yet there was, I just had this sense about him, that this just was not quite fitting with... I don't know if it was body language or what it was, and it just didn't feel real honest, and so, I said to him, you know, it was like two in the morning and I was shaving him and getting him all ready and I said, "Now listen, you think there's anything we should talk about?" And he said, "Well, you, know, it's not like I'm going

19

to die or anything." And he started laughing. And I... and it was just like this bell went off right in my head, and I, I just looked at him and I said, "You know, I think we need to talk about that."

When is a laugh more than a laugh? When do we, as nurses, need to look beyond the laughter to hear what our clients are really saying? This experienced nurse described caring for a patient prior to a kidney transplant when fears becsme unspeakable, when the possibility of death was truly in front of him. How can patients communicate this entire spectrum of emotion? What is the language that expresses fear, lost hope, frustration, and doubt? At times like these, words alone may not adequately communicate what is needed, and oftentimes laughter becomes a new language.

As this story continues, the nurse explains:

We went through this whole thing about what his life had been like and he really wasn't afraid of dying but he was afraid of going to sleep. He was afraid of being put under. So we went through this whole conversation about how that's a normal fear and issues surrounding control . . . .

Here, an experienced nurse listens to a client prior to undergoing transplant surgery. The patient laughs when he talks about the possibility of dying during the procedure. Instead of changing the topic or ignoring the comment, this nurse is able to detect that something else is of concern and elicits conversation about the real issue this patient is unable to discuss (i.e., his fear of anesthesia).

Nurses often interact with patients and families during times of emotional or physical breakdown; i.e., worsening symptoms, exacerbations, traumatic events, and death. During these times, patients often find themselves in an unfamiliar environment with uncertain schedules. Their bodies have become unpredictable and unreliable. What was once familiar and comfortable is now foreign. How can patients communicate any of this with their health care providers? There are times when our language of verbal communication is deficient. Although patients engage in polite dialogue with their nurses, the real issues of concern are rarely spoken. Humor then becomes an acceptable mechanism whereby patients can express the real issues. Humor becomes the "how" of asking. It is through this language, the nonverbal language of laughter, that patients can speak the unspeakable and ask the unspoken questions. Humor becomes a way to communicate.

Sharing Who We Are

In her book Humor and the Health Professions, Robinson (1991) discusses the importance of social context as it relates to humor. She states, "Humor depends on a knowledge of the actual situation or events and a shared experience" (p. 48). From a patient's viewpoint, who would seem the most likely person to understand the actual situation, what is happening psychologically as well as physiologically? Who would most likely understand the delicate fabric that holds a family together during times of stress? Most often, patients rely on the nurse, and frequently humor helps form that special bond.

Nurses tell how humor helps them bond with their patients and families in a variety of ways. Many nurses describe using humor through self-disclosure as part of that bonding:

"Part of humor is sharing a part of yourself that kind of gives a little self-disclosure so it's not so risky for the other person. When I feel like I'm doing something humorous with a patient, I'm usually telling them something about my family or myself."

She goes on to tell how a patient questioned her about a funny incident relating to her children:

Well, you know, one of the nurses told me a story about your children. And I wanted to know if that was true ... and there had been a bond there placed with that person that I didn't even know that, and they knew this self-disclosure about me. So I think that there's some self-disclosure stuff that happens in humor, especially if you give it about personal things about yourself.

Humor, as self-disclosure, can be subtle, so subtle that it can be overlooked by the novice nurse. Instead of a hearty belly laugh, this type of humor may be as elusive as a smile, or a passing comment that communicates a level of personal understanding and connection between patient and nurse. One nurse working in oncology describes how humor as self-disclosure helped a young woman who was near death:

You share a little bit of your life experiences with them to help them cope with the experiences they are going through. I can remember a hospice patient that we had that was on the unit, and she was about the same age as myself, probably mid-thirties. Had a brand new baby and had only been married for a couple of years, and was dying of cancer. The baby was probably nine months old. And [she] was given a matter of days, weeks to live. And was very uncomfortable with the fact that she hadn't made any preparations for the funeral, hadn't done a will, and was upset that her husband was having to do all of these things. And I just sat down with her and told her that there are very few people our age that have sat down and made those life-long goals completed. I don't think typically a 30 year old person goes out and wonders what type of casket they are going to get buried in. It's just not one of those things, and that was okay in that situation and she just needed to talk to her husband as much as she could and let him know what her wishes were. She was also much more acutely ill but she was able to smile and make small comments. But the level of humor utilized with her was much more indirect humor.

In this situation, humor as self-disclosure involves sharing commonalities of early adulthood. In saying, "I don't think typically a 30-year-old person goes out and wonders what type of casket they are going to get buried in," the nurse discloses that, "I'm not prepared either"; no 30-year-old is prepared for their own mortality. In so doing, the nurse is able to communicate the absurdity and irony of the patient's situation. The patient recognizes this and smiles. For that moment, she is at peace.

Humor, as self-disclosure, serves a reciprocal function. Once patients feel comfortable and trusting that you are willing to share a part of who you are, they too will use humor and share a part of who they are. One nurse eloquently states:

I think it [humor] has allowed me to be able to make bonds with a lot of patients, and a lot of patients I am really close to. I think a lot of that is through the humor and they will disclose things to me that they may not disclose to another nurse.

Self-disclosure can be risky for both the nurse and the patient. Yet, as health care providers, we have come to expect that patients will routinely and freely discuss every aspect of their health care despite how personal it may be. Humor as self-disclosure provides a safe vehicle to disclose, to express fears and anxiety. Humor invites and expresses closeness and intimacy. As part of self-disclosure, another nurse talks about sharing information with clients just as one would a friend:

A friend is somebody you share with; well, I share with my patients. I share their lives, I share their misery. By the time I get through admission, I know lots of things about them that a lot of other people don't know. Consequently, I share little things about myself, like how we just got back from Florida, my husband is going to retire, and little joking things about my child. I never really thought about it . . . my patients are my friends.

It takes time to establish a relationship in which patients feel safe to express their concerns. Using humor in an appropriate and mutually acceptable manner can make patients feel relaxed and more at ease. Being able to laugh with another person reflects a certain "one-on-one" level of closeness, as patients and nurses work together to share concerns that may otherwise have gone unspoken.

Humor as Asking

Laughter is socially acceptable, much more so than crying. Laughter is also more socially acceptable than discussions about dying, sexuality, loss of control, or suicide. Laughter has been conceptualized and understood as either a positive or negative "coping mechanism." "Coping" is something that patients do independently, which nurses can support. Laughing, however, is a part of sharing and connecting. Laughing is fundamentally not being alone. If our understanding of humor and laughter goes no further than a coping mechanism, then we will never hear the language of laughter, or hear what patients may be asking through their humor. Humor becomes the "how" of asking and laughter the language of closeness.

One nurse describes how a gentleman she cared for used humor to ask about and try to make sense of a night when he was acutely ill and began to hallucinate. In this situation, using humor as part of asking reveals one's own individual vulnerability and loss of control. Humor becomes the vehicle whereby this patient can ask for reassurance.

Humor is a part that's more socially acceptable, readily available, entertaining, for people to be able to understand when he tells the story because it's easier for him to relay that story to kind of laugh about it than it is to say how scared he was that night because he was hallucinating and he was seeing me roam around the room and how he didn't know what was real and what wasn't real. It's just real interesting that humor becomes the way to talk about some of that stuff. Humor is just another way of nurses and patients connecting on a very serious level and that's the part that's easy for patients to talk about is the humor part. Because the humor is just one part of a very strong relationship with these people because we shared this moment and time together.

Another nurse describes preparing a man for an orchiectomy:

One man I worked with was going in for an orchiectomy, and I went in after he had already signed the permit and everything and he was just kind of waiting for the surgical team to come down and get him and I went in to see if there was any more questions and I said, "Do you fully understand what the doctor is going to do?" And he looked at me and said, "Oh, yes, the doctor is going to change me from a rooster to a hen." And I think a lot of people might have said, "Oh, isn't that marvelous that he's still got this wonderful sense of humor." And yet to me that was a real signal that there were some concerns about his sexuality and it opened the door very nicely to the fact that we could talk about his concerns, and he did have some concerns. He was really worried about a few issues related to the sexuality, but using that kind of statement, had I not responded correctly, he has the "out" of saying, "Oh, I was only joking, I was only kidding" and has a way out. I think patients are using this all of the time, it's just that we are not always catching the messages.

Listening to the laughter provides an opportunity for nurses to become engaged with their patients in a way that may not be possible if humor is viewed as merely a coping mechanism or a "way out." By listening beyond the laughter to what is being asked, meaningful, engaged conversation becomes possible.

The Language of Laughter

Laughter, as the language of closeness, involves intimacy and connection. When used in a way that is congruent with the relationship established between the nurse and patient, the language of laughter connects in an intimate way. If the language is used in a way that does not reflect the experience of the relationship, then the humor feels uncomfortable, similar to touching someone's body inappropriately. Humor communicates much differently, and in some instances much more deeply than words convey. In this regard, humor can be used as conversation between the nurse and the patient when they are alone, but it can also be an intimate way of communicating and connecting in the midst of a frightening situation or in a room full of strangers. Sometimes, humor masks fear and anxiety. So nurses must remain vigilant to what is actually being communicated.

As part of the language of closeness, humor needs to be thoughtfully implemented, with careful use, timing, and depth. This includes both initiating humor with clients as well as responding to humor. The subtle nuances of the language communicate closeness and connection. Because of the imprecision of the language, however, the messages conveyed can be confusing for patients and families who sometimes misinterpret the level of intimacy that the humor is meant to reflect.

One nurse describes a situation in which it is difficult to define the individual personal boundaries reflected by the type of humor utilized:

I remember a situation where I was very close with a patient and the family and friends. . . I got to know them all. The family member kind of like pinched my bottom as I walked by the bed. . . She was doing it totally as a joke because she laughed about it, but my way of dealing with that situation was that it was inappropriate, and I think she could tell by the response that she got from me. It was a very non-verbal response but it was just like "that was just a little too far."

Learning the boundaries of the language takes time and expertise. Nurses who use humor talk about "getting it wrong" before they "get it right" and the role expertise plays in knowing the difference. Despite its imprecision, laughter provides an opportunity for patients to communicate when they find themselves at the margins of their existence. Laughing becomes a releasing moment, "an answer to a boundary situation" (Plessner, 1970). Plessner describes laughing (and crying) as two boundary reactions; i.e., the limits of human behavior. Through laughing and crying, Plessner postulates that individuals directly demonstrate their humanity: "to be able to deal with something at the point where nothing further can be done" (p.142).

This is often where nurses interface with patients at the margins of their existence. One nurse tells a story about a woman who had received a kidney transplant. Her husband had been staying with her during her early convalescence, which had been fraught with complications. The nurse says:

. . . so she always tells the story about how I tripped over her husband one night.

I didn't realize he was sleeping in the room, you know. And I tripped over her husband and kind of landed on the cot with him, they just think that's the funniest story. And yet it's Fran that was hemorrhaging really bad one night that I had the "fellow" come in and that Fran will say to me when we are alone, "You know, I have my kidney today because you were there." But it's so funny to think that [for] so many of these people, the bond of humor . . . was also a bond of extreme crisis in their life.

Another nurse says:

Kim, he's also a patient of ours now, and he will come and tell the story about how he calls me the Irish Catholic Girl and he and his wife, they'll like leave you little presents when they come in the clinic, weird little stuff, like St. Patrick's Day stuff you know, because supposedly I'm Irish, and he'll tell weird stories about how I was dancing down the hall with him in the middle of the night and stuff like that but it's also Kim who sits in the smoking lounge and also tells people that I saved his life one night. Do you know what I mean?

Laughing can be the language that communicates the boundaries of our existence. When nothing else can be done, all one can do is laugh. The challenge for nurses lies in understanding the riddle.

Summary

Nurses have the opportunity to provide, encourage, and support laughter everyday as we interact with patients and their families. Laughing together can be revitalizing. By laughing, a momentary release is found from the intensity of what would otherwise be an overwhelming situation. Laughing provides an opportunity to reframe the situation. Through laughter, individuals find a means of "staying" in what would otherwise be an intolerable situation.

Laughter is a language of closeness, intimacy, and connectedness-just as laughing directly demonstrates our humanity. Nurses are in a unique position to interact with patients in a manner that reflects our understanding that a laugh may be more than a laugh, and that we are truly listening beyond the laughter.

Bibliography

Plessner, H. (1970). *Laughing and crying: A study of the limits of human behavior.* Evanston, IL: Northwestern University.

Robinson, V. M. (1991). *Humor and the health professions*, 2nd edition. Thorofare, NJ: Slack.

CHAPTER III

THE MISSING ELEMENT IN HEALTH CARE: HUMOR AS A FORM OF CREATIVITY

by Florence Ditlow, RN, BS

What is Creativity?

Creativity. . . . the humble human counterpart of God's creation. Human creativity uses what is already existing and available and changes it in unpredictable ways. It brings about a desirable enlargement of human experience, liberating us from conditioning and usual choices. The creative work may make us laugh when we are confronted with something new, which is witty and comical; may offer us aesthetic pleasure, when we are in the presence of works of art; may give us a feeling of transcendence, as in the fields of philosophy and religion; or may provide the qualities of usefulness, understanding and predictability as scientific innovations do.
S. Arieti, Creativity: The Magic Synthesis

Necessity is the mother of invention.
William Wycherly (From Bartlett's Familiar Quotations)

The multitude of problems presented to human beings calls for every kind of coping skill. While testing out new ideas, humanity learns and evolves. In this process of change, creativity happens. Our civilization moves forward when problems show us the need for new ideas. We are well aware that change is needed regularly in the routine of health care delivery. This relates to or involves not only client and caregiver, but the institution or setting in which the care takes place. While virtually all institutions view change as being imperative, unfortunately, most do not view creativity as being vital to their growth.

Creative thinking, followed by action, brings us to a new understanding, and changes the way we live; but there is an element of risk involved. Taking a risk means facing our own fears, learning from the criticism of others, and devoting time and effort to that which begins as an inspiring idea.

Creative Thinking
Creative thinking is based, not on "genius," but on ordinary thought processes.
Weisberg, Creativity Beyond the Myth of Genius, 1993, p. 23.

27

Weisberg believes that the mind of the "creative person" operates as does the mind of the average person. Rather than simply being blessed with a gift of genius, the creative individual is more willing to take the action required to nurture new ideas. Such activity includes taking advantage of skills and experiences. Commitment to the goal is coupled with a desire to work toward that goal. Taking these qualities and framing them with yet another quality, that of a flexible nature, gives us the portrait of a creative individual.

The expression of creativity requires energy. Inventors and artists who have come to be known as creative believe that unlimited creative energy is available to those desiring it. The provision for relaxation starts the process of setting that energy in motion. Various thinking styles are available to place us in a creative state of mind, including meditation, visualization, prayer, journal writing, and brainstorming. The first three are introspective activities, centered around deep relaxation intended to clear the mind for optimal functioning. The latter two are active techniques which allow the conscious mind to empty its thought content. In so doing, new ideas flow and we unveil insights. When these thinking styles are practiced with dedication, we release the vast inner strengths which fuel the creativity of humanity.

The "special of the day" on the menu of creative thinking is humor. The experience of humor provides relaxation, release, and the possibility of perspective at any time and in any place. As nurses, we may rely on it as an active skill that we can easily learn to employ as various stresses erode our energy. In the echo of laughter, tension dissolves, providing mental clarity and, along with that, a creative state of mind.

Creativity — The Open Mode of Thinking

Creativity lives in paradox: serious art is born from serious play. We must work at learning to play. Creativity must be freed from the narrow parameters of capital A Art and recognized as having much broader play. In order to nurture our creativity, we require a sense of festivity, even humor.
J. Cameron, The Artist's Way, 1992, p. 112.

What is the open mode of thinking? It is a relaxed, alert, playful state of mind in which innovative concepts can be created by the imagination. The ability to see the problem/situation, as a neutral observer would see it, is another property of the open mode. The problem is an opportunity for creativity. Throughout the creative process, humor can provide the open mode state of being because it can dissolve anxiety. Knowing we can cope by our own sense of humor gives a sense of sanity; it can even bolster our faith in the future!

28

The day we learn to laugh at ourselves is the day we grow up.
Ethel Barrymore, quoted in Warner, 1992, p.169.

It has been said that the greatest form of self-esteem is attained when we learn how to laugh at ourselves. This means that we are mature enough not only to tolerate trial and error, but to learn from our mistakes. Both are part of the search for creative solutions.
Do not fear mistakes — there are none.
Miles Davis, quoted in Cameron, 1992, p.194.

The Use of Humor for Creativity in Health Care - A Literature Review

We experience humor as a feeling state. John Cleese, comedian and producer of business training films, teaches about humor's positive effect on all body organs causing a "gut reaction" (Cleese, 1989). He believes that educators who employ humor in their teaching are effective because the message is felt in body as well as in the mind. Humor also provides a means for easier retention of new material.

Nursing education often benefits from the creative technique of cartoons. We can use this vehicle to say volumes in a small amount of space. For students, cartoons provide stress reduction and promote group cohesion (Pease, 1991). This medium offers a means to reframe our ideas. Instructors who utilize humor are highly rated by students for their ability to create an atmosphere where release of tension is allowed in the presence of even the most difficult subjects (Uchuck, 1984). Cartoons and other forms of humor allow a view of chaos from a safe distance. This perspective seems to help us transform tragedy into comedy.

Humor also has therapeutic value as a means of gaining perspective. Rothenberg's (1991) work in psychoanalytic treatment cites the "creative use of irony," in which humor lends a feeling of safety, allowing self-discovery to take place. "Flashes" of insight by the patient aid the therapist in choosing appropriate therapeutic interventions.

Humor is an enjoyable aspect of self-care for bedside nurses. Nurses who see humor as a positive emotion and integrate it into their usual communications find new perspective. Patients also use humor in get-well cards to deal with fear, pain, and embarrassment (Simon, 1989). When pain is reduced, hope comes to terminal patients. They desire access to the power found through humor which is reflected in joy, relaxation, and hope (Herth, 1990).

When humor techniques are applied therapeutically, creating laughter becomes a release mechanism. We can then look at our own difficulties and see them from a more neutral position. Whether from the perspective of patient or nurse, humor allows us to

29

view ourselves with new clarity and trust. When we experience humor on a regular basis, it can be used to strengthen the belief in our own future creative ability.

What is Humor?

Humor is a subject which is challenging to define. Yet, people from every culture and strata of society eagerly have the answer for, "What is funny to you?"
Life does not cease to be funny when people die, anymore than it ceases to be serious when people laugh.
George Bernard Shaw, quoted in John-Roger & McWilliams, 1990, p.104.
Humor is a phenomenon healing both body and mind. Release, more than any other word, describes what transpires during and after an amusing experience. To know humor is to be acquainted with what Cousins (1989) called "positive emotions." These are laughter, love, hope, faith, will to live, festivity, purpose, and determination. He called laughter a "metaphor" for these positive emotions. His research at the University of California School of Medicine shows how emotions guide our beliefs about our health. Cousins summed up his findings with the statement, "Belief becomes biology" (p.229).
Dr. William Fry, humor researcher for thirty years, sees it as an exercise for the body. The hearty laugh affects the diaphragm and lung, circulating blood faster than our resting heart rate (Fry, 1977). Like aerobic exercise, laughter tends to reduce blood pressure, leaving muscles relaxed. With a facial muscle workout, we often "laugh so hard, we cry." This change in the blood circulation affects every body system. Studies show that humor has a positive effect on the immune system (Dillon, 1985) and the autonomic nervous system (Averill, 1969). Smiling, laughing, and delightful play strengthen human beings both physiologically and psychologically. Reviewing these research efforts in the context of the interconnection of all body systems, one comes to appreciate the impact of the mood on the total picture of health.
It appears that humor is closely associated to other feeling states such as "the good cry," the cardiovascular effect of exercise, and some forms of meditation. Indeed, each experience works in its own way, leaving the formerly stressed person with a sense of satisfaction and release. Literature substantiating the healing power of humor says that smiling, laughing, and delightful play strengthen human beings both physiologically and psychologically. Feeling this enjoyment is that part of the human spirit at play. Curiously, the very root of the word humor, "hu" is an ancient sound for the higher power (John-Roger & McWilliams, 1990). This healing property appears in patients as a shift from their "sick" mode into one of acting out wellness. When a positive attitude is present, patients feel better, and focus outside the illness.
To be amused is to experience spiritual diversion. A muse is a spirit which has the

power to breathe life into creative endeavors. Whoever uses humor on a regular basis knows that it breathes life into our thinking. Amusement has an aura of freedom, of surrender to relaxation. In the amusement brought on by our own response and individual sense of humor, subsequent relaxation allows the perspective needed by the imagination in order to bring about new ideas. Indeed, successful comedians make a living looking at life's situations in a humorous light. Viewing life from this perspective distances us from tragedy and it is a way of coping with reality.

The Value of Humor to our Clients

When humor is used therapeutically, the client momentarily begins to feel relaxed in the presence of the one who initiates the humor. For instance, the personal nature of humor helps the patient deal with the impersonal nature of wearing the patient gown and numbered ID band. Through the eye of humor, this attire and "jewelry" becomes more tolerable. Embarrassing questions and uncomfortable tests are more bearable. Gilda Radner (1989), speaking of her fight against cancer, said, "I have a theory that cancer cells hate laughter, jokes, songs, and dancing ... joy makes them want to move out" (p.208).

Smiles potentiate other nurturing measures such as therapeutic touch (Ditlow, 1990). Using humor as a means to motivate, the client overcomes anxiety or pain. This unexpected dividend anchors rapport between the caregiver and patient. Progressively, the patient is more likely to show initiative as a team member. Caretakers are most comfortable when applying their own sense of humor. Our laugh and smile-inducing behavior are perceived as more intelligent when related to the subject at hand, rather than to mimic a professional comedian.

"Every joke is a tiny act of rebellion"
George Orwell, quoted in Mindess, Miller, Turek, Bender, & Corbin, 1985, p.91.

I have used the following anecdote to address the embarrassment of the patient and in some cases relieve the tension associated with surgery:

Nurse: Mr. Smith, please change into this hospital gown for your test.
Mr. Smith: OK, I guess it's a necessary evil.
Nurse: Never mind that you have to give up all your street clothes.
Mr. Smith: What?
Nurse: Never mind that it exposes all of the posterior. This is a gown especially designed for the movies!
Mr. Smith: How's that?
Nurse: Well, it's rated "G" in the front and "X" in the back.

Patient gowns are not happy garments. They are disliked by most everyone. Patients in my practice welcome the chance to poke fun at this dreary garb; better yet, to laugh with a nurse who understands how patients feel. Nurse and patient have used the gown as a vehicle for rapport, and in the process the "institutional setting" takes on a more comfortable tone.

In the individualization of patient care, the nurse may question whether a client is a candidate for therapeutic humor. It is generally advisable to avoid humor in situations of emergency, acute physiological or psychological pain. When the caregiver feels unsure about the risk of creating humor, these two questions can help decide the issue:
1. Is there a need for motivation or energy in this patient's care?
2. If the answer is yes, go a step further and ask the patient, "Would you like to be cheered up?"
This approach makes your intentions clear for both the client and caregiver.

> *One inch of joy surmounts of grief a span*
> *because to laugh is proper to the man.*
> Franìois Rabelais, quoted in Black, 1984, p. 2995.

Therapeutic humor is a lively two-way street, fun for both giver and receiver. Patients declare their need of it as a welcome relief from the usual tests and high pressure atmosphere experienced in the hospital. It dispels fear of the unknown, uniting the patient and caregiver as a healing team. The cementing of this bond with humor makes way for change.

The Value of Humor to the Caregiver

As in other forms of communication, humorous messages are sent, and then there is a reaction to the message. A joke is as funny as the surprise at the end, the punch line. The element of surprise provides a welcome relief from serious or mundane interactions that accompany illness. Clients as well as caregivers say that creating humor is difficult for them; however, this has not reduced their desire to experience this elusive state of being. *"Just as you can learn to express your anger or your love, or to become more capable of coping with anxiety or despair, you can also learn to release and expand or to modify and control your sense of humor, but not without effort and perseverance"* (Mindess et al., 1985, p.89).

A regular dose of humor in the personal life of the caregiver has a striking effect on mood. A consistent "payment" of humorous experiences to the stressed caregiver gives dividends in the form of relaxation, better sleep, greater self awareness; and, of course, problem-solving capacity gains the dimension of creativity. Humor enhances image in that the one sharing the humor is in control of the situation (Ditlow, 1989).

When the caregiver sees a need for humor in the course of care delivery, unexpected and delightful results can happen. The nurse who dispenses humor will begin to find greater ease in establishing rapport, and clients will be motivated to take part in their own care. Caregivers who regularly uses humor as a tool will notice that people seek them out to exchange stories or jokes. "When people laugh, they are listening; when they are listening, they may be influenced" (LeBoeuf, 1987, p.50).

Information can be efficiently packaged through humor. In 1980, future president Reagan's age was a campaign issue. He turned the tables on his competitors with the clever comment, "I am not going to exploit for political purposes my opponent's youth and inexperience" (Orben, 1987, p.4). Thanks to wit and perceived wisdom, Reagan was viewed not only as in control but succeeded to attract voter empathy, and went on to win the election.

Many tasks on a medical-surgical unit are stress-producing. Tedious, often hourly treatments in an acute care setting is one example. In this case, both nurses and patients experience discomfort and tension. When the nurse initiates a joke or tells a story, tension for the moment is nonexistent or forgotten. New behaviors, such as painful movement after surgery, are viewed differently through the lightness of humor.

Discharge teaching demands concise communication and instant rapport with family. Quotes and cartoons can brighten handouts and return demonstrations. When dealing with time-consuming phone calls and a myriad of other distractions, the smile can indeed be a creative umbrella between ourselves and stressful fallout. When nurses feel in control, they feel effective, happy to be who they are and where they are.
Humor signifies the triumph not only of the ego but also of the pleasure principle.
Sigmund Freud, quoted in Mindess et al., 1985, p.91.

The Value of Humor to the Health Care Institution

Where is the need for humor in health care institutions? Every problem is actually an opportunity for creativity, whether it be staffing, budgeting, or interdepartmental relations. With large numbers of patients to be served, hospitals hunger for creative minds. Will humor be ever taken seriously in the health care environment? Many farsighted institutions have recognized the value of humor for recovery from illness and its positive effect on the human spirit. In the words of a very caring and intelligent nurse, "Humor has a ripple effect throughout the hospital" (D. Rege, personal communication, January 1991).

Let's follow a laugh around the hospital!

If a staff member shares a laugh while working with a patient, that patient then shares this feeling of pleasure with another patient or employee. Productivity increases whenever morale improves, and a playful frame of mind encourages creative thinking. Like a good hospital rumor, humor filters everywhere. Into the staff education

33

department it goes, facilitating learning and giving a sense of control or power. Serendipitously, hospital employees find the use of humor to be an enjoyable coping skill. Patients find that the physiological and psychological benefits speed healing. They commend their caregivers for giving them permission to deal with illness through expression of their emotion. They recover and return home to "humor" their relatives with what they learned from the hospital. This is the life cycle of a laugh; in reality, it never dies.

"And by God, she is smart! Good operating nurse. Got a sense of humor" (Boylston, 1937, p. 109). In the world of high-tech health care, humor is the one thing that is easy to relate to. Health care institutions advertising their interest in providing humor as a caring skill will have a large, interested audience that knows that laughter is the best medicine.

Expect the best; convert problems into opportunities; be dissatisfied with the status quo; focus on where you want to go, instead of where you're coming from and most importantly, decide to be happy, knowing it's an attitude,a habit gained from daily practice, and not a result or payoff. Denis Waitley, quoted in Hayward, 1984, p.119

Many have wondered how an individual may have access to a supply of humor. Increasing our access to laughter, like other pursuits, requires intention. We will find more humor by seeking it. Proven ways to attract humor are offered in the next section.

The Humor Quest: How to Find and Create Humor

Humor Chest: Lots of laughs are stored in the chest. They are more valuable when
    released.
Humor Desk: A desk that invites you to enjoy working. Perhaps this is accomplished
    by the pencil you use or your answering machine message.
Humor Fest: Use of an object which creates laughter. An example would be juggling
    while on your break.
Humor Guest: A visit with a friend who laughs with you. This works even while on the
    phone.
Humor Jest: Your own brand of kidding. Allowing the "kid" in you to surface can be
    more powerful than a dozen professional comedians.
Humor List: Checking for the newest humor bestsellers at your local bookstore.
Humor Pest: Kidding oneself while feeling negative. An example is, when late for work,
    exaggerating the effect on the world ("Why, this will be in the evening paper!").
    The object of this technique is to stay in perspective while releasing frustration.
Humor Request: If you want a laugh, asking a friend for it may be the speediest way to
    reach it. A source of humor and creativity resides within each of us. Experienc

ing humor with regular hilarity is likely to unleash creativity.

Humor Rest: Taking a break with your favorite comedian by bringing a tape player to work.

Humor Test: Making an attempt to acquire humor skills such as joke telling or cartooning.

Humor Vest: A funny button or clothing disguise delights patients who have come to regard hospitals as humorless places; e.g., Groucho glasses.

An entire book could be devoted to humor programs. Like other programs, success depends upon quality planning, interest of a group, and dedication. Groups interested in having an ongoing program are advised to educate themselves and then educate their fellow staff members. When this approach is taken, eventually the concept of humor will be much clearer to the patients in the care of these staff members. Surveys will point out where the staff's interests lie, as well as who will make a commitment to the success of the program.

In the initial planning of humor education, an employee group will want to select a medium in which to express their humor. Unlike other high-tech operations, failure is rare. As with other group endeavors, participation is required–even to create humor. One group may choose to devote a bulletin board to humor, encouraging patient participation. A less visually oriented group may meet for lunch to exchange funny stories. Still others may assign April Fool's Day as "Funny Sock Day." Staff members find more enjoyment when there is group participation.

A unique humor program exists at Mary Hitchcock Hospital (Hanover, NH). It was originated by Cathy Johnson, RN. In baskets, she packaged assorted fun items like postcards for patients to send and funny items such as Mr. Rubber Chicken. These baskets are an inexpensive therapeutic means to bring humor to the bedside and help patients cope with illness. "The Humor Basket allows me to provide the human touch I was looking for in my work," says Johnson (C. Johnson, personal communication, August 12, 1992). Humor Baskets successfully motivate patients to laugh and to affect change through creativity. Moving the patients toward positive action promotes healing.

If you are interested in enjoying the benefits of therapeutic humor, commit to carrying out your plan for at least six months. Humor programs reap benefits when, like medications, they are followed up to see how they benefit people the most. It all begins with our imaginations. Imagine a visitor walking through a hospital where humor is created and enjoyed. The first impression is that the hospital cares about its patients and staff. Then imagine us joining patients and fellow employees in sharing your own sense of humor, so that you may approach your work with some special sense of joy, which builds toward a sense of peace.

35

Summary

Human creativity uses what is already available, changing it in unpredictable ways. Creativity is an option for client, caregiver, and institution. It is likely to occur in the open mode of thinking where alertness, relaxation, and playfulness coexist. Humor is a desirable avenue to creative thinking for health promotion. The release and relaxation of humor benefits client and caregiver both physiologically and psychologically. Tension eases for patients, while nurses gain a new sense of control through the use of their own sense of humor. A source of creativity resides within each of us. Experiencing humor with regular hilarity is sure to release our creativity.

Bibliography

Arieti, S. (1976). *Creativity: The magic synthesis.* New York: Basic Books.

Averill, J. (1969). Autonomic response patterns during sadness and mirth. *Psychophysiology*, 5(4), 399-414.

Bartlett's Familiar Quotations. (1937). New York: Little, Brown.

Black, D. (1984). Laughter. *Journal of the American Medical Association*, 252(21), 2995-2998.

Boylston, H. (1937). *Sue Barton, senior nurse.* New York: Scholastic Book Services.

Cameron, J. (1992). *The artist's way.* New York: Tarcher, Perigree Books.

Clese, J. (1989). Humor is not a luxury (videotape). Northbrook, IL: Video Arts Video Presentation.

Councill, M. (1988). Creating inspiration. *Journal of Creative Behavior*, 22(2),123-131.

Cousins, N. (1989). *Head first.* New York: Penguin.

Dillon, K. (1985). Positive emotional states and enhancement of the immune system. *International Journal of Psychiatry in Medicine*, 15(1), 13-18.

Ditlow, F. (1989, April/May). Humor is a serious remedy for stress. *Imprint*, 80.

Ditlow, F. (1990). Humor enhances health (videotape). Newton, MA: Joke Poke Video.

Ditlow, F. (1993). The missing element in health care: humor as a form of creativity. *Journal of Holistic Nursing*, 11(1), 66-79.

Fry, W. (1977). The respiratory components of mirthful laughter. *Journal of Biological Psychology*, 19, 39-50.

Goodman, J. (1989). To wit your appetite. In The positive power of humor and creativity (handout). Available from The Humor Project, 110 Spring St., Saratoga Springs, NY 12866.

Hayward, S. (1984). *A guide for the advanced soul.* Crows Nest, NSW (Australia): In Tune Books.

Herth, K. (1990, January/February). Contributions of humor as perceived by the terminally ill. *American Journal of Hospice Care*, 36-40.

Jevne, R., & Levitan, A. (1989). *No time for nonsense.* San Diego: LuraMedia.

John-Roger, & McWilliams, P. (1990). *You can't afford the luxury of a negative thought.* Los Angeles: Prelude Press.

Joke Poke, Inc. (1992). The serious work of humor rooms. Unpublished survey.

LeBoeuf, M. (1987). *How to win customers and keep them for life.* New York: Berkely.

Mindess, H., Miller, C., Turek, J., Bender, A., & Corbin, S. (1985). *The Antioch humor test: Making sense of humor.* New York: Avon.

Orben, R. (1987). Why humor? *Current Comedy* (pp. 1-4). Wilmington, DE: Comedy Center.

Pease, R. (1991). Cartoon humor in nursing education, *Nursing Outlook*, 39(6), 262-267.

Radner, G. (1990). *It's always something.* New York: Avon.

Rothenberg, A. (1991). The Janusian process in psychoanalytic treatment. *Contemporary Psychoanalysis*, 27(3), 422-453.

Simon, J. (1989). Humor techniques for oncology nurses. *Oncology Nursing Forum*, 16(5), 667-670.

Uchuck, G. (1984). Creative teaching techniques. Seminar for Nurses at East Tennessee Baptist Hospital, Knoxville.

Warner, C. (1992). *The last word: A treasury of women's quotes.* Englewood Cliffs, NJ: Prentice-Hall.

Weisberg, R. (1993). *Creativity beyond the myth of genius.* New York: Freeman.

37

CHAPTER IV

SICK, BLACK AND GALLOWS HUMOR AMONG EMERGENCY CAREGIVERS, OR-ARE WE HAVING ANY FUN YET?

by Lisa Rosenberg, PhD, RN

A paradoxical thing is that in making comedy, the tragic is precisely what arouses the funny. . . we have to laugh due to our helplessness in the face of natural forces and [in order] not to go crazy.
Chaplin, 1966, p. 327.

The great comedian, Charlie Chaplin, understood that an important dimension of humor is its value in dealing with tragedy. In so many instances of adversity, the flipside of the grim or the horrible is joking and laughter. It would be as if Mary Poppins and The Texas Chainsaw Massacre were billed as a double feature at the same movie theater. The juxtaposition is so incongruous that we are forced to laugh. This is, indeed, what happens to emergency caregivers. The nature of emergency and critical care is extremely serious. To say that people's lives are at stake is not a mere exaggeration, it is reality. Appropriate recognition and response to patients' physical and emotional problems, existential confrontation with death and dying, and realization of social inequities (i.e., poverty, abuse of children and the elderly) are just some of the issues which make emergency health care a serious, if not depressing, affair. To inject humor into this arena is truly unexpected, surprising, incongruous. Kuhlman (1988) describes the use of humor as a coping mechanism in "scaffold settings." These settings are characterized by "the presence of unremitting or inescapable stressors over which there is minimal control and a sense of existential incongruity" (p. 1086). The entire milieu of emergency caregiving thus provides the perfect environmental setting for the use of gallows humor; the grave and demanding nature of the work makes it so. Professional comedians have long profited from the axiom, "Reality makes a great straightman." It is no less true here.

Within an environment conducive to the expression of incongruous emotions, the use of black or sick humor serves many functions. It is important, however, to first understand the unique stressors of emergency care since they influence how and when humor is used. The next section will discuss those stressors followed by the presentation of work which supports the use of morbid humor among emergency care providers.

39

The Nature of Emergency Health Care

Unlike other professions, the health professions are faced with stressors that involve perceptual, cognitive, and affective mediating processes (Hammer, Mathews, Lyons, & Johnson, 1986). "The pressures of assuming responsibility for another's life, chronic time urgency, or contact with a large number of patients are among the stressors of these professions" (p. 536). Emergency and critical care specialties usually involve interacting with people who are acutely suffering, in a state of physical and emotional decompensation. Appropriate recognition and efficient response to patients' physical and emotional problems are imperative, yet made more difficult by their distress. There is tremendous pressure to make "correct" decisions quickly, since incorrect ones may prove life-threatening. There is no time to prepare for critical events; one must be able to "gear up" rapidly to meet the mental and physical demands of the job. Maintaining a sense of calm and control over oneself and the emergency care environment is vital for the provision of competent health care under conditions of high stress.

Perhaps the most profound stress of emergency and critical care is that tragedy is often the nature of the work. There is no way of minimizing the impact of death. Paramedics especially, "encounter death and dying routinely in the course of their jobs. Many times the death is not a clean and sterile occurrence but is witnessed and/or participated in under the most trying physical and emotional conditions" (Palmer, 1983, p. 83). The reality of death often underscores the discrepancy between actual practice and the myth of the "superhuman" health care provider (Keller & Koenig, 1989). Experiencing feelings of both omnipotence and impotence in dealing with patients' life problems can result in emotional highs and lows for staff (Lipson & Koehler, 1986). The phenomenon of burnout can be the painful result of this unrealistic, self-imposed expectation of omnipotence (Henderson, 1984).

Several factors related to contact with death and dying lead to increased tension and grief among emergency personnel. Typical staff members are not well equipped to deal with the frequency of death and tragic events. In addition, many emergency personnel are young and personally unthreatened by ill health. One must also consider the social and personal impact of having to clean up the results of what often are viewed as devastating and unnecessary horrors. It is not difficult to envision the enormous impact such events create (Rosen & Honigman, 1988). Furthermore, emergency personnel are frequently required to give care to the person responsible for the accident or injury (such as the drunken driver with hardly a scratch who caused a head-on collision that fatally injured others). For some, this may require expending tremendous emotional energy in order to maintain self-control and a caring attitude.

Another source of grief is the unacceptability of death in the young or otherwise "undeserving" (Rosen & Honigman, 1988). Emergency personnel can usually deal adequately with the death of an elderly person who suffers a stroke or cardiac arrest. It is much more difficult to cope emotionally with a SIDS (Sudden Infant Death Syndrome) infant or a child fatally injured through abuse. Feelings of horror, rage, and frustration can erupt in response to the innocence and unfulfilled nature of the life taken. Emergency caregivers deal with many unpleasant and unfortunate circumstances in the course of their work. They are most moved, however, by the tragedy of those victims who do not appear to have deserved their fate. The existential nature of this experience often leads critical care personnel to question why bad things happen to good people. Kushner (1981) addresses this wrenching subject and asks, "Can you accept the idea that some things happen for no reason, that there is randomness in the universe? Some people cannot handle the idea" (p. 46). For those who are deeply affected by these tragic events, awareness and consideration of these issues are vital to lessen the inner sense of distress and disillusionment.

The impact of stress on clinical performance provides the major reason for concern. Stressed providers may be less able to maintain their objectivity in their compassionate attitude toward the patients. They often exhibit a numbing of emotions, excessive self-criticism, a cynical attitude, and ultimately a dissatisfaction with the field (Strauss & Glaser, 1970). Another study (Hammer et al, 1986) of emergency department personnel identified four dimensions of an occupational stress syndrome: (a) organizational stress characterized by a negative attitude about one's place of employment and coworkers; (b) negative attitudes toward patients, including insensitivity to their physical and emotional needs; (c) job dissatisfaction and discontent with one's current position; and (d) somatic distress, including fatigue, increased illness, and self-medication to relax.

Several studies have been crafted to investigate the particular occupational and response stressors encountered by paramedics. Mason (1982) reported that role conflict and role ambiguity were the most commonly identified occupational stressors. A stable set of situational stressors were also found to exist in the study population. These included infant death, dealing with mass casualties, and childbirth with complications. Another study (Cox, 1980) sought to identify the occupational stressors which characterize the work of two types of emergency personnel: paramedics and emergency medical technicians (EMTs). For both groups, pediatric trauma ranked as a persistently high stressor. Paramedics, however, evidenced more occupational strain in a variety of ways than did EMTs. Role confusion, conflict with administration, fatigue, emotional involvement in work, and increased responsibility for human life characterized paramedic perceptions and complaints. Although both groups were similar as to trait anxiety, paramedics were significantly higher on state anxiety as well as exhibiting more psychological distress, fatigue, and a higher incidence of negative feelings at work than

41

did the EMTs. Paramedics overwhelmingly identified intrinsic as opposed to extrinsic rewards and motivators in their work. This study recommended the implementation of stress prevention and management programs for fire departments concerned about reducing the harmful social, psychological, and physical impact of work stress on this population.

Use of "GaSBag" Humor among Providers of Emergency Care

As described above, there is ample evidence to indicate that the provision of emergency care is uniquely stressful. GaSBag humor is one coping mechanism used by the providers of emergency care. GaSBag is a playful but useful pseudo-acronym for Gallows, Sick and Black humor as these terms are used somewhat interchangeably in the literature and my own research. GaSBag jokes allude to death, disease, deformity, accidents, or content of a grim or morbid nature. Perhaps it is also a metaphor for the "anesthetizing" effects of GaSBag humor, the distance or momentary transcendence one is able to achieve when confronted with a disturbing event.

In their work on humor, Mindess, Miller, Turek, Bender, and Corbin (1985) discovered that doctors and nurses, especially those assigned to emergency units, often had a particular liking for sick jokes. "They tend to indulge in such humor as a way of relieving the tension of dealing on a daily basis with accident victims and horrifying events" (p. 71). The use of black humor allows people to defend themselves from the things that frighten them (Feinberg, 1978; Ziv, 1984). Black humor can be seen as a sort of challenge to frightening phenomena. This challenge carries a number of messages. "First, the very naming of the phenomenon indicates that a person has it within [their] power to face it. Furthermore, not only [are they] not paralyzed by fear; they even contend that the phenomenon is not really that frightening-and, in fact, that it is rather ridiculous and even funny. Their laughter testifies to a sense of victory and control over the situation" (Ziv, 1984, p.52).

Black humor may frighten people who have not directly experienced a specific traumatic situation. Out of context, it is difficult to see anything funny in the grim, spontaneous humor of the emergency room. However, black humor fulfills the function of encouragement for those who do provide emergency care. "These individuals encourage themselves with the aid of a nonserious approach to very serious matters, which neutralizes the horror and makes it possible to rise above it . . . . In this aspect of self-encouragement, there is a sort of provision of strength for coping with the tragic situation" (Ziv, 1984, p.54). Although reality cannot be altered, one's attitude or perception about it can be temporarily modified so that effective coping behaviors are facilitated.

42

Humor use has been reported as helpful by a variety of critical care and emergency personnel (e.g., nurses, physicians, paramedics). Metcalf (1987) described humor as helping to develop the "fluidity and flexibility needed to survive in an environment of rapid change, trauma, and difficulty" (p. 20). In a paper presented at the Second International Conference on Humor, Lindsey and Benjamin, two emergency physicians, explained how humor is indispensable in the emergency room (cited in Morreall, 1984). By distancing themselves through humor from the serious life and death situations they encounter, emergency personnel are able to offset anxiety, depression, and mental exhaustion and allow their skills to operate maximally. These observations receive empirical support from a study investigating the management of stress and prevention of burnout in emergency physicians (Keller & Koenig, 1989). Two coping methods were demonstrated to have a strong statistical relationship with high levels of job satisfaction and personal accomplishment: drawing on experience and trying to see humor in the situation.

Critical care and emergency nursing also identify humor as a useful coping strategy. Keller (1990) investigated the coping strategies of emergency nurses. She reported that trying to see humor in the situation was one of two short-term coping methods significantly correlated with feelings of personal accomplishment. According to Robinson (1991), in areas of high stress, such as emergency and critical care, GaSBag humor is used more frequently. "There is a need to reduce the strain, the seriousness and the feeling of pain, despair and hopelessness which could paralyze and overwhelm the professional and lead to burnout" (p.80). In a study cited by Leiber (1986), a comparison was made between the humor use of intensive care unit (ICU) nurses and oncology unit nurses. Nurses in the ICU reported using significantly more humor among themselves and with other staff than did nurses on the oncology unit. Specifically, critical care nurses used it most frequently among themselves as a means to cope with job-related tension, frustration with "the system," stress, and anger. With patients, nurses reported using humor most often to help with adjustment to hospitalization and the "sick role," to reduce stress and anxiety, to combat depression, and for distraction during unpleasant procedures (Leiber, 1986, p. 166).

In another study (Hutchinson, 1987), critical care nurses were interviewed in order to determine their job stress strategies. Humor was identified as a self-care strategy which facilitates the use of other major stress-buffering strategies used by nurses, such as acting assertively employing catharsis. The unique subculture of the psychiatric emergency room has also been described in the literature (Lipson & Koehler, 1986). Humor was identified as the mainstay of work and the major coping mechanism of staff members. This subculture allowed staff to adapt to system overload and maintain morale in the face of increased stress and a worsening economic situation.

The use of humor by paramedics has been noted in the literature as well (Palmer, 1983; Zierke, 1988). When used appropriately, it can be effective in reducing patient anxiety to relieve their own tension. The paramedics also use humor after a stressful call. Research using a participant-observer approach revealed that humor is one of six principal coping methods that assist paramedics in their response to death and dying (Palmer, 1983). This observation is supported in the literature by others who describe humor as an effective coping/defense mechanism in dealing with death and disaster (Burkle, 1983; Lattanzi, 1984; Thorson, 1985; Weinrich, Hardin, & Johnson, 1990). The frequency with which most people engage in sick or black humor has much to do with the content of their daily experiences. Most people are far removed from a steady diet of direct contact with illness, accidents, death, and social inequities. This, however, is the nature of emergency care. The occupational world of emergency care is a skewed microcosm of human beings (and the environment) functioning at their best and worst. Simply stated, the opportunities that emergency personnel have to laugh at things that are basically frightening or sad protects their mental health. One need only spend a short period of time with a group of emergency caregivers to discover they possess the capacity to use humor as a coping strategy in dealing with their occupational duties. Similar to police, firefighters or soldiers, emergency care providers use humor to deal with a wide range of difficult emotional, cognitive, and physical events.

How is it that emergency personnel come to use GaSBag humor? How do they describe it as helpful? In a qualitative investigation of paramedics (Rosenberg, 1989), these subjects richly portrayed their use of humor within the Emergency Medical Service (EMS) environment. The attributes which best describe EMS humor are its frequent use in dealing with stressful situations, joke content that is often morbid or sick, and its wide use and support in the EMS environment. As one paramedic eloquently stated, "Humor is built into the fabric of the [EMS] environment and people who work in crisis situations" (p. 170).

There is an EMS humor subculture among emergency personnel. Paramedics have alluded to this subculture in the following comments:

As you get to know more EMS people, a pattern of humor comes out that you plug into. The more you are surrounded by those people [ER nurses, MDs], the more you pick up that personality. It becomes easier to make a joke and see the lighter side of things-you can more easily adapt to a situation. You learn that it is acceptable to joke about sick things. During the training experience, by riding with other paramedics, humor is handed on like a trait, it's learned (Rosenberg, 1991, p. 199).

Paramedics readily acknowledge the presence and use of GaSBag humor with other emergency care providers. Experienced paramedics seem to use GaSBag humor more than newly trained paramedics and much more than individuals not exposed to emergency health care. This tells us something very important about the use of humor as a flexible stress buffer; depending on the cause of tension, humor can be molded to fit the situation. The content of what one experiences and must deal with provides the material for the type of humor individuals express. Emergency caregivers may find an immediate outlet through GaSBag humor from their steady exposure to illness, trauma, death, and social crises they encounter.

The sensitive nature of GaSBag humor makes it imperative to discuss where and with whom this type of humor is appropriately used. Robinson (1991) addresses this issue by asking whose needs are being met when gallows humor is used. She describes gallows humor as relieving the tensions of the health professional and, although ". . . it may seem inappropriate to others, [it] provides a balance for the individual involved" (p. 80). Paramedics emphasize that the GaSbag humor used with other emergency personnel is not readily shared with family and friends. It is difficult to share humor which is based on experiences the listener has not had. This lack of understanding of the emergency care experience results in a ". . . corresponding loss of empathy and appreciation for the joke and its context" (Rosenberg, 1991, p. 199). This is certainly compounded by the fact that the humor itself is often sick or morbid. As one paramedic stated, "Other people would not appreciate it or get the point; they would think you were sick" (p. 199). Thus, the use of GaSBag humor is context-specific and produced spontaneously within the situation. One needs to participate in the experience from the point of view of the caregiver in order to "get the joke."

An important implication of the above is that the benefits of GaSBag humor are linked to its production within the immediate emergency care environment. The health care provider must be able to make spontaneous, situationally relevant jokes when under stress. It is not just the capacity to appreciate this humor but the ability to produce it which contributes to stress reduction. Other researchers have found this to be an important factor in both laboratory and real-life conditions (Bizi, Keinan, & Beit-Hallahmi, 1988; Fay, 1983; Martin & Lefcourt, 1983). In short, the use of GaSBag humor among emergency care providers is situational, produced spontaneously and experiential in nature.

Experienced paramedics are quite articulate about the purposes of GaSBag humor among emergency personnel:

> Humor allows you to forget, to not obsess about the last [case], to prepare for the next [case]. Humor returns you to a normal frame of mind. It puts the situation in a different perspective to change your way of thinking [in order] to decrease the seriousness of the situation. Humor allows you to go on to the next [case] and be effective; it may be used to get past a tragic event. Humor gives you a mental break (Rosenberg, 1991, p. 200).

45

These statements focus on the coping/defense mechanism functions of GaSBag humor. Collectively, these functions provide emotional and cognitive refocusing--the ability to momentarily transcend a situation and improve one's perspective. This is humor used as Freud (1959), Mindess (1971), and others have conceptualized it: to produce a psychologically liberating effect. What emergency personnel tend to gain from engaging in sick or black humor is a distancing from both a critical situation and their own emotions, objectivity, and continuing mastery over themselves and the environment. Emergency care providers need a means to reframe the pain and depression inherent in what they encounter. Humor allows an immediate deflection of the emotional impact of serious events to enable continuing competent performance.

Can humor ever be overused in the emergency care setting? There is general agreement that humor has its limits. Frequently cited circumstances of negative humor use are when:

A. It is used inappropriately or insensitively without regard to the situation, timing or individuals present,
B. It becomes annoying or tiresome,
C. It interferes with job performance, or,
D. There is an overreliance on humor use for stress relief to the exclusion of other coping strategies (Rosenberg, 1991, p. 201).

Problems of an intrapersonal or interpersonal nature are likely to arise when humor of any type is overused or misused. Humor use is generally a shared, social experience, affecting the listener either positively or negatively. Inappropriate use of GaSBag humor is apt to rankle and may even offend coworkers. Intrapersonally, the singular use of GaSBag humor, to the exclusion of other coping strategies, could delay or deny any real introspection of a problem or sensitive issue.

The discussion in this chapter focuses on the use of a very specific brand of humor among the providers of emergency health care. It is important to note that emergency personnel also find the use of a more general, comforting humor with patients to be indispensable. Appropriate humor use helps to relax patients and put them at ease. It also helps to "break the ice" with individuals who must be administered to promptly and in often highly stressful situations. Emergency personnel are quick to point out, however, that the humor shared with patients is very different from that used among coworkers. This differentiation underscores the distinctive purposes of humor for different individuals in what may seem to be the same stressful situation.

Conclusion

Humor is a readily accessible coping strategy for almost all individuals, supporting a healthy aspect of their emotional functioning. We are socialized to use humor purposefully to relieve tension in a number of situations (as a social icebreaker, or to defuse embarrassing moments). The "generic" humor use in daily life naturally carries over to the workplace. Thus, the use of humor as a coping strategy is not the exclusive domain of emergency personnel. The humor used by the providers of emergency care is unique because of the emergency care experience itself. Most people just don't undergo the physical, emotional, and existential bombardment that emergency personnel do in their occupational lives. With clinical experience, the emergency care provider's use of humor molds to the situational demands of the job and the surrounding EMS milieu.

There is a goodness of fit between how the provision of care induces stress in the emergency care environment and how the use of humor intervenes in that process. Emergency personnel experience a wide spectrum of serious events: trauma, life-threatening illness, chaotic emotional situations — often all at the same time. There is no time to emotionally prepare for these events, and little time to ventilate afterwards or "decompress." The spontaneous way in which humor can be produced in almost any situation, and its instantaneous stress-reducing effects are well suited to the emergency care experience.

Bibliography

Bizi, S., Keinan, G., & Beit-Hallahmi, B. (1988). Humor and coping with stress: A test under real-life conditions. *Personality and Individual Differences*, 9, 951-956.

Burkle, F. M. (1983). Coping with stress under conditions of disaster and refugee care. *Military Medicine*, 148, 800-803.

Chaplin, C. (1966). *My autobiography*. New York: Pocket.

Cox, J. D. (1980). Occupational stress and individual strain: A social-psychological study of emergency medical personnel. Dissertation Abstracts International, 41, 2768.

Fay, R. J. (1983). The defensive role of humor in the management of stress. Dissertation Abstracts International, 44, 1028.

Feinberg, L. (1978). *The secret of humor*. Amsterdam: Rodopi.

Frankl, V. (1959). *Man's search for meaning*. New York: Pocket.

Freud, S. (1959). *Jokes and their relation to the unconscious* (J. Strachey, Trans. and Ed.). New York: Norton.

Hammer, J. S., Mathews, J. J., Lyons, J. S., & Johnson, N. J. (1986). Occupational stress within the paramedic profession: An initial report of stress levels compared to hospital employees. *Annals of Emergency Medicine*, 15, 536-539.

Henderson, G. (1984, October). Physician burnout. *Hospital Physician*, 8-9.

Hutchinson, S. (1987). Self-care and job stress. *Image-The Journal of Nursing Scholarship*, 19, 192-196.

Keller, K. L. (1990). The management of stress and prevention of burnout in emergency nurses. *Journal of Emergency Nursing*, 16, 90-95.

Keller, K. L., & Koenig, W. J. (1989). Management of stress and prevention of burnout in emergency physicians. *Annals of Emergency Medicine*, 18, 42-47.

Kuhlman, T. L. (1988). Gallows humor for a scaffold setting: Managing aggressive patients on a maximum-security forensic unit. *Hospital and Community Psychiatry*, 39, 1085-1090.

Kushner, H. S. (1981). *When bad things happen to good people.* New York: Schocken.

Lattanzi, M. E. (1984). Professional stress: Adaptation, coping, and meaning. *Family Therapy Collections*, 8, 95-106.

Leiber, D. B. (1986). Laughter and humor in critical care. *Dimensions in Critical Care Nursing*, 5, 162-170.

Lipson, J., & Koehler, S. (1986). The psychiatric emergency room: Staff subculture. *Issues in Mental Health Nursing*, 8, 237-246.

Martin, R. A., & Lefcourt, H. M. (1983). Sense of humor as a moderator of the relation between stressors and mood. *Journal of Personality and Social Psychology*, 45, 1313-1324.

Mason, J. H. (1982). Stress in paramedics. Dissertation Abstracts International, 43, 1428.

Metcalf, C. W. (1987). Humor, life, and death. *Oncological Nursing Forum*, 14, 19-21.

Mindess, H. (1971). *Laughter and liberation.* Los Angeles: Nash.

Mindess, H., Miller, C., Turek, J., Bender, A., & Corbin, S. (1985). *The Antioch humor test: Making sense of humor.* New York: Avon.

Morreall, J. (1984). *Taking laughter seriously.* Albany: State University of New York Press.

Palmer, E. C. (1983). A note about paramedics' strategies for dealing with death and dying. *Journal of Occupational Psychology*, 56, 83-86.

Robinson, V. (1991). *Humor and the health professions*, 2nd edition. Thorofare, NJ: Slack.

Rosen, P., & Honigman, B. (1988). Life and death. In P. Rosen, F. J. Baker, R. M. Barkin, G. R. Braen, R. H. Dailey, & R. C. Levy (Eds.), *Emergency medicine: Concepts and clinical practice.* St. Louis: Mosby.

Rosenberg, L. (1991). A qualitative investigation of the use of humor by emergency personnel as a strategy for coping with stress. *Journal of Emergency Nursing*, 17,

197-203.

Rosenberg, L. (1989). An Exploratory Investigation of the Use of Humor as a Coping Strategy for Dealing with Stress Among Paramedics. Unpublished doctoral dissertation.

Strauss, A., & Glaser, B. (1970). Awareness of dying. In B. Schoenberg, et al. (Eds.) *Loss and grief.* New York: Columbia University Press.

Thorson, J. A. (1985). A funny thing happened on the way to the morgue: Some thoughts on humor and death, and a taxonomy of the humor associated with death. *Omaha Death Studies*, 9, 201-216.

Weinrich, S., Hardin, S. B., & Johnson, M. (1990). Nurses respond to Hurricane Hugo victims' disaster stress. *Archives of Psychiatric Nursing*, 4, 195-205.

Zeirke, J. (1988, February). A funny thing happened on the way to the call. *Emergency*, 62.

Ziv, A. (1984). *Personality and sense of humor.* New York: Springer.

CHAPTER V

HUMOR-AN EDUCATIONAL STRATEGY

by
Kathleen S. Cannella, RN, CS, MN, MS, PhD
Sandra Missroon, EdD, MSN, RN
and
Margaret P. Opitz, EdD, MSN, RN

Throughout their careers, nurses recognize education as an essential component of effective practice. Education is also essential to the well-being of nurses and their clients. Broadly defined, nursing education encompasses basic, graduate, and doctoral academic programs, continuing education, and staff development. The inclusion of humor in nursing education leads to the inclusion of humor in the education of patients, families, and communities (i.e., clients).

Detailed in each section of this chapter are the relevant factors that educators need to know to use humor as an educational strategy, ranging from the benefits and deterrents of humor to considerations for the educator, environment, and learner. Concepts and processes are supported with research. Appropriate educational settings for using humor include academic programs, continuing education and staff development workshops and programs, and even client education sessions and programs.

A review of various definitions of humor, the amount of literature focused on humor, the development of theories devoted to humor, and the use of humor in the health sciences-especially nursing-illustrates the importance and relevance of humor to people in general and nursing in particular. This review should facilitate understanding the benefits of humor and its application in educational endeavors.

Definitions of Humor

Humor is a complex phenomenon that has been difficult to define. There is no universally accepted definition of humor (Robinson, 1991). Humor has often been defined in relation to laughter. For instance, in her pioneering chapter on humor, Robinson (1970) defined humor as "... that which produces laughter" (p. 132). Although the words humor and laughter are often used as descriptors for each other, they are

51

different. Laughter is a behavior that occurs for a variety of reasons, many of which-such as nervousness or laughing gas are not related to humor. Expanding on her earlier definition, Robinson (1977) defined humor as "... any communication which is perceived by any of the interacting parties as humorous and leads to laughing, smiling or a feeling of amusement" (p. 10). Some define humor as a cognitive, as well as an emotional, process (McGhee, 1979; Wandersee, 1982); others have incorporated the idea of intentionality in their definition of humor (Long & Graesser, 1988). Still others have defined their own humor-related terms, such as humor-eliciting stimuli, using published definitions of humor (Wyer & Collins, 1992).

Although definitions of humor continue to evolve, a general consensus has yet to be reached. While the lack of consensus helps prevent premature closure of ideas during these still early stages of work, it also means that readers must be careful to note the definition of humor used by various authors. For instance, the reader needs to ask whether humor was defined as a stimulus or a response. And, whether humor was defined as a stimulus or a response, must it be associated with a stimulus intended to be or result in humor (the notion of intentionality)? For the purposes of this chapter, Robinson's (1977) definition of humor will be used.

Perspectives on the Scholarly Literature on Humor

Consideration of the body of literature on a particular topic contributes to a holistic perspective. The quantity of published literature on a particular topic reflects the perceived relevance and importance of that topic to a discipline at that time. Searching relevant indexes has been one way to identify literature on particular topics. The computerization of these indexes has greatly facilitated such searches in recent years.

Computer searches of relevant databases were used to assess the literature focusing on humor. Five databases were searched. Four databases were accessed through SilverPlatter 3.11: CINAHL® (1982 to August 1994), MEDLINE EXPRESS® (1982 to October 1994), PsycLIT (1974 to June 1994), and ERIC (1982 to June 1994), and one database, Dissertation Abstracts Ondisc (1861 to September 1994) was accessed using ProQuest version 4.10. Using the key words "humor or wit" and "nurse or nursing" as text words, 587 citations were identified. The CINAHL® and Medline databases contained the most citations, 243 and 258, respectively. The remaining databases, ERIC, PsychLIT, and Dissertation Abstracts International (DAI), contained 23, 5, and 58 citations, respectively. Using the above key words as subject headings whenever possible, suggesting that those key words are a major focus of the citations identified, 141 citations were identified: 43 from CINAHL®, 92 from Medline, 4 from PsycLIT, and 2 from ERIC.

Humor has been even less a focus of nursing education than of nursing in general. This is evidenced by the relative lack of published literature in this area. Searching the same five databases, only 108 citations were identified using the text words "humor or wit," "nurse or nursing," and "education," and 64 citations were identified using the text words "humor or wit" and "nursing education." When these key words were used as descriptors rather than as text words, 42 citations were identified.

An examination of the nature of the content related to humor in these publications added further insights into the perceived relevance and importance of humor to the discipline of nursing. There has been a shift in the content, as well as the amount, of published literature in nursing related to humor. Presentations of humorous materials, themselves, are no longer the sole form of content. Increasing numbers of scholarly discussions and research focusing on humor in nursing have been reported.

Reports of research studies comprise part of this literature. One measure of research on humor is the number of doctoral dissertations. The DAI database was reexamined using the key words "humor or wit" as text words. From January 1861 through December 1981, a 121-year period, 622 citations were identified. Over the next 7 years, through December 1987, 549 citations were identified. During the next 6 years, through December 1992, 551 citations were identified, while 234 citations were identified over the past year and a half, from January 1993 through June 1994.

Information regarding humor-focused literature, including research literature, can also be obtained from literature reviews. Goldstein and McGhee (1972) systematically reviewed all articles written in English addressing psychological theory and research on humor published in the 1900s; they located only 376 articles. At that time, the major theoretical base used for humor research remained Jokes and Their Relation to the Unconscious by Sigmund Freud. Originally published in 1905, an English translation of this work was published in 1960. McGhee (1989) described the difficulty Goldstein and he had in finding potential contributors for their 1972 book, The Psychology of Humor. Since the early 1970s, the amount of research on humor has grown steadily. The importance of humor as a legitimate topic for research was evidenced by the appearance of conferences, books, and organizations devoted to humor (McGhee, 1989). In fact, the number of research articles increased so much that the publication of a new humor journal, the International Journal of Humor Research, began in 1988.

The increasing number of publications focusing on humor supports its vital place in nursing, in both education and practice settings. Robinson (1991) stated that there had been a major change in the acceptance, recognition, and use of humor since the publication of her first book in 1977. And yet, there remains relatively little emphasis on humor in both nursing education and practice settings. Perhaps this reflects a lack of perceived value of humor in professional practice and education. Asking if there is a value to humor interventions within the health care system, Ruxton and Hester (1987) asserted that humor is not found in the indices of textbooks that are required reading for health professionals, and is only briefly mentioned in literature on coping. Further efforts to describe, explain, and publicize the value of humor to nursing education and practice are needed to enhance its incorporation in nursing education and practice settings.

Historical Perspectives on Humor

Sigmund Freud, the founder of psychoanalysis, was one of the earliest social scientists to theorize about humor. How delightfully appropriate, when Freud is both a noun and a name meaning *joy* in German. In the 1960 translation of his 1905 book, Freud asserted that, "Joking activity should not, after all, be described as pointless or aimless, since it has the unmistakable aim of evoking pleasure in its hearers" (p. 95). Freud's theory has been a major framework used to study humor. The theories of Freud and others have been categorized as arousal theories; e.g., theories postulating tension relief as the function of humor and laughter (Lefcourt & Martin, 1986).

In contrast, incongruity and incongruity-resolution theorists have postulated that humor results from sudden and surprising shifts in cognitive processing, while superiority theorists have proposed that humor results from the feelings of superiority associated with the disparagement of others or oneself (Lefcourt & Martin, 1986). Lefcourt and Martin (1986) asserted that these theoretical views are more complementary than contradictory, and that their combination provides a more comprehensive theoretical foundation for understanding humor.

Interest and research in the area of humor increased during the 1970s and 1980s. Chapman and Foot's (1976) edited book described current thinking and research in the area of humor and laughter. McGhee, either alone or with colleagues, published several important works during this period: a book on the origin and development of humor (1979), a two-volume edited handbook of humor research (1983), and an edited book focusing on humor and aging (1986). Lefcourt and Martin (1986) published a book describing their program of studies on the relation of humor to stress.

For the most part, humor has not been considered particularly relevant to the educational and work experiences of nurses in this country. In its early days, nursing education focused on apprenticeship in hospital diploma programs. Nurses worked long hours for low pay. Duties of staff nurses ranged from direct patient care to supportive services, such as mopping the floors and preparing food. In these kinds of atmospheres, psychosocial concepts such as humor received little or no attention.

Robinson (1970) decried the lack of humor in nursing education and nursing practice. She emphasized that humor has an " . . . important and unexploited place in nursing" (p. 129). Robinson (1970) was also the first to encourage the use of humor in nursing education. She recommended humor because it can enhance learning, establish warmth, reduce stress, and release anger. However, she recognized that faculty often treat nursing as too serious a business. She encouraged nursing faculty to cultivate the planned use of humor in their lectures and make use of situational humor in the classroom.

Despite this and other evidence on the use of humor, the health professions, including nursing, largely ignored its use until the publication of Norman Cousins' book, Anatomy of an Illness (1979). This book increased awareness of the value of humor and laughter. Cousins cited humor as one coping mechanism that helped him recover from a collagen disease, ankylosing spondylitis, in 1964. Twenty years later, he again described the important role humor played in recovering from heart disease in The Healing Heart (1983). In each instance, humor and laughter were described as important to the treatment process. Cousins' two books are unique in their documentation of how humor played a significant role in a person's recovery process from two distinct illnesses. Using programmed sessions of laughter as one of several therapeutic approaches, Cousins believed his humor strategy was an important part of the healing process. Cousins' books publicized the use of humor as an important part of his therapy, promoting the credibility of humor as a therapeutic intervention and a topic of research.

Cousins' beliefs have been supported by the work of Fry (1977, 1986, 1992), a Stanford University psychiatrist who has committed his life to studying the physiological benefits of laughter. He has described cardiovascular, respiratory, endocrine, and neurological effects of laughter, concluding that laughter is good exercise, similar to stationary jogging.

Robinson's Humor and the Health Professions was first published in 1977. This book provided an overview of theories and research, issues and controversies in the field of humor; descriptions of current uses of humor in health settings and by health professionals; and beginning guidelines for cultivating the use of humor.

During the early and mid 1980s, more nurses discussed the importance of humor in nursing. Herth (1984) described her use of humor as a nursing intervention, including her assessments of patients' receptivity to humor with the "funny bone history" she developed and several cases in which humor was an effective intervention. In her 1985 book, Snyder discussed humor as an independent nursing intervention, including basic concepts, humorous techniques, and measurement of their effectiveness. Moses and Friedman (1986) discussed using humor in evaluating nursing students' laboratory performance.

Contemporary Nursing Perspectives on Humor

Humor is a common, yet complex and controversial phenomenon (Robinson, 1991). Much of the recent work devoted to humor exemplifies this. Recent work in nursing can be viewed as focusing on humor in relation to the nursing discipline, nursing practice, and nursing education. Ferguson and Campinha-Bacote (1989) examined the concept of humor in relation to nursing practice using concept analysis. They delineated four defining attributes of humor: tension reducer, form of therapeutic communication, behavioral response, and learning enhancer. They demonstrated these attributes using five different types of constructed case reports. They also identified antecedents and consequences of humor, and defined the empirical referents of humor, visual and vocal cues that indicate the occurrence of humor. They identified two priorities whose accomplishment would foster progress in theory construction related to the use of humor in nursing practice. First, increased research needs to be conducted on the use of humor in all areas of nursing practice, focusing on the cultural and spiritual as well as the psychodynamic, physiological, and sociological aspects of humor. And second, humor needs to be examined in relation to other concepts, such as the earlier work of Warner (1984) comparing the relationships between humor and self-disclosure.

Other authors have focused on laughter, one aspect of humor (Davidhizar & Bowen, 1992; Dugan, 1989). Dugan (1989) emphasized the importance of laughter and tears in managing personal and professional stress. Davidhizar and Bowen (1992) also focused on laughter, describing its assessment and benefits, as well as the causes and dynamics of inappropriate laughter.

The recognition of humor as a basic human need and the importance of this need have also been emphasized (Yura & Walsh, 1988; Yura-Petro, 1991). Yura-Petro (1991) suggested several researchable questions focused on humor. She also identified three new nursing diagnoses related to humor. In two phenomenological studies, Parse synthesized common elements emerging from descriptive expressions of the lived experience of laughter (1993b) and laughter and health together (1994) in persons over 65 years old. Rose (1990) identified using humor as one of nine essential themes characterizing the way women in a phenomenological study experienced inner strength, defined as psychological well-being or mental health.

Applications to Nursing Practice

Recent literature has focused on humor as an intervention. Recently, second editions of Robinson's (1991) book, Humor and the Health Professions, and Snyder's (1992) book, Independent Nursing Interventions were published. Buxman (1991b) described the benefits of "humor rooms" to settings, and identified strategies to design and gain support for humor rooms. In a progress report on their Humor Intervention Project, Ruxton and Hester (1987) described their assessment of humor, suggested strategies for adding humor to work, home, and relationships, and identified positive effects of humor interventions.

The uses of humor with particular client populations have also been discussed and studied. Like Parse (1994), Simon (1988a, 1988b, 1990) and Tennant (1990) focused on the relation of humor to the well-being of older adults. Simon studied humor in relation to perceived health, life satisfaction, and morale, while Tennant studied the impact of a humor program on well-being. Herth (1993) studied older adults' definition, regard, and use of humor. Both Bellert (1989) and Simon (1989) discussed the use of humor as a therapeutic approach in oncology nursing. Bellert addressed the role of humor from the perspective of the nursing process, and included a list of questions used in assessing humor. Both authors identified a variety of humor interventions. Gaberson (1991) studied the use of humorous distraction on preoperative anxiety, and Parfitt (1990) studied the effectiveness of humorous preoperative teaching on recall of postoperative exercise routines.

Several nurses discussed the use of humorous interventions in different populations with some form of mental illness. Buxman (1991a) discussed the chronically mentally ill, Sumners (1988) focused on those recovering from addiction, and both Sullivan and Deane (1988) and Lapierre and Padgett (1991) focused on geropsychiatric patients. Pasquali (1990) discussed humor and how it could be incorporated into psychotherapeutic interventions. As an example, she described a humor program she developed for primarily chronically mentally ill clients in a psychiatric day treatment center.

The use of humor among nurses themselves has been encouraged. Simon (1989) supported the use of humor as a stress management strategy for oncology nurses. White and Howse's (1993) survey of nursing staff revealed that nurses believed that humor might reduce the stress associated with some, but not all, work situations. Sumners (1990) studied the professional nurses' attitudes toward humor in personal and profes-sional settings. Rodgers (1988) discussed the value of humor and laughter for nurse executives. Describing stressful conditions under which nurses work, Eccles (1990) advocated that nurses use humor to relieve stress, and described resultant benefits. Schaefer and Peterson (1992) studied the coping strategies of critical care and noncritical care staff nurses, and recommended a sense of humor among other stress management strategies.

Applications to Nursing Education

The authors of this chapter believe that humor in educational settings typically remains minimal. Robinson (1991) declared that there has been little attempt to deliberately use humor in the education of professionals. Yet, it has been increasingly recognized in the literature that humor is a most effective teaching strategy. Ziv (1988) said that research on humor in education is relatively new. While many authors have praised the value of humor as an educational strategy in teaching, few research projects have tested this empirically. Noting an absence of humor-related content in teacher training, Ziv reviewed 14 well-known educational psychology textbooks, finding none had a reference to humor.

Like their colleagues in the field of education, many nurse educators have described the usefulness of humor in educational endeavors. The use of humor in nursing education has markedly increased during the past 5 years in both academic and continuing nursing education programs. Rosenberg (1989) focused on the relevance and importance of humor to nursing education in addition to nursing practice. In contrast to Watson and Emerson's (1988) focus on humor as content and intervention with sophomore nursing students, Warner (1991) studied senior nursing students' use of humor as a coping response. Pease (1991) described her use of cartoons and cartoon-writing exercises as teaching/learning strategies in a BSN completion program. Parkin (1989) described the stressfulness of the nursing student experience, the benefits of humor as a teaching strategy, and educators' hesitancies in deliberately using humor in educational settings.

Leidy (1992) and Wright (1993) advocated the incorporation of humor and laughter into learning experiences such as the required review of certain information periodically to reduce stress and burnout among nursing staff. Leidy also said that reductions in stress and burnout may decrease absenteeism, enhance productivity, and reduce turnover. Mooney (1993) used humor to educate nurses how to teach psychomotor skills using performance checklists. Wooten (1992) studied the effects of a humor workshop on nurse burnout. Nurses who took this workshop, as compared with nurses working nearby at a small community hospital who had not taken this workshop, experienced increased humor appreciation.

The educational benefits of humor have not received much attention, although the notion that humor is beneficial has gained some notoriety in both the popular and professional literature. Humor's appeal to the health professions has been traced to Norman Cousins (1976), who related how laughter played a major role in his recovery from a serious collagen disease. These beneficial effects can be categorized in terms of health, the learner, the learning environment, and the teacher. While these beneficial effects are considerable, deterrents to using humor as an educational strategy have lessened its use.

The Effect of Humor on Health

The health-promoting effects of laughter evoked by humorous material have been well publicized in the works of Cousins (1979, 1983), Fry (1977, 1986, 1992), Haig (1986), and Simonton, Simonton, and Creighton (1978), among others. These effects include improved physical functioning (increased arterial and venous circulation with reduced venous stasis, increased ventilation and clearing of mucus, increased tissue oxygenation and nutrition, improved immune system functioning, increased muscle conditioning followed by muscle relaxation), and improved psychosocial functioning (increased alertness and memory, enhanced perspective and insight, improved healing of emotional wounds, increased interpersonal responsiveness, and increased recognition and gratitude for positive life experiences) (Fry, 1986, 1992; Haig, 1986; Simonton, Simonton, & Creighton, 1978). Slowly, nurses are beginning to recognize the importance of including humor as part of their professional practice. Nurses should keep in mind that, when they choose to use humor as an intervention, it should be for therapeutic reasons. The use of humor can be inappropriate if it results in sarcastic jokes and laughter made at the expense of others. Inappropriate humor can result in hurt feelings, anxiety, hostility, and embarrassment.

Recent literature reflects an increasing emphasis on the effect of humor as a therapeutic intervention in clinical settings, with studies yielding mostly positive findings (Gaberson, 1991; Leiber, 1986; Napora, 1984; Parfitt, 1990; Raber, 1987; Simon, 1988a,b,c; Smith, 1986; and Tennant, 1990). Simon's (1988a) research regarding the use of humor (situational and coping) suggested that humor may influence the older adult's perception of perceived health, life satisfaction and morale, and may help people age successfully. Findings from these studies suggested that laughter and humor decrease agitation and loneliness, and increase feelings of well-being in older adults. Humor has been found to offer many physiological and psychological benefits which nurses need to consider in helping clients. Smith (1986) found humor to be effective in helping children cope with mild or moderate pain, although other researchers such as Gaberson (1991) and Parfitt (1990) found that humor was not effective as a preoperative teaching strategy. Their findings lend support to the need for subsequent studies to further investigate the effects of humor, as in learning recall and retention of knowledge by clients in health care settings.

Another important dimension in humor education is teaching nurses to teach clients

59

themselves how to use humor as an intervention to cope with stressful or painful situations and enhance health and wellness. Nurses can encourage clients to cultivate their sense of humor, teaching them the importance and relevance of humor in their everyday lives. Humor carts and rooms further facilitate clients' use of humor by providing humorous stimuli. Humorous greeting cards also exemplify the value of humor in coping with the tension of hospitalization and illness.

Nurses can also learn to use humor as a strategy to cope with stressful situations encountered in their nursing practice. Working in high stress areas such as operating rooms, delivery rooms, and emergency departments, nursing personnel frequently deal with frightened and perhaps angry patients, anxious relatives, and tense physicians and nursing colleagues. Stressors also include severe time constraints, long hours, changing shifts, and lack of sleep. Thus, humor and laughter have been increasingly presented in the nursing literature as facilitating effective management in health care settings. Dugan (1989) advocated laughter and tears as natural resources for managing personal and professional stress. He suggested that the practical and appropriate integration of laughter and tears into nursing care could increase work satisfaction and foster emotional healing.

The Effect of Humor on the Learner

It is generally accepted that nursing education is stressful for the student not only because of learner anxiety associated with testing, grades, and deadlines, but also because of the intensity of the clinical laboratory experiences. These clinical experiences often require late night preparation of nursing care plans and mountains of paperwork. In addition, in clinical settings, students care for clients who are often encountering life-threatening health problems and disruptions in individual and family situations. In this context, learners experience additional demands, leading to symptoms of the stress response in their attempt to cope with the resultant anxiety. Anxiety connected with the learning process has been described as causing a multiplicity of stress-related symptoms including somatic complaints, decreased attention span, selective listening, narrowed perception, and impaired judgment.

In the clinical setting, nurses encounter stressors from a variety of sources, including organizational factors, client conditions, and family and/or significant other responses. Working in high acuity areas, where nurses are responsible for managing unstable client populations, is a frequent source of stress for professionals. Added to the stress associated with caring for acutely ill clients is the stress that may occur in encounters with anxious family members and tense physicians. Finally, today's bottom-line organizational climate has added a new nuance to the multiplicity of variables that confront the professional practitioner and contribute to symptoms of the stress response.

Used appropriately, humor can be a valuable therapeutic tool useful in releasing emotional tension, resolving conflicts, creating bonding among individuals, and establishing a mental approach for constructive problem-solving. Robinson (1991) asserted that humor, used appropriately as a coping strategy, decreases fear, establishes trust, reassures, relieves stress and tension, and even provides an acceptable outlet for aggression. Other authors have contended that humor used as a coping strategy helps students relieve anxiety, stress, and tension, and release hostility and anger (Hutchings, 1987; Parkin, 1989). Humor can offer a new perspective on an event by providing a temporary relief from the rules and restrictions common to educational situations. Parkin (1989) suggested that humor could be used to alleviate anxiety connected with achievement in the learning process.

The use of humor during teaching processes affects the stress surrounding learning experiences, helping allay tensions and fears, and thus enhancing learning. Incorporating humor into an educational session can also enhance communication by breaking down barriers, by making people feel good and closer to one another. Establishing humor in the learning environment allows for a non-threatening atmosphere, promoting expression and the exchange of ideas among learners. Thus, individuals ask questions they may otherwise not ask, and hear instructions they may otherwise be too anxious to hear. Used in a group, shared laughter indicates a common perception. It provides an instantaneous link between virtual strangers, enhancing group cohesiveness and problem-solving abilities. The risk of self-disclosure is feared less and a sense of belonging and control ensues.

When humor is an integral part of the teaching-learning process, a caring and trusting environment is created. In this environment, learners have permission not to be perfect and mistakes are tolerated, directly fostering student participation in the learning process. In this accepting and caring milieu, there is freedom to explore and try new options, thus leading to enhanced critical thinking skills.

The Effect of Humor on the Learning Environment

Humor in education sets the tone for a caring environment that promotes openness and facilitates communication. McGhee (1979) said that creating a humorous atmosphere probably improves the mood and willingness of students to express original ideas. Students are then more willing to shift patterns of thinking, generate creative solutions to problems, perceive double meanings, understand analogies, and examine paradoxes. Flexible and creative ways of thinking emerge; the corollary benefits are critical thinking and independent problem-solving.

61

Humor enhances the learning process by promoting an environment conducive to open discussion. Laughter can help students deal with the anxiety and stress associated with the learning process. Parkin (1989) asserts that employing humor strategies in the classroom setting might serve as a retention mechanism, eliminating students' self-image trauma. If students come with a sense of humor, then using humor as a teaching strategy may further reinforce the idea that the learning environment is friendly. From a sociological standpoint, humor reduces social distance and establishes rapport between people (McGhee, 1979). Groups of students laughing together form an immediate bond or cohesiveness within the group, promoting solidarity and establishing relationships, thus stimulating learners to participate in the learning process.

Humor as a Characteristic of Effective Teachers

Teachers who purposefully and appropriately use humor in education view it as a valuable teaching strategy. Robinson (1991) characterized a teacher who uses humor as ". . . a facilitator of learning, a warm, caring person who is open" (p. 116). Rogers (1969) viewed humor as an essential quality of teachers. Appropriate use of humor by teachers promotes the teacher-student relationship and establishes an environment conducive to learning by relieving tension and enhancing communication.

Parkin (1989) identified the stress-reducing benefits of humor as worthwhile not only in reducing students' stress associated with the learning process, but also in enhancing instructors' performance. Research by Yasko (1983) and Jenkins and Ostchega (1986) suggested a positive relationship between perceived level of stress and burnout. Using humor in creative educational strategies, educators may diminish burnout and also enhance job satisfaction and performance.

A survey of evaluations from 113 nursing continuing education programs involving 2,877 participants and 41 different faculty members provided further support for the positive effects of humor on instructors' performance (Eason & Corbett, 1994). Participants' written comments regarding preferred characteristics of continuing education faculty were reviewed, resulting in the identification of 130 attributes considered desirable. Sense of humor was one of 20 attributes identified most frequently.

Interestingly, while professionals' opinions of humor have been positive, the mixed findings from studies of the effectiveness of using humor in teaching provide a curious contradiction in the literature. Bryant and Zillmann (1989) identified most claims for success in teaching as resulting from studies focusing on elementary and secondary teachers. In contrast, they reported that most negative or insignificant findings came from studies of college students.

Deterrents to Using Humor in Education

There are several deterrents to the effective use of humor in educational endeavors. These include the misuse or nonproductive use of humor, the lack of appreciation of the relevance of humor to education, the lack of time to develop humor as a teaching strategy, and discouragement of creativity in the teaching process.

The value of unrelated humor in the classroom is a subject of debate in the literature with differing viewpoints about its effect in the educational experience. While it might be argued that the use of unrelated humor will make the listener more attentive in general, this issue has not been directly evaluated in college-age students. Other scholars argue that unrelated humor distracts the student from course content, thereby making it less likely for material to be noted and learned in the first place. According to this analysis, directly related humor might be expected to facilitate learning if it served to direct the student to the material that was to be learned. Robinson (1991) noted that, "Unrelated or irrelevant humor by the teacher detracts from the student-teacher rapport and has detrimental effects on the acquisition of information" (p. 114). According to Robinson, the use of related humor, however, may lead to superior retention of content and also enhanced student-instructor relationships. Support for the use of unrelated humor is engendered by those who feel that, although unrelated humor may not contribute to the educational experience, any use of humor-whether related or unrelated-enhances student-instructor relations, thus increasing student learning (Gorham & Christophel, 1990).

Another deterrent to using humor in education may be the lack of appreciation of the relevance of humor to education. Educators may feel that they take the risk of appearing fallible, imperfect, and human if they display their sense of humor. Perhaps another reason for educators' lack of attention to humor is the belief that one must display a serious demeanor while teaching so as to convey a professional image. This lack of humor in educational sessions may impart an image of detachment to the student who, in turn, may interpret this detached and serious manner as a way of maintaining professional credibility when relating to patients.

Another reason for inattentiveness to humor as an instructional strategy is the significant amount of time required to incorporate meaningful humor into the educational event. While there is a proliferation of resources available to educators in most content areas, humorous strategies are rare, necessitating time-consuming preparation and creativity by educators in finding the right humorous message or creating the humorous situation that will effectively convey the educational message. For instance, Pasquali (1990) found that it took 4 weeks to identify appropriate humor for a humor intervention program for psychiatric day treatment clients.

Nurse educators in all settings can be encouraged to use humor as an effective instructional strategy because of the commonalities experienced by nurses in their professional role development. The common language and culture, inherent in the nursing profession can ease the expression and reception of humorous strategies.

Humor as Content in Nursing Education

The idea of humor as content to be studied and learned has received little attention in nursing education. Historically, nursing education has been based on the medical model, which resulted in curricula emphasizing medical diagnoses and treatments and related dependent nursing activities. More recently, nursing education has shifted to a conceptual approach that focuses on a nursing process model. This approach promotes the inclusion and emphasis of concepts relevant to nursing — such as humor — in nursing curricula. Such concepts would not have been deemed relevant to nursing curricula based on the medical model.

Robinson (1970) was the first to describe humor as a nursing intervention. She presented a case example in which humor was used as an intervention in the nursing care of an elderly woman who had become depressed, lethargic, and unwilling to participate in her own care following major surgery. The patient responded well to the consistent use of humor as an intervention in her nursing care, and traditional psychiatric nursing approaches to depressed patients were not needed (Robinson, 1970). Robinson (1977, 1978, 1991) has continued to advocate the use of humor as a nursing intervention. Other nurses have joined with Robinson in calling for this use of humor. In using humor as an intervention, Snyder (1985, 1992) emphasized five considerations: patient assessment, techniques, measurement of effectiveness, functions, and precautions. She also identified related topics for research. In her discussion of humor as a nursing intervention, Hunt (1993) described relevant research studies and emphasized the need for careful assessment to determine the appropriateness of humor interventions. She described humor as a skill that needs to be learned, practiced, and developed in order to be used effectively. Kolkmeier (1988) emphasized the importance of incorporating play and humor into nursing care through the use of the nursing process, using case studies to further illustrate their use and importance.

Further support for humor as a nursing intervention is its identification as such by the Iowa Intervention Project (Iowa Intervention Project [Iowa], 1992, 1993). The focus of this project has been the development of a taxonomy of nursing interventions. Bulecheck and McCloskey (1987) defined nursing interventions as concepts, rather than discrete activities, that consist of groups of independent, science-based actions that nurses do to benefit patients/clients by resolving actual problems, preventing potential problems, and/or promoting higher levels of wellness. Operational definitions have been used to empirically verify the concepts identified as nursing interventions. Particular nursing interventions are selected and used based on nurses' clinical decision-making about their relevance to nursing diagnoses and goals in specific situations.

Level 1 of the taxonomy consists of six domains of nursing interventions: basic physiological, complex physiological, behavioral, family, health system, and safety. Each domain contains a number of separate and distinct classes. These 26 classes comprise Level 2 of the taxonomy. Each class contains a number of separate nursing interventions, which is Level 3 of the taxonomy. Each intervention contains a number of discrete activities deemed to be critical, rather than merely supportive, to the intervention.

Humor is one of 357 distinct nursing interventions identified thus far. The nursing intervention of humor was operationally defined (Iowa, 1992) as . . . facilitating the patient to perceive, appreciate, and express what is funny, amusing, or ludicrous in order to establish relationships, relieve tension, release anger, facilitate learning, or cope with painful feelings" (p. 297). It has been placed in the class of coping assistance-defined as "interventions to assist another to build on own strengths, to adapt to a change in function or achieve a higher level of function" (Iowa, 1993, p. 191) and in the behavioral domain-defined as "care that supports psychological functioning and facilitates life style changes" (Iowa, 1993, p. 190).

Humor as Process in Nursing Education

Beyond the focus on humor as content in the education of nurses, it is essential that humor be integrated into the process of nursing curricula. This integration serves three major purposes. First, the intentional use of humor with learners, both spontaneous and planned, can enhance their learning through a variety of mechanisms, including reduced anxiety, increased attentiveness, increased retention, and sharpened critical thinking skills. Second, the intentional use of humor with learners fosters their perception of humor as valuable both personally and professionally. Third, attitudes of openness to humor, ready perception and expression of overt appreciation of ideas, events, etc., as humorous, as well as the intentional use of humor with learners, serve to model these behaviors for them. In return, the atmosphere fostered is conducive to increased risk-taking behaviors by learners, enabling them to perceive, appreciate, express, and use humor intentionally in the relatively safe atmosphere of the educational setting. Such practice fosters the development of skills in the intentional use of humor, and facilitates learners' successful use of humor in their clinical practice. This promotes the likelihood that learners will choose to use humor as a nursing intervention in relevant client (patient, family, and/or community) and staff situations.

65

The use of humor in the process of nursing education has been advocated by a number of authors (Moses & Friedman, 1986; Parkin, 1989; Rosenberg, 1989; Warner, 1991; Watson & Emerson, 1988), beginning with Robinson in 1970. At this time, Robinson suggested role-playing, the planned use of humor in lectures, and the use of situational humor. She especially advocated cultivating humor as a means of enhancing its use. Throughout her later works, Robinson (1977, 1991) has continued to emphasize the importance of integrating humor into educational endeavors.

Using Humor in the Process of Teaching

With creativity, educators can capitalize on the benefits of humor to make learning and teaching more memorable and enjoyable; i.e., more fun in all settings. Humor can be used to arouse, motivate, and stimulate thinking (Bellert, 1989; Cohen, 1990; Klein, 1992). Humor can be used to address a variety of objectives in each of the three learning domains (see Table 1).

Table 1.

Objectives for Using Humor	
Learning Domain	Objectives
Cognitive	Facilitate understanding
	Enhance recall
	Enhance short and long term memory
	Increase attention
	Stimulate divergent thinking
Affective	Relieve anxiety and tension
	Decrease perceived intimidation of subject matter, educator, and/or fellow learners
	Establish positive relationships and rapport
	Establish positive classroom climate
	Acknowledge students' feelings

Table 1 continued	Promote positive feelings re:
	Learning and education
	Topic under study
	Process of studying
	Humor
	Relieve feelings such as anger, aggression, and hostility in a socially acceptable manner
	Promote learners' valuing, development, and use of humor
Psychomotor	Promote increased coordination
	Promote increased dexterity

Humor can be conceptualized as a form of serious play. Discussing the relevance of serious play to classroom learning, Wasserman (1992) postulated that serious play is a process for serious learning, a process that supports " . . . the development of knowledge, of a spirit of inquiry, of creativity, of conceptual understanding-all contributing to the true empowerment of children" (p. 133). Play promotes the cognitive and creative development of children through its generative nature; facilitates risk-taking, which encourages thinking and trying new ideas and actions; prevents failure and fear of failure by having no standards of right and wrong; encourages autonomy; and involves hand movements which actively engage the mind (Wasserman, 1992). Wasserman recommended using serious play to teach important concepts at all levels, from kindergarten to graduate school, and to design and implement curricula in which important concepts are actively learned through serious play.

One strategy for using humor employs puns as an attention-getting device during a session. For example, in orienting new employees, humor can be easily incorporated into a session which focuses on relating institutional goals and attitudes by presenting attendees with candy bars with messages that correlate with the topics addressed below:

Bit O'Honey	"Compliments and praise are motivators"
Carefree Gum	"Because when we produce we can all relax"
Mounds Bar	"We've eliminated mounds of paperwork"
Butterfingers	"Let's not let opportunities slip through our fingers"
Good & Plenty	"That's the kind of opportunity you have with this company"
Crunch	"Motivate us during tough times"
PayDay Bar	"If we do our job, every day becomes a pay day"
Baby Ruth	"We ask for home runs from all of you"
Whoppers	"We don't boast about what we're going to do, we do it"

(Original source unknown).

This activity lends itself to many variations, but the idea is to put a little fun and laughter into a training session. Hunt (1993) described the work of a staff nurse who uses puppetry to communicate humor and caring as she provides care. This approach could also be used in educational settings. It might be particularly helpful when learners' stress and anxiety are high.

Stories. While a student in her basic nursing program, the first author of this paper (Cannella) was routinely bored by the anatomy and physiology reviews during systems lectures. Despite required anatomy and physiology courses during the student's freshman year, such lectures invariably preceded the presentation of health problems and nursing care related to that system. Stimulated by the idea that learning should be fun and enjoyable, she took advantage of the opportunity to enter a writing contest for senior nursing students and received the third place award for a humorous drama entitled, The Trip (Silva, 1970). The Trip was a humorous futuristic account of the microscopic voyage of a group of nursing students and their instructor through someone's ear in the year 2525. This comedy provided a review of the anatomy of the ear. As such, it could replace a dry nonhumorous oral review.

Staff development instructors have incorporated humor into teaching strategies in creative ways to stimulate nurses' and other learners' interest in and facilitate their learning and retention of annual mandatory topics, such as job hazards and safety. After brainstorming, Wright (1993) "magically" turned an annual update about safety in the workplace from an unexciting program into a memorable and enjoyable event by incorporating the traditional content into a fairy tale theme. Bonheur (1994) wrote a comical narrative story with visual images to teach the signs and symptoms of impending cardiac arrest and appropriate interventions, two concepts that are part of the American Heart Association's basic life support course.

Prose. Humorous prose can be used to present information in a fun and enjoyable way. Gross (1994) effectively used this technique in her examination of uses and misuses of overheads and overhead transparencies. Her humorous descriptions of misuses maintains attention and promotes retention of this material. Johnson (1991) called attention to the stressfulness of undergraduate nursing education in her humorous account of a fictitious research study investigating stress in baccalaureate nursing students. Lefraniois' (1972) book on learning theories, written as a report by an extraterrestrial being named Konger M-III 216, 784, 912, IVKX4, is an excellent example of the use of humorous prose, as is his educational psychology book (1979). Lefraniois used humorous prose augmented by cartoons in these educational psychology texts.

Poetry. Humorous verse often playfully distorts particular life experiences, social situations, and conceptual schemes. As such, it conveys associated positive and/or negative feelings and perceptions, attracts and maintains attention, and emphasizes particular points. For instance, Wabschall (1993) used a humorous poem to describe the effectiveness of different leadership styles in nursing. She emphasized that the appropriate leadership style varies with the situation.

Cartoons. Cartoons, the most frequent type of humor used as an educational strategy, can be used as an attention-getter and to make an educational point by the use of example. Getting the reader's attention may be only the first step in a chain of communication events that continues on through comprehension, acceptance, recall, and finally the use of the new information.

For instance, stereotypical thinking can be examined with the use of cartoons either by including the caption or showing a cartoon without a caption on an overhead and then asking the group to speculate what they think the caption should be. Showing the group the real caption in this activity facilitates the examination and discussion of mind-sets and preconceptions about a certain group. Cartoons can promote group cohesion by assuring class members that others share similar frustrations.

In her editorial "Cartoons: Glimpsing Paradoxical Moments," Parse (1993a) introduced a cartoon series as a regular feature of the journal Nursing Science Quarterly. She aptly described cartoons and their relevance to the advancement of nursing:

> A cartoon has been, historically, a preparatory sketch or tracing, preliminary to a painted fresco, an illustration that tells a story in art. Today it is a humorous sketch symbolizing, satirizing, or caricaturing some person, idea, object, or situation. The cartoonist brings to life paradoxical moments through juxtaposing words and images in ways that can engage the viewer in a mirthful experience that may be anywhere from a smile to a deep belly laugh. . . . The cartoon as an art form represents complex ideas in simple line and few words shedding a different light on something. . . . Shifts in rhythms, flashes of insight, discovery of new possibilities, and more flexible stances can move us along our journey in the advancement of nursing science. (p.1).

The present authors have used humor in the form of cartoons, visual puns, and verbal exaggerations throughout research courses with undergraduate and graduate nursing students to enhance the learning process and promote recall and retention of research content (Cannella, Opitz, & Missroon, 1993). The following examples are illustrative of the humor used in teaching these courses.

When the class focused on the ethical considerations in conducting research, a cartoon showing a person using a periscope to spy on others was used with the caption, "I'm secretly very interested in life." Building on the simplistic message reflecting the unawareness of the subjects of being watched, the instructor focused the class discussion on ethical principles underlying full disclosure and informed consent.

Another cartoon focused attention on and encouraged understanding of the concept of internal validity in conducting research. In this example, a cartoon showing a caricature drawing of a middle-aged couple eating dinner at a restaurant with a sign posted on the wall, "Today's Special: Frog Legs." The couple is staring at a group of tiny frogs in wheelchairs filing past them from another room. The caption on the caricature is "Don't accept the findings at face value." After mirthful laughter, the instructor can use the message projected by this cartoon to discuss the tendency to assume causal relationships among variables without exploring alternate explanations for the findings.

Whenever the topic of the literature review is explored, a visual pun can illustrate the concept of writing style. An illustration of a man talking to a woman depicts the man with a flower dangling from his mouth and the woman with a slice of cake on her head. The caption shown is "What good is it if I talk in flowers........While you're thinking in pastry?" The topic of scientific communication is then explored and the class focuses their discussion on guidelines for writing the research report.

Photoons. Photoons are humorous combinations of pictures and captions. While neither the pictures nor the captions alone may be humorous, their selective combination is designed to create humorous messages. In a text designed for use in an introductory educational research course, Gay (1987) illustrated a major concept of each unit with a photoon. For instance, the unit on subjects and sampling is illustrated with a picture of a sea monster threatening two sailors in a boat and the caption "... every individual has the same probability of being selected and selection of one individual in no way affects selection of another individual" (p. 98).

Activities. Humorous activities can be developed to enhance learning, as evidenced by the work of Froman and Owen (1991). They offer a series of activities designed to teach reliability and validity concepts to groups of nurses, pharmacists, physicians, and nursing students in a fun way. They suggest that a sense of humor and a blackboard are helpful additions to the rubber bands, string, and rulers needed for these activities. The activities include collecting and recording data and answering a 10-item test. A discussion of problems and issues that arise from the activities and concepts of reliability and validity concludes these activities.

Games. Gaming is an educational strategy that promotes laughter and feelings of amusement as well as learning in a fun way. Games have been focused on a variety of concepts and processes in academic and continuing nursing education programs.

Capitalizing on the benefits of humor, Leidy (1992) described a game called "Not So Trivial-Protective Pursuit" developed by staff development educators to review policies, procedures, and responsibilities for the use of protective devices. This game, used with all nursing service employees during annual review classes, encouraged

70

mirthful laughter in a supportive fun atmosphere. Petersen (1994) used a fortune cookie contest to increase staff's awareness of the nursing department's standards. Dols (1988) used a card game to reinforce nurses' understanding and application of the language and basic rules of writing care plans.

Games have been used successfully to teach nursing students basic concepts about fluids and electrolytes (McDougal, 1992), endocrine disorders (Hermann & Bays, 1991), diabetes (Sprengel, 1994), nutrition (Corbett & Lee, 1992), pharmacology (Black, 1992), pathogenic microorganisms (Gruca & Douglas, 1994), germs (Ishida, McKnight, Solem, Tanaka, & Wong, 1994), old age (Halloran & Dean, 1994), research (Blenner, 1991), nursing diagnoses (Weber & Smith, 1991), and clinical judgment (Haak, Burton, Birka, Carlin, Davey, & Hujes, 1990; Weber, 1994). In these situations, gaming-which can be adapted to any topic-was used as a stress-reduction strategy and made the learning experience enjoyable. Three additional games suitable for classroom instruction were described by Johanson (1992).

In using gaming as an educational strategy, effective results will be realized if well-known games, whose format is known by most participants, are used — such as Jeopardy or Trivial Pursuit. Participation in a gaming teaching strategy increases group cohesiveness in a non-stressful environment that frequently results in mirthful laughter as groups compete with one another. Incorporating laughter and humor into an educational program using games challenges educators to use their creativity in designing meaningful learning experiences.

Many prepackaged games are available in the marketplace to help reduce instructional preparation time. By using pre-made game pieces, preparation time can be sharply decreased, as preparation can then be reduced to adding customized information to the game.

Riddles. Pyrczak's humorous statistics workbook (1989) is an example of how riddles can be incorporated into the world of statistics, a topic which many learners dread. In this humorous workbook and study guide, 60 worksheets are included, each based on a humorous riddle. Letters and words associated with the results of computation problems and statistical questions are used to decode the answers to the riddles. If, in completing the worksheet, the answer to a riddle does not make sense, learners know they need to check their computations. An example of one of the riddles follows:

Riddle: Why is it NOT true that ants are the busiest animals?

Answer: They always have time to go to picnics.

(Worksheet #35)

Puzzles. Word searches, word scrambles, and crossword puzzles, can be humorous in and of themselves or used in a way that facilitates humor. For instance, assigning learners to work on a puzzle as a group often facilitates humorous interactions within the

71

group.

Since solving puzzles requires high-level cognitive skills, puzzles are less effective in presenting new information than in reinforcing or evaluating learning. Humorous puzzles can be developed to assess students' application of knowledge by incorporating absurdities or incongruities. Word processing or specialized computer software programs can be used to develop crossword and other word puzzles (Bloom & Trice, 1994).

Jokes. Health professionals frequently resort to a type of joking, identified as gallows humor by Robinson (1991), to cope with and relieve anxieties associated with the tragedies prevalent in professional practice. Joking is a form of humor that many times can turn an unpleasant situation into a more tolerable one by relieving tension and establishing an accepting attitude. Frequently, individuals vent their frustrations by using joking as a verbal shield for job-related aggravations.

In poking fun, one needs to be sensitive to the individuals involved in the situations to avoid offending anyone. Blumenfeld and Alpern (1986) suggest the following four guidelines to avoid offense when using joking:
1. Don't joke about something that reflects negatively about an individual's personality or work performance.
2. Joke about yourself, not the other person.
3. Share humor that is related to your job or the profession in general, keeping it off the personal level.
4. Find out the "in" jokes and work them into your educational sessions, poking fun at frustrations and problems common in the organization (pp. 97, 98, 117).

To develop awareness of using jokes as a humorous intervention, students can be encouraged to keep a journal of jokes which are periodically shared with others. In clinical situations, clients can also be instructed to keep a diary of jokes for a specified period of time to be shared with others.

Songs. Humorous songs combine music with humor. Often the lyrics to popular or traditional songs are changed in a humorous fashion (i.e., a parody). Such songs may be particularly effective in relieving anxiety and tension. Students and faculty often engage in these endeavors. For instance, in "An Anthem for Nurses in Graduate School" set to the music of "My Country, 'tis of Thee" or "God Save the Queen," Jacques (1987) satirized graduate student research.

Like poetry, songs can also be used to introduce more serious topics. An all-RN barbershop quartet, the Nursing Notes, has written songs and parodies of familiar songs about nursing and health issues. They have been said to put the "SING" in nursing. Humorist and singer/songwriter Peter Alsop's recordings, tapes, and videos have won numerous awards. His songs are used by professionals to facilitate the discussion of issues such as codependency, chemical and sexual abuse, disability, and death.

On a more serious note, Pedersen (1987) described how she used humorous songs when caring for an elderly woman with pneumonia, decubiti, and end-stage chronic brain syndrome. This patient did not speak and had been communicating only with screams. While changing the soiled bed linens, Pedersen began singing one of Elizabeth Kubler-Ross's favorite songs to relieve the stress of the patient's continuing screams:

> Row, row, row your boat,
> Gently down the stream.
> Fooled you. Fooled you.
> Fooled you. Fooled you.
> I'm a submarine. (p. 19)

Pedersen noticed that the patient had stopped screaming. As a matter of fact, the patient smiled and grinned in response to Pedersen's singing. Whereas previously she had been screaming whenever she was touched, she grinned in response to Pedersen's songs, even when being fully turned. The use of humorous songs enabled Pedersen to establish a caring relationship with this patient. Pedersen concluded "Smiles and songs can be another language of caring" (p. 19).

Teaching Humor as Content

In addition to using humor as an instructional process, humor can be used and taught as content to students and nurses. In this context, emphasis is placed on the use of humor in nursing practice. The nursing process provides a framework for teaching and incorporating humor into nursing practice, in clinical as well as classroom settings. Humor-focused data, such as sense of humor and humor preferences (see Table 2), can be elicited by using informal humor-focused observation and questioning. In addition, more formal assessment tools/instruments (see Appendix) may be used with the individuals and/or groups and situation(s) of interest.

Table 2.

Assessment Data and Nursing Diagnoses Related to Humor

Humor-Focused Assessment Data:
Attitude towards humor
Appropriateness of sense of humor and/or family laughter
Past uses of humor
Ability to perceive and understand humor (auditory/visual stimuli, reading ability, mental status)
Preferences for specific types and forms of humor
Topics considered taboo
Preferred comedian(s)
Time of day most receptive to humor
Information about typical response(s) to humor (laughter, smiles)
Prior use of humor as coping strategy
Physical limitations which would influence participation in activities

Nursing Diagnoses (Potential or Actual):
Coping, ineffective individual
Anxiety
Powerlessness
Hopelessness
Altered thought processes, depression
Dysfunctional grieving, bereavment
Alteration in comfort, pain
Activity intolerance
Impaired physical mobility
Diversional activity deficit
Altered health maintenance
Lack of humor, disturbance of humor*
Excessive inappropriate humor*

*Identified by Yura-Petro (1991)

Regardless of the method(s) used, humor-focused assessments should be specific and thorough, since neither the interacting individual(s) nor situation(s) can be anticipated and specific variables related to humor may vary considerably within and across situations as well as gender and cultural groups (Snyder, 1992; Sullivan & Deane, 1988). Analysis of these data and data focused on other human responses forms the basis for identifying pertinent nursing diagnoses (see Table 2, above), and developing individualized goals and objectives. Humor interventions may be appropriate for a variety of goals and objectives in the cognitive, affective, and psychomotor learning domains, as previously described (see Table 1), as well as goals and objectives pertaining to biological, physiological, psychological, social, cultural, and spiritual responses.

Recognizing the appropriateness of humor interventions for a variety of nursing diagnoses and objectives enables nurses and nursing students to plan their use in clinical and classroom settings. One of the most effective ways to facilitate the use of humor as an intervention is to develop humor resources that are readily available for use when their appropriateness is identified (see Table 3). While some of these resources, such as videotapes, are relatively expensive (usually costing $20 to $150 per videotape), others — such as collections of cartoons or jokes — cost only a few dollars but require a more substantial investment of time.

Table 3.

Humorous Interventions: Resources and Strategies

Resources:
Develop a humor scrapbook of cartoons from books, magazines, newspapers
Collect "funny faces"
Collect interactive toys (wind-ups, noisemakers, etc.)
Develop a library of jokes, stories, greeting cards, bumper stickers, puzzles, poems, songs
Develop a library of humorous videos, audiotapes, or comedy films
Develop a humor basket, cart, room
Maintain a unit bulletin board of humorous drawings, cartoons, sayings, etc.
Keep a file of local magicians and comedians
Keep a personal humor journal or diary
Keep a unit-based journal or log, encouraging staff and clients to record humorous incidents, etc.
Subscribe to/collect issues of humor newsletters and journals, such as the Journal of Nursing Jocularity

Strategies:
Cultivate a sense of humor in yourself, others
Role model humorous responses to life
Share humor with others
Make humorous remarks or comments, such as pointing out humorous incongruity in a situation
Tell humorous stories or jokes
Encourage visualization with humor
Encourage clients to create humor, by sayings, writings, and/or drawings that the client perceives as humorous-provide specific suggestions or supplies as needed
Share greeting cards, cartoons, bumper stickers, puzzles, poems, songs
Post funny cartoons, drawings, sayings, signs
Arrange for a clown to visit the unit
Invite a comedian or magician to perform
Teach clients magic tricks
Send singing telegrams
Play dress-up on holidays or special days
Encourage clients to keep personal humor journals

Planning also involves identifying one's own humor style and preferences, and developing skills in using humor as an intervention. Using humor as a nursing intervention takes time, continued feedback, and self-assessment. Responding positively to client-initiated humor gives clients permission to use and respond to humor. As such, it is an important part of using humor as an intervention. One's comfort and skill in using particular humor strategies should also be considered in choosing strategies to apply to particular client situations. For instance, if one has difficulty remembering the punch lines of jokes, alternative strategies to verbally telling jokes to clients are likely to be more effective. Considering assessment data, diagnoses, and objectives in relation to available resources and personal humor preferences and skills, decisions can be made regarding the appropriateness and relevance of particular humor strategies, whether they are spontaneous or planned. A variety of forms of humor activities or strategies can be used appropriately in clinical and classroom settings (see Table 3, above).

Implementing humor interventions also involves using empathy and sensitivity to assess the potential appropriateness of both spontaneous and planned interventions. Humor designed to laugh with people rather than at them, and to be easily perceived and understood, is appropriate as an intervention (Bellert, 1989; Cohen, 1990; Davidhizar & Bower, 1992; Erdman, 1991; Gibson, 1994; Hunt, 1993; Kolkmeier, 1988; Pasquali, 1990; Snyder, 1992). Timing of humor, receptiveness of clients, and context of the humor are important factors in determining the appropriateness of humor and laughter in given situations (Davidhizar & Bower, 1992; Cohen, 1990; Leiber, 1986). Furthermore, certain mental states-such as confusion, depression, and paranoia-may impair the reception of humorous stimuli, and thus hinder or preclude the use of humor as an intervention (Davidhizar & Bower, 1992; Leiber, 1986; Sullivan & Deane, 1988). In contrast, humor that is disparaging or put-down in nature, including ridicule, generally is not considered appropriate for use as an intervention (Bellert, 1989; Cohen, 1990; Davidhizar & Bower, 1992; Erdman, 1991; Hunt, 1993; Pasquali, 1990; Snyder, 1992). This type of humor may be used to mask manipulation or feelings such as aggression and hostility (Hunt, 1993; Yura-Petro, 1991).

Together with empathy and sensitivity, evaluation is essential to the use of humor as an intervention. The effectiveness, including the appropriateness, of humor is largely determined by the success of the interaction in which humor is attempted. Clients' outcomes, their responses to humor strategies, as well as their attainment of objectives, should be evaluated and documented. Positive responses from clients may include humor-focused responses such as further development of humor awareness and sense of humor, increased perception of humor in everyday events, increased expression of smiling and laughing behaviors, increased creation and expression of humor, as well as reduced subjective severity of target symptom(s) (anxiety, discomfort, pain, etc.), decreased social distance, increased closeness and trust in interpersonal relationship(s), enhanced communication, increased insight, changes in perspective, enhanced learning, improved coping, and a generalized sense of health and well-being (Bellert, 1989; Cohen, 1990; Davidhizar & Bower, 1992; Erdman, 1991; Hunt, 1993; Pasquali, 1990; Snyder, 1992, Yura-Petro, 1991). In contrast, negative responses, such as reduced self-esteem and confidence, impaired interpersonal communication and relationships, decreased learning, feelings of stress, anxiety, pain, embarrassment, shame, anger, and hostility, decreased coping effectiveness, and a reduced sense of health and well-being may also be observed (Bellert, 1989; Cohen, 1990; Davidhizar & Bower, 1992; Erdman, 1991; Kolkmeier, 1988; Pasquali, 1990; Snyder, 1992). On the other hand, particular humor strategies should be discontinued if they are deemed ineffective.

Case Examples Using Humorous Strategies in Educational Endeavors

The following two case examples focus on the use of humorous strategies in educational endeavors. They deal with some of the common, yet complex, situations that occur in education.

Case Example 1: Using humorous strategies in teaching nursing research
Teaching nursing research is challenging for most faculty. Students are often very anxious about such courses, typically because they are concerned about the expectations of this unfamiliar nursing subject and its perceived lack of relevance to their clinical practice. The present authors have found that using cartoons and humorous comments related to the learning situation has been effective in reducing the stress associated with such courses.

During the first class, the present authors have used a cartoon strip showing Charlie Brown watching Woodchuck who is flying a kite which soon gets tangled in a tree. Charlie returns home to tell Lucy, "I hate to admit it, but I just saw something that makes me feel real good." Students readily laugh at this cartoon, for they can easily relate to this situation. This provides an opening for faculty to guide a discussion regarding students' anxious feelings related to this course.

Cartoons and humorous comments were used throughout the course to illustrate major research concepts. For instance, the concept of purpose in research was illustrated using a cartoon depicting a puzzled man going around in a circle with a net trying to catch an elusive purpose and captioned, "Of course I have a purpose — to find a purpose!"

Case Example 2: Using humorous strategies in teaching nursing skills

Educators at one hospital (Bradbury-Golas & Carson, 1994) used the innovative format of a skills fair to offer nursing staff a variety of fun ways to learn or review particular nursing skills. Using a circus/fair theme to emphasize that learning can be fun and nonthreatening, opportunities for nursing staff to practice and demonstrate 22 commonly used and critical skills were provided at 2-hour intervals on all three shifts during a 24-hour period. Each skill comprised one station. Station presenters were given the autonomy to choose the optimal teaching strategy for their station. "Miss Universal Precautions" was used to present concepts of infection control. At the arterial blood gas station, nursing staff participated in a flip chart game to review the interpretation of ABGs. Nursing staff self-selected the stations they attended. Refreshments and door prizes were provided, significantly contributing to the relaxed and carefree atmosphere. This skills fair, involving very active, self-selected, and fun learning experiences, was positively evaluated by the approximately 150 nursing staff who attended it.

The Ripple Effect of Using Humor in Teaching and Learning

Humor is important to the discipline of nursing. Because humor has not been a focus of nursing, it is essential to incorporate humor in the continuing education, practice, and research of nursing faculty and clinical educators.

The ramifications of the use of humor in educational efforts need to be explored from the perspective of learners and teachers. The goals for learners are to improve their knowledge, attitudes, and skills related to humor, its effects and its relevance; promote increased valuing of humor; sharpen their understanding and appreciation of the relevance of humor to health and wellness; expand their perception of humor; refine their appreciation of humor; improve their expression and use of humor in teaching and other professional as well as personal interactions; and increase their ability to use humor, both spontaneous and planned usage. For teachers, the goals are to incorporate what they have learned about humor into their educational strategies and practices, increasing their use of humor in their work.

It is important for those with expertise in the area of humor to share their knowledge, attitudes, and skills with others to maximize humor dissemination. Humorous ways should be used to teach such material, so that humor is reflected throughout both the content and process of the educational endeavor.

The initial focus of humor education is on faculty and clinical educators, first as learners and then as teachers. As learners, faculty and clinical educators learn from experts in humor; as teachers, they then teach humor to students and nursing staff. The second focus is on students and nursing staff as learners, and then as teachers. Students and nursing staff learn about humor from faculty and clinical educators; then, they teach

79

patients, families, and communities. The final focus is on patients, families, and communities as learners, and then as teachers. Patients, families, and communities learn about humor and health care from students and nursing staff; in turn, these same patients, families, and communities teach others. In this way, the knowledge, attitudes, and skills of humor scholars and experts can be disseminated in much the same way that water ripples in a circle outward from the spot where a pebble drops.

The Future of Humor in Education

Progress has been made in the study and use of humor, particularly over the past 25 years. Continued progress in this area is hindered by the relative lack of funding for the needed research on humor in nursing education. However, increasing nurses' recognition of the positive effects of appropriate humor in enhancing learning, stimulating creativity and divergent thinking, promoting health and wellness, and improving stress management will facilitate the incorporation of humor in education and, ultimately, in clinical practice.

Bibliography

Bellert, J. L. (1989). Humor in oncology nursing. *Cancer Nursing*, 12(2), 65-70.

Black, R. L. (1992). Pharmacology instruction: A game approach for students. *Nurse Educator*, 17(2), 7-8.

Blenner, J. L. (1991). Researcher for a day: A simulation game. *Nurse Educator*, 16(2), 32-35.

Bloom, K. C., & Trice, L. B. (1994). Let the games begin. *Journal of Nursing Education*, 33, 137- 138.

Blumenfeld, E., & Alpern, L. (1986). *The smile connection: How to use humor in dealing with people.* Englewood Cliffs, NJ: Prentice-Hall.

Bonheur, B. B. (1994). Creating a new learning experience: "The Story of Art" and "Prudent Art." *Journal of Continuing Education*, 25, 237-240.

Bradbury-Golas, K., & Carson, L. (1994). Nursing skill fair: Gaining knowledge with fun and games. *Journal of Continuing Education in Nursing*, 25(1), 32-34.

Bryant, J., & Zillmann, D. (1989). Using humor to promote learning in the classroom. *Journal of Children in Contemporary Society*, 20(1/2), 49-77.

Bulechek, G. M., & McCloskey, J. C. (1987). Nursing interventions: What they are and how to choose them. *Holistic Nursing Practice*, 1(3), 36-44.

Buxman, K. (1991a). Humor in therapy for the mentally ill. *Journal of Psychosocial Nursing*, 29(12), 14-17.

Buxman, K. (1991b). Make room for laughter. *American Journal of Nursing*, 91(12), 46-48.

Cannella, K. S., Opitz, M, & Missroon, S. (1993, February). The effectiveness of humor as a teaching strategy in initial research courses. Paper presented at the Southern Nursing Research Society, Birmingham, AL.

Chapman, A. J., & Foot, H. C. (Eds.). (1976). *Humour and laughter: Theory, Research and Applications.* London: Wiley.

Cohen, M. (1990). Caring for ourselves can be a funny business. *Holistic Nursing Practice*, 4(4), 1-11.

Corbett, R. W., & Lee, B. T. (1992). Nutriquest: A fun way to reinforce nutrition knowledge. *Nurse Educator*, 17(2), 33-35.

Cousins, N. (1976). *Anatomy of an illness as perceived by the patient.* New England Journal of Medicine, 295, 1453-1463.

Cousins, N. (1979). *Anatomy of an illness.* Boston: Hall.

Cousins, N. (1983). *The healing heart.* New York: Norton.

Davidhizar, R., & Bower, M. (1992). The dynamics of laughter. *Archives of Psychiatric Nursing*, 6, 132-137.

Dols, J. D. (1988). An innovative strategy for teaching care plan writing. *Journal of Continuing Education in Nursing*, 19, 131-133.

Dugan. D. (1989). Laughter and tears: Best medicine for stress. *Nursing Forum*, 14(1), 18-26.

Eason, F. R., & Corbett, R. W. (1991). Effective teacher characteristics identified by adult learners in nursing. *Journal of Continuing Education in Nursing*, 22, 21-23.

Eccles, A. M. (1990). Using humor to relieve stress. *Point of View*, 27(1), 8.

Erdman, L. (1991). Laughter therapy for patients with cancer. *Oncology Nursing Forum*, 18, 1359- 1363.

Ferguson, S., & Campinha-Bacote, J. (1989). Humor in nursing. *Journal of Psychosocial Nursing*, 27(4), 29-34.

Freud, S. (1960). *Jokes and their relation to the unconscious.* (J. Strachey, Trans. and Ed.) New York: Norton. (Original work published 1905)

Froman, R. D., & Owen, S. V. (1991). Teaching reliability and validity: Fun with classroom applications. *Journal of Continuing Education in Nursing*, 22, 88-94.

Fry, W. F. (1986). Humor, physiology, and the aging process. In L. Nahemow, K. A. McCluskey-Fawcett, & P. E. McGhee (Eds.), *Humor and aging* (pp. 81-98). Orlando, FL: Academic Press.

Fry, W. F. (1992). The physiologic effects of humor, mirth, and laughter. *Journal of the American Medical Association*, 267, 1857-1858.

Fry, W. F., & Rader, C. (1977). The respiratory components of mirthful laughter.

Journal of Biological Psychology, 19, 39-50.

Fry, W. F., & Salameh, W. A. (Eds.) (1987). *Handbook of humor and psychotherapy: Advances in the clinical use of humor.* Sarasota, FL: Professional Resource Exchange.

Gaberson, K. B. (1991). The effect of humorous distraction on preoperative anxiety. *AORN Journal,* 54, 1258-1264.

Gay, L. R. (1987). *Educational research: Competencies for analysis and application,* 3rd edition. Columbus, OH: Merrill.

Gibson, L. (1994). Healing with humor. *Nursing 94,* 24(9), 56-57.

Goldstein, J., & McGhee, P. (1972). *The psychology of humor.* New York: Academic Press.

Gorham, J., & Christophel, D. M. (1990). The relationship of teachers' use of humor in the classroom to immediacy and student learning. *Communication Education,* 39, 46-61.

Gross, G. J. (1994). Epidemic: Overheaditis. *Journal of Continuing Education in Nursing,* 25, 46- 47.

Gruca, J. A. M., & Douglas, M. R. (1994). Bug of the week: A personification teaching strategy. *Journal of Nursing Education,* 33, 153-154.

Haak, S. W., Burton, S., Birka, A. M., Carlin, A. M., Davey, S. S., & Hujes, M. (1990). Clinical judgment: An instructional game for nursing. *Nurse Educator,* 15(4), 11, 20-28.

Haig, R. (1986). Therapeutic uses of humor. *American Journal of Psychotherapy,* 40, 543-553.

Halloran, L., & Dean, L. (1994). Old for an evening: An experiential learning game. *Journal of Nursing Education,* 33, 155-156.

Hermann, C. P., & Bays, C. L. (1991). Drawing to learn and win. *Journal of Nursing Education,* 30, 140-141.

Herth, K. A. (1984). Laughter: A nursing treatment. *American Journal of Nursing,* 84(8), 91-92.

Herth, K. A. (1993). Humor and the older adult. *Applied Nursing Research,* 6, 146-153.

Hunt, A. H. (1993). Humor as a nursing intervention. *Cancer Nursing,* 16(1), 34-39.

Hutchings, P. (1987). Break out, be there! Thoughts on teaching creativity. *College Teaching,* 35(2), 47-48.

Iowa Intervention Project (Iowa), J. C. McCloskey, & G. M. Bulechek (Eds.) (1992). *Nursing Interventions Classification* (NIC). St. Louis: Mosby.

Iowa Intervention Project (Iowa). The NIC taxonomy structure. (1993). *Image: Journal of Nursing Scholarship,* 25, 187-192.

Ishida, D., McKnight, P., Solem, S., Tanaka, J., & Wong, L. (1994). Multimodal teaching strategies: A "student friendly" approach. *Journal of Nursing Education*, 33, 163-165.

Jacques, S. (1987). An anthem for nurses in graduate school. *Nursing Research*, 36, 380.

Jenkins, J. F., & Ostchega, Y. (1986). Evaluation of burnout in oncology nurses. *Cancer Nursing*, 9, 108-116.

Johanson, L. S. (1992). Three games for classroom instruction. *Nurse Educator*, 17(5), 6-9.

Johnson, L. W. (1991). Homeostasis conservation among undergraduate nursing students. *Nursing Research*, 40, 118-119.

Klein, A. (1992). Storybook humor and early development. *Childhood Education*, 68, 213-217.

Kolkmeier, L. G. (1988). Play and laughter: Moving toward harmony. In B. M. Dossey, L. Keegan, C. E. Guzzetto, & L. G. Kolkmeier (Eds.), *Holistic nursing: A handbook for practice* (pp. 289-304). Rockville, MD: Aspen.

Lapierre, E. D., & Padgett, J. (1991). What is the impact of the use of humor as a coping strategy by nurses working in geropsychiatric settings? *Journal of Psychosocial Nursing*, 29(7), 41-43.

Lefcourt, H. M., & Martin, R. A. (1986). *Humor and life stress: Antidote to adversity*. New York: Springer.

Lefranıois, G. R. (1972). *Psychological theories and human learning*: Konger's report. Monterey, CA: Brooks-Cole.

Lefranıois, G. R. (1979). *Psychology for teaching: A bear sometimes faces the front*. Belmont, CA: Wadsworth.

Leiber, D. B. (1986). Laughter and humor in critical care. *Dimensions of Critical Care Nursing*, 5, 162-170.

Leidy, K. (1992). Enjoyable learning experiences: An aid to retention? *Journal of Continuing Education in Nursing*, 23, 206-208.

Long, D. L., & Graesser, A. C. (1988). Wit and humor in discourse processing. *Discourse Processes*, 11 35-60.

McDougal, J. E. (1992). Bringing electrolytes to life: An imagery game. *Nurse Educator*, 17(6), 8-10.

McGhee, P. (1979). *Humor: Its origin and development*. San Francisco: Freeman.

McGhee, P. E. (1988). Introduction: Recent developments in humor research. *Journal of Children in Contemporary Society*, 20(1-2), 1-12.

McGhee, P. E., & Goldstein, J. H. (Eds.) (1983). *Handbook of humor research, vol. I, Basic issues*. New York: Springer.

Mooney, N. E. (1993). Juggling performance checklist. *Journal of Continuing*

Education in Nursing, 24, 43-44.

Moses, N., & Friedman, M. (1986). Using humor in evaluating student performance. *Journal of Nursing Education, 25,* 328-333.

Nahemow, L., McCluskey-Fawcett, K. A., & McGhee, P. E. (1986). *Humor and aging.* Orlando, FL: Academic Press.

Napora, J. (1984). A study of the effects of a program of humorous activity on the subjective well-being of senior adults. Doctoral dissertation, University of Maryland Baltimore Professional Schools. Dissertation Abstracts International, 46, 276A.

Parfitt, J. M. (1990). Humorous preoperative teaching. *AORN Journal, 52,* 114-120.

Parkin, C. J. (1989). Humor, health and higher education: Laughing matters. *Journal of Nursing Education, 28,* 229-230.

Parse, R. R. (1993a). Cartoons: Glimpsing paradoxical moments. *Nursing Science Quarterly, 6,* 1.

Parse, R. R. (1993b). The experience of laughter: A phenomenological study. *Nursing Science Quarterly, 6,* 39-43.

Parse, R. R. (1994). Laughing and health: A study using Parse's research method. *Nursing Science Quarterly, 7,* 55-64.

Pasquali, E. A. (1990). Learning to laugh: Humor as therapy. *Journal of Psychosocial Nursing, 28*(3), 31-35.

Pease, R. A. (1991). Cartoon humor in nursing education. *Nursing Outlook, 39,* 262-267.

Pedersen, K. A. (1987). Another language. *Nursing 87, 17*(7), 19.

Petersen, J. (1994). Increasing standards awareness through a fortune cookie contest. *Journal of Continuing Education in Nursing, 25,* 48.

Pyrczak, F. (1989). *Statistics with a sense of humor: A humorous workbook and comprehensive guide to statistics study skills.* Los Angeles: California State University.

Raber, W. (1987). The caring role of the nurse in the application of humor therapy to the patient experiencing helplessness. *Clinical Gerontologist, 7*(1), 3-11.

Robinson, V. (1970). Humor in nursing. In C. Carlson & B. Blackwell (Eds.), *Behavioral Concepts and Nursing Interventions* (pp.129-151). Philadelphia: Lippincott.

Robinson, V. (1978). Humor in nursing. In C. Carlson & B. Blackwell (Eds.), *Behavioral Concepts and Nursing Interventions,* 2nd edition (pp.191-210). Philadelphia: Lippincott.

Robinson, V. M. (1977). *Humor and the health professions.* Thorofare, NJ: Slack.

Robinson, V. M. (1991). *Humor and the health professions,* 2nd edition. Thorofare,

NJ: Slack.

Rodgers, J. A. (1988). An invitation to laugh. *Journal of Professional Nursing*, 4, 314.

Rogers, C. (1969). *Freedom to learn.* Columbus, OH: Merrill.

Rose, J. F. (1990). Psychologic health of women: A phenomenologic study of women's inner strength. *Advances in Nursing Science*, 12(2), 56-70.

Rosenberg, L. (1989). A delicate dose of humor. *Nursing Forum*, 24(2), 3-7.

Ruxton, J. P., & Hester, M. P. (1987). Humor: Assessment and intervention. *Clinical Gerontologist*, 7(1), 13-21.

Schaefer, K. M., & Peterson, K. (1992). Effectiveness of coping strategies among critical care nurses. *Dimensions of Critical Care Nursing*, 11(1), 28-34.

Silva, K. A. (1970). The trip. *RN*, 33(11), 56-58, 60-64, 66.

Simon, J. M. (1988a). Humor and the older adult: Implications for nursing. *Journal of Advanced Nursing,* 13, 441-446.

Simon, J. M. (1988b). The therapeutic value of humor in aging adults. *Journal of Gerontological Nursing*, 14(8), 9-13.

Simon, J. M. (1988c). Therapeutic humor. *Journal of Psychosocial Nursing,* 26(4), 9-12.

Simon, J. M. (1989). Humor techniques for oncology nurses. *Oncology Nursing Forum,* 16, 667- 670.

Simon, J. M. (1990). Humor and its relationship to perceived health, life satisfaction, and morale in older adults. *Issues in Mental Health Nursing,* 11, 17-31.

Simonton, C., Simonton, S., & Creighton, J. (1978). *Getting well again.* Los Angeles: Tarcher.

Smith, D. (1986). Using humor to help children with pain. *Children's Health Care*, 14, 187-188.

Snyder, M. (1985). *Independent nursing interventions.* New York: Delmar.

Snyder, M. (1992). *Independent nursing interventions,* 2nd edition. New York: Delmar.

Sprengel, A. D. (1994). Learning can be fun with gaming. *Journal of Nursing Education*, 33, 151- 152.

Sullivan, J. L., & Deane, D. M. (1988). Humor and health. *Journal of Gerontological Nursing,* 14(1), 20-24.

Sumners, A. D. (1988). Humor: Coping in recovery from addiction. *Issues in Mental Health Nursing*, 9, 169-179.

Sumners, A. D. (1990). Professional nurses' attitudes toward humor. *Journal of Advanced Nursing*, 15, 196-200.

Tennant, K. F. (1990). Laugh it off: The effect of humor on the well-being of the older adult. *Journal of Gerontological Nursing*, 16(12), 11-17.

Wabschall, J. M. (1993). Leadership styles. In C. Kenefick & A. Y. Young (Eds.), *The *best of nursing humor* (p. 102). Philadelphia: Hanley & Belfus. Note: This is cited as being reprinted from Nursing Forum, 1984, 21(2), 91.

Wandersee, J. H. (1982). Humor as a teaching strategy. *American Biology Teacher*, 44, 212-214.

Warner, S. L. (1984). Humor and self-disclosure. *Journal of Psychosocial Nursing*, 22(4), 17-21.

Warner, S. L. (1991). Humor: A coping response for student nurses. *Archives of Psychiatric Nursing*, 5(1), 10-16.

Wasserman, S. (1992). Serious play in the classroom: How messing around can win you the Nobel prize. *Childhood Education*, 68, 133-139.

Watson, M. J., & Emerson, S. (1988). Facilitate learning with humor. *Journal of Nursing Education*, 27, 89-90.

Weber, J. R. (1994). Using a gaming-simulation to teach students how to collect data and make clinical judgments. *Nurse Educator*, 19(1), 5-6.

Weber, J. R., & Smith, D. I. (1991). Name that nursing diagnosis: A gaming simulation. *Nursing Diagnosis*, 2, 79-83.

White, C., & Howse, E. (1993). Managing humor: When is it funny — and when is it not? *Nursing Management*, 24(4), 80, 83, 86, 88, 92.

Wooten, P. (1992). Does a humor workshop affect nurse burnout? *Journal of Nursing Jocularity*, 2(2), 42-43.

Wright, D. (1993). The princess and the chemo spill — A policy magically turned into a fairy tale. *Journal of Continuing Education in Nursing*, 24, 37-38.

Wyer, R. S., & Collins II, J. E. (1992). A theory of humor elicitation. *Psychological Review*, 99, 663-688.

Yasko, J. (1983). A survey of oncology clinical nursing specialists. *Oncology Nursing Forum*, 10, 25-30.

Yura, H., & Walsh, M. (1988). *Nursing process*, 5th edition. Norwalk, CT: Appleton-Lange.

Yura-Petro, H. (1991). Humor: A research and practice tool for nurse scholar-supervisors, practitioners, and educators. *Health Care Supervisor*, 9(4), 1-8.

Ziv, A. (1988). Teaching and learning with humor: Experiment and replication. *Journal of Experimental Education*, 57(1), 5-15.

CHAPTER VI

HUMOR IN EVALUATING PERFORMANCE

by Nancy Moses, MSN, PhN, RN

I wish to acknowledge my humor mentor, Dr. Vera M. Robinson, and my thesis advisor at Cal State, Dr. Marilyn Friedman, who significantly contributed to the development of this project.

One of the most difficult types of clinical evaluations in nursing education is when the procedure to be evaluated is both complex and technically demanding. In these cases, most students are highly anxious and, because of their increased anxiety, tend to perform more poorly than when more relaxed. Procedures noted which provoke heightened anxiety in the beginning Associate Degree nursing student include oral and intramuscular medication administration, sterile dressing changes, and gastric gavage (nasogastric tube feedings).

Concern about how to help students perform more adequately when being evaluated in stress-producing situations led to consideration of alternative strategies that instructors might use. Believing that heightened anxiety was the "culprit" that often compromised students' ability to perform in evaluation situations, a possible and promising teacher strategy, albeit untested in nursing evaluation, is the use of humor. As both the layman and professional know, humor is a recognized tactic for helping people relax (Bernard, 1954; Robinson, 1977). Hence, it was reasoned that the deliberate use of humor in evaluating student performance could be an effective mechanism for reducing student tension and anxiety in stressful clinical evaluation situations.

This chapter describes the researcher's investigation of this clinical evaluation question. More specifically, the focus of this study was to investigate the effects of deliberate teacher humor on anxiety and performance during evaluation among beginning nursing students in a simulated stress-producing performance situation. In order to study the impact of deliberate use of humor during evaluation on students' anxiety level and task performance, the gastric gavage procedure was selected. Use of humor in the study referred to any communication which is recognized by the students as humorous, leading to laughing, smiling, or a feeling of amusement (Robinson, 1977). Anxiety is defined as those self-reported verbal indications of response to threatening conditions in the environment as measured by Spielberger's (1970) State Anxiety Inventory. Performance refers to the extent to which the student was able to carry out a nursing procedure, in this case the nasogastric tube feeding procedure, as measured by a researcher-generated observation performance checklist.

The potential significance of this study is that, if using humor during evaluation of stressful clinical procedures reduces anxiety and enhances performance, then the addition of this evaluative strategy into the educator's repertoire of tactics for evaluating student performance will serve to augment effectiveness in evaluation.

Theoretical Framework

Freud (1928) was the first theorist to describe and analyze people's behavior into a single meaningful framework. He discussed the central role that humor plays as a coping mechanism in reducing anxiety and suggested that humor is tension reducing.

Based on the writings of Bernard (1954), Coombs and Goldman (1975), Freud (1928), and Smith, Ettingel and Nelson (1971), it was theorized that humor could be used as a means of intervening in the emotional process of heightened anxiety. Spielberger (1966) elaborates on the notion of what anxiety is and explains the relationship between anxiety and performance. He conceptually distinguishes anxiety as an emotional reaction involving both a transitory state (state anxiety) and a relatively stable personality attribute (trait anxiety). State anxiety is precipitated whenever a person perceives a particular situation as threatening (such as in the evaluation situation being studied).

Spielberger's theoretical perspective (that heightened anxiety involves both state and trait components) evolved from his recognition that heightened anxiety is a major problem for college students. High anxiety is seen by Spielberger (1972) as compromising learning and performance, in that highly anxious people become more concerned with the evaluation of their performance than with the performance itself. Sarason, Davidson, Lighthall, Waite, and Ruebush (1960) theorized similarly. They asserted that, when evaluative anxiety becomes heightened, the anxiety causes concerns about possible failure in testing; hence, the student is often unable to satisfactorily deal with the demands at hand. Spielberger further contended that, if an individual's high anxiety state can be lowered to a moderate level, improved learning is likely to ensue.

Spielberger's theoretical explanation of how anxiety affects performance can be summarized as follows. He postulates that, when an individual experiences an anxiety reaction (rise in anxiety to a moderate/high level), this leads to a cognitive reappraisal of the situation which is that the situation produces stress. This leads to primarily defensive or avoidance type responses. However, if the individual's anxiety level can be lowered, the cognitive reappraisal will be that the potentially stress-producing situation is less threatening. This "reframing" of the situation leads to increased coping (positive problem-solving) behavior rather than primarily defensive or avoidance type responses.

Greater coping and problem-solving responses enhance students' performance levels.

In summary, the specific theoretical propositions underlying this study were that: (a) the deliberate use of teacher humor as an intervention in a stressful simulated task performance situation leads to a reduced anxiety state level among beginning nursing students, and (b) this reduced anxiety level, in turn, results in improvement of task performance.

Review of the Literature

There has been considerable interest in the concept of anxiety and its influence on learning, as evidenced by the increasing documentation of research in this area. However, nursing in general, and nursing education in particular, has only recently demonstrated an interest in studying the role of humor. Robinson (1977), in a pioneering book in this area, reviews the functions of humor in health care settings and incorporates some guidelines for utilizing humor in teaching. Other health care professionals are beginning to promote the use of humor as a therapeutic tool; this has been best exemplified by the work of Norman Cousins, the eminent former editor of the Saturday Review and author of Anatomy of an Illness (1979). Despite these initial efforts to promote the use of the positive functions of humor, no research in nursing education relating to the use of humor as a teaching or evaluation strategy could be located. Even in the more general health area, published research is very limited.

The precise nature of humor has defied description since man began to communicate. Webster (1981) defines humor as "that quality which appeals to the sense of the ludicrous and absurdly incongruous" (p. 1102). The Encyclopedia Britannica (1977, pp. 5-11) defines humor as "that type of stimulation that tends to elicit the laughter reflex" and further classifies humor as either verbal or situational. Verbal humor includes puns, comic verse, jokes, anecdotes, satire, and allegory. Situational humor refers to the practical joke, impersonation and parody, comedies, tickling, visual arts, and music. Anthropologists and sociologists view humor as a means of reducing interpersonal tensions in a socially acceptable way. Humor may develop from a need for the sudden release from tension (Bergson, 1900/1960; Fry, 1963; Koestler, 1964).

Robinson (1977) identified humor as a complex coping mechanism operative in several areas: relief of anxiety, stress, and tension; release of hostility and anger; denial of reality; and as a means of coping with disabilities and death. With respect to humor operating to reduce anxiety and tension, Coombs and Goldman (1975) conducted a qualitative research study observing the use of humor by the hospital intensive care staff. They found that personnel commonly used humor to handle the emotional stress of caring for the critically ill and dying patients. Lightheartedness seemed to contribute to the quality of performance of the staff by reducing the emotional pressure and anxiety created by the constant contact with life-threatening circumstances. Coombs and Goldman (1975) suggested that laughter freed the individual from the burden of anxiety, confusion, cruelty, and suffering. Humor operates in terms of psychic economy and offers ego comfort through its meaning: "Look here! This is all that this seemingly dangerous world amounts to. Child's play — the very thing to jest about!" (Freud, 1905/1960, p. 220). Hence, the findings of this investigation demonstrated that the use of humor is an effective method for managing stress.

One of the potential problems concerning the use of humor in teaching and evaluation is that what is humorous to one individual may not be humorous to another. Research (cf. the Antioch Humor Test) has validated these differences in humor preference. It has also been observed personally that cross-cultural differences in humor are significant; thus, I believe that it is important to consider these differences when working with ethnically diverse groups of students.

Anxiety and Performance

Sarason et al. (1960) found that, in testing children: (a) high test anxiety interfered with performance on school tests or other "test-like" situations; (b) the greater the test-like characteristics of the task, the more the child's anxiety was manifested and the more it interfered with performance; and (c) conversely, reduction in the test-like characteristics of a task reduced the impairing effects of anxiety. Based on the above findings, we speculated that the use of humor in teaching and evaluation would attenuate the test-like characteristics of the evaluation session, and thus reduce the detrimental effects of anxiety.

Turning to other studies which focused on the relationships between anxiety and performance, Spielberger (1966) examined the effects of anxiety on academic performance among college students. The students were grouped according to low, middle, and superior abilities, based on their psychological examination scores. The highly anxious middle-ability students showed poorer performance than did the minimally anxious students. For the very superior students, increased anxiety levels appeared to enhance performance. Hence, the effects of anxiety levels seem to differentially affect students depending on their intellectual ability.

The general consensus among educational researchers is that the extent to which performance is affected by anxiety depends primarily upon task complexity and the level of ego involvement (Gaudry & Spielberger, 1971; Mandler & Sarason, 1952; Sarason et al., 1960; Sinclair, 1965). Peplau (1952) discussed how ego involvement increases the likelihood of anxiety in interpersonal relationships, especially in situations where

90

prestige and dignity are threatened by those from whom one cannot escape. She commented that, when one's performance is not perceived as strongly threatening to the ego, an individual's anxiety level is generally lower. However, as ego involvement increases, anxiety level also increases with resulting alterations in performance. Likewise, when the task is complex, increases in anxiety are reflected in alterations in performance.

Use of Humor in Testing Situations

Two studies were found which examined the effects of humorous tests with high, middle, and low anxiety groups of students. Smith, Ascough, Ettinger, and Nelson (1971) studied the tension-reduction effects of humor on the academic test performance of college-level students. During the first week of a psychology course, all students were given the Sarason Test Anxiety Scale. Control and experimental test groups were similarly apportioned by sex and anxiety level. At midsemester, the experimental group was administered a course examination containing humorous content items, and their performance was compared with that of the control group who received a form of the examination containing matched nonhumorous items. Both groups of students were told that results would contribute 50% to their course grade. Results indicated that high test-anxiety students receiving the non-humorous test form performed at a significantly lower level than did the high test-anxiety students who received the humorous test form.

In a second study related to use of humor in a classroom test situation, Townsend and Mahoney (1981) ranked students according to gender and anxiety level, and then randomly assigned them to either the humorous or non-humorous test groups. The humorous tests differed in Townsend and Mahoney's (1981) study (when compared to the Smith et al.'s 1971 study). In this case, Townsend and Mahoney included humorous supplements unrelated to the actual content of the test. In contrast, the Smith et al. test items themselves were humorous. The findings of Townsend and Mahoney's study differed from those of the previous study. Highly anxious students in this sample had lower achievement scores on the humorous test than the highly anxious students taking the non-humorous test. The reason for this conflicting finding, according to the authors, may be that the unrelated humorous content appeared as quite distracting to the highly anxious student.

In summary, humor has been shown to reduce anxiety and tension (Coombs & Goldman, 1975; Freud, 1928). Moderate to high anxiety has been shown to result in diminished performance when students are of middle ability (Spielberger, 1966), when tasks are complex (Sinclair, 1965), and when extensive ego involvement is present (Peplau, 1962; Sarason, 1956). Humorous tests, where humor was injected into the actual test items, were demonstrated to be helpful for highly-anxious students (Smith et al., 1971). No research studies were found which focused on the effectiveness of teacher's use of humor in clinical evaluations. Hence, this research was conducted to extend the present body of knowledge of clinical evaluation strategies applicable for nursing educators.

Current Study

The setting for this study was a community college in a large metropolitan area in southern California. All of the entering class of nursing students in an Associate degree program were invited to participate in the study. The actual sample included all 30 students who were enrolled, although one student was ill when the testing occurred and so did not participate. Thus, 29 subjects constituted the sample. All students were female but one, and all were Caucasian with the exception of one Asian. The ages for the subjects ranged from 23 to 38 years with a mean age of 28.3 years. Sixty-five percent of the sample subjects were or had been married. Eight subjects reported prior nursing experience, but none at a level higher than nursing assistant.

A quasi-experimental design was used to study the effects of deliberate teacher humor on anxiety and performance levels (see Table 1). It was not possible to randomly assign students to groups. Students were arbitrarily preassigned by the college to a basic nursing skills class and divided into three groups on a random basis. These groups were utilized as the experimental and control groups in this study.

Table 1

STUDY DESIGN

Groups	Pre-Intervention Procedure		Intervention	Post-Intervention Procedure
Control Group (R1) (traditional evaluation)	1. Demographic data form 2. Informed consent form 3. Spielberger's State Anxiety Instrument (all of these procedures to be completed prior to intervention)	NASOGASTRIC TUBE FEEDING LECTURE AND DEMONSTRATION	During return demonstration traditional evaluation strategy utilized (no intervention)	1. Performance evaluation concurrent with return demonstration carried out by both evaluator and observer. 2. Spielberger's State Anxiety Instrument (administered immediately following completion of performance evaluation)
Experimental Group (R2) (pause intervention)	Same as above		During return demonstration pause intervention utilized	Same as above
Experimental Group (R3) (humorous intervention)	Same as above		During return demonstration humor/pause intervention utilized	Same as above with one addition: the research assistant interviewed students relative to their reactions to humorous intervention immediately following completion of anxiety instrument.

92

The author carried out the experiment at the time in which each group was normally studying the Nutrition Module (where the procedure for nasogastric tube feeding was taught). The first group starting the Nutrition Module became the control group (R1), and received traditional teaching and demonstration, followed by traditional evaluation. The second group starting the Nutrition Module became the first experimental group (R2) which received the traditional teaching and demonstration approach, followed by an evaluation in which two pause periods were interjected during the evaluation to simulate the pause periods inherent in the humorous evaluation group (R3). The last group of students starting the Nutrition Module became the second experimental group (R3), and received the traditional teaching and demonstration followed by evaluation where humor was interjected at the beginning of evaluation as well as during the two pause periods.

Students were told at the end of the teaching and demonstration presentation that they could familiarize themselves with the equipment without instructor assistance, and that the first student's task performance evaluation would begin in approximately 30 minutes, with the remainder of the students following one by one. For the control group (R1), the subjects were asked to perform the nasogastric tube feeding procedure one at a time as demonstrated, without any pauses or humorous inserts by the instructor. For the pause-intervention group (R2), the task was performed sequentially in a nonhumorous environment with two intervening one- to two-minute pauses. The first of two pause interventions was introduced between the preparation (part 1) and the performance (part 2) on the performance checklist. The second pause intervention occurred approximately at the end of the feeding procedure (part 2) and the beginning of the closure (part 3). The two pause periods were structured to be approximately of the same duration as occurred for the introduction of humor with the humor/pause intervention group (R3). For the third (humor/pause) group (R3), the procedure paralleled that for the second group except that the one to two minute pauses included instructor-interjected humor. The first exposure that the students had to humor was via a humorous doctor's order. At the times corresponding to the two pause periods outlined for the pause-intervention group, a humorous anecdote was shared by the instructor with the student. Humorous responses of participants in the humor/pause group was noted and recorded on the performance checklist by the evaluator and observer.

Directly following the student's completion of the performance evaluation, a trained research assistant gave each student the Spielberger State Anxiety Inventory (1970) to complete. The students in the R3 (Humor/pause intervention) group was then asked by the research assistant to give their reactions to the humorous interventions. Five questions were asked:
1.   Did you notice any difference in the way the evaluation was conducted?
2.   If so, what was the difference and what was your reaction?

3. If not, some humorous anecdotes were made during the evaluation. What was your reaction to these?
4. Did this affect the way you felt?
5. Do you think this affected your performance?

Any humorous response, as evidenced by smiling, laughing, chuckling, or other visible expression of amusement, was noted on the performance checklist at the specified intervals by the observer and evaluator as described above. A maximum of one positive response constituted sufficient evidence that the student perceived the evaluator's behavior to be humorous.

Instruments for Data Collection

The instruments for data collection were (a) Spielberger's State Anxiety Inventory, Form X-1, which measures state anxiety only, and (b) a performance observation checklist.
1. The State Anxiety Inventory, published in 1970, measures state anxiety levels and has acceptable reliability and validity. The state anxiety scale has been shown to indicate actual levels of anxiety induced by stressful procedures when administered during or immediately following the stressful situation.
2. A performance observation checklist was developed by the author to assess performance level of clinical skills relative to nasogastric tube feeding. This checklist was based on procedures taught in the standard modular teaching/learning framework used in the course. The evaluation procedure exactly followed the content and format of the preceding lecture and demonstration.

Discussion of Findings

The following discussion of the data analysis and findings includes both quantitative and related qualitative results. Comparisons of the effects of the teaching strategy on state anxiety were performed using three separate measures. First, ANOVA compared the unadjusted posttest state anxiety scores of the three groups. Second, ANOVA procedure using pretest state anxiety scores as a covariate was used to compare the posttest state anxiety scores of the three groups. Third, ANOVA was utilized to compare the state anxiety change scores of the three groups. There were no statistically significant differences among the experimental and control groups for any of these comparisons on state anxiety. However, trends toward a significant difference in state anxiety change scores between groups R2 and R3 and between groups R1 and R2 were found. Although the required significance level of .05 was not reached, further evaluations using t-test gave

94

a probability of 0.084 which was sufficiently high to indicate a likelihood of significance using larger group samples. This indicates that the pause intervention group (R2) had a significantly higher state anxiety posttest score than did either group R1 or group R3. The pause intervention strategy was specifically designed to isolate the effects of the humor strategy from the effects of a pause or supportive opportunity to "regroup" or "collect one's thoughts." Such an opportunity was expected to contribute to the evaluative situation a nonthreatening, caring milieu. Although the subjects in the pause group (R2) did not appear any more anxious or uncertain than did the subjects in the other groups, the state anxiety reaction was higher; this might be due to the students' perception of the pauses as being perplexing or disturbing, rather than supportive.

Even though no significant quantitative group differences in state anxiety scores were demonstrated (i.e., the humorous intervention teaching strategy did not appear superior), pertinent subjective comments were made by five of nine students in the humorous intervention group, suggesting that humor had possible positive effects. For example, comments include "it calmed me"; "it let me know everyone is human and makes mistakes"; "the humorous stories put me at ease"; "I feel more at ease"; "I thought they [the evaluators] were trying to add a little levity to make me feel less anxious."

Turning to the question of whether humor assisted students to perform better, ANOVA procedures were performed. Among the three student groups, the humor/pause group (R3) showed the best overall performance, while the no-intervention group (R1) showed the next best performance, and the pause/intervention group (R2) performed most poorly. More specifically, comparison of task performance between groups R2 and R3 using ANOVA showed a significant between-group difference. A similar comparison between groups R1 and R2 evidenced statistical significance using a t-test. Also, comparison of groups R1 and R3 indicated a near significance at $p = 0.065$ using a t-test. Although the study failed to demonstrate the required level of statistical significance ($p = <.05$) in performance between the R1 and R3 students, there was a sufficient difference to indicate a likelihood that with a larger sample, statistical significance could have been demonstrated.

Qualitatively, the research assistant did indicate that humor was reported as helping five out of nine students during the task performance. Nevertheless, it is not possible to separate out the effects of the humor (true experimental effects) in one group R3 from the possible unintended effects of the pause in the R2 group. It should also be noted that the humor/pause students (R3) were initially uncertain about how to respond to the "doses" of humor. If the evaluator had introduced the anecdotes with a phrase such as "let me tell you something funny that happened to another student," the subjects in the humorous intervention group might have perceived a sense of permission to respond with a smile, chuckle, or laugh. Moreover, although the anecdotes were specifically related to task performance, beginning nursing students may not have been able to distinguish between those experiences which were humorous and those which were inappropriate.

Additionally, Pearson correlational coefficients were computed to assess the association between (a) posttest state anxiety scores and performance, and (b) state anxiety change scores and performance. No association between these variables was found; hence, the expected positive relationship between anxiety and performance did not materialize.

In searching for reasons why the humorous intervention did not have any demonstrable quantitative effect on anxiety, there are several possible explanations. One certainly may have been the small sample size. In addition, since humor is extremely individualized, the humorous insertions may not have been perceived as funny to all the students. Third, the humorous insertions were related to, but not an integral part of, the actual task/activity, and as Townsend and Mahoney (1981) demonstrated, these humorous insertions may have been distracting to some students, thereby cancelling out any possible effects on anxiety.

Implications

Based on these rather suggestive findings, there are implications relevant to nursing education in both the academic and practice settings. The nurse educator needs to be aware that humor may be effective as a cognitive strategy to assist students in stressful situations to gain control over anxiety, thus increasing their ability to demonstrate necessary competencies. The nursing inservice educator should also be aware that humor may be useful in helping instructors and staff alike deal with stressful performance evaluations. The qualitative findings, in particular, lend support to the idea that this additional evaluative strategy may enhance the nurse educator's effectiveness in carrying out stress-producing evaluations.

In the ten years since this research was done, much has been written about the benefits of laughter and humor as an aid to retention (Leidy, 1992), to promote learning (Watson & Lewis, 1990; White & Emerson, 1988), as an avenue to creative thinking (Ditlow, 1993; Gelazis, 1990), and to reduce stress (Leidy, 1992; Parkin, 1989; Warnock, 1989). Humor is being deliberately incorporated into educational programs through gaming, riddles and puzzles (Leidy, 1992), cartoons (Pease, 1991), anecdotes, skits, and humor profiles or diaries (Gelazis, 1990; White & Lewis, 1990). Yura-Petro (1991) also urges nursing professionals at every level to incorporate the human need for humor into the theoretical bases for practice. A concept analysis of humor for nursing practice has been developed by Ferguson and Campinha-Bacote (1989), attempting to clarify its use, nature, and properties. The defining attributes of humor have been identified as: (a) a tension reducer, (b) a form of therapeutic communication, (c) behavioral responses, and (d) a learning enhancer. Qualitative findings from the above research example do suggest that these attributes are relevant. In a study on the benefits of humor in reducing threat-induced anxiety, Yovetich, Dale and Hudak (1990) found that a sense of humor had a beneficial effect on self-reported anxiety. However, since both high sense of humor and low sense of humor subjects benefited from humor, these authors suggest that the artificial conditions for humor in a lab/research situation may inhibit the cognitive restructuring necessary to ameliorate negative experiences.

Another descriptive study was found (Warner, 1991) that examined senior nursing students' use of humor to cope with clinical experiences in a psychiatric setting. This study demonstrated that when students were encouraged to share humorous experiences, they did report utilizing humor to cope with stressful person-environment situations.

Bibliography

Bergson, H. (1960). Laughter. In J. J. Enck, E. T. Forster, & A. Whitley (Eds.), *The comic in theory and practice*. New York: Appleton-Century-Crofts. (Originally published, 1900).

Bernard, H. W. (1954). *Psychology of learning and teaching*. New York: McGraw-Hill.

Coombs, R. H., & Goldman, L. J. (1975). *A situation of distressed arousal and strategies of emotional detachment*. In L. Lofland (Ed.), Doing social life. New York: Basic.

Cousins, N. (1979). *Anatomy of an illness*. New York: Bantam.

Ditlow, F. (1993). *The missing element in health care: Humor as a form of creativity*. *Journal of Holistic Nursing*, II(1), 66-79.

Encyclopedia Britannica, Inc. (1977). *Encyclopedia Britannica*, 15th edition, vol. 9 (pp. 5-11). London/Oxford: Author.

Ferguson, S., & Campinha-Bacote, J. (1989). Humor in nursing. *Journal of Psychosocial Nursing*, 27(4), 29-34.

Freud, S. (1960). *Jokes and their relation to the unconscious*. (J. Strachey, Trans. and Ed.). New York: Norton. (Originally published, 1905).

Freud, S. (1961). *The complete works of Sigmund Freud*. (J. Strachey, Trans. and Ed.). vol. 21. London: Hogarth. (Originally published, 1928).

Fry, W. F., Jr. (1963). *Sweet madness*. Palo Alto, CA: Pacific.

Gaudry, E., & Spielberger, C. D. (1971). *Anxiety and educational achievement*. New York: Wiley.

Gelazis, R. (1990). Creative strategies for teaching care. *NLN Publication*, 41-2308, 155-165.

Koestler, A. (1964). *The act of creation*. New York: Macmillan.

Leidy, K. (1992). Enjoyable learning experiences-An aid to retention? *Journal of Continuing Education in Nursing,* 23(5), 206-208.

Mandler, G., & Sarason, S. B. (1952). A study of anxiety and learning. *Journal of Abnormal and Social Psychology,* 47, 166-173.

Mindess, H., Miller, C., Turek, J., Bender, A., & Corbin, S. (1985). *The Antioch Humor Test: Making sense of humor*. New York: Avon.

Parkin, C. J. (1989). Humor, health, and higher education: Laughing matters. *Journal of Nursing Education,* 28(25), 229-230.

Pease, R. A. (1991). Cartoon humor in nursing education. *Nursing Outlook,* 39(6), 262-267.

Peplau, H. E. (1952). *Interpersonal relations in nursing*. New York: Putnam.

Robinson, V. M. (1991). *Humor and the health professions*, 2nd edition. Thorofare, NJ: Slack.

Sarason, I. G. (1956). The effect of anxiety, motivational instructions, and failure on serial learning. *Journal of Experimental Psychology,* 51, 253-260.

Sarason, S. B., Davidson, K. S., Lighthall, F. F., Waite, R. R., & Ruebush, B. K. (1960). *Anxiety in elementary school children*. New York: Wiley.

Sinclair, K. E. (1965). The influence of anxiety and level of ego involvement on classroom learning and performance. Unpublished doctoral dissertation, University of Illinois.

Smith, R. E., Ascough, J. C., Ettinger, R. F., & Nelson, D. A. (1971). Humor, anxiety, and task performance. *Journal of Personality and Social Psychology,* 19(2), 243-246.

Spielberger, C. D. (Ed.). (1966). *Anxiety and Behavior*. New York: Academic Press.

Spielberger, C. D. (Ed.). (1972). *Anxiety: Current trends in theory and research*. New York: Academic Press.

Spielberger, C. D., Gorsuch, R. L., & Lushene, R. E. (1970). *State/trait/anxiety inventory*. Palo Alto, CA: Consulting Psychologists Press.

Townsend, M. A. R., & Mahoney, P. (1981). Humor and anxiety: Effects on class test performance. *Psychology in the Schools,* 18(2), 228-234.

Warner, S. L. (1991). Humor: a coping response for student nurses. *Archives of Psychiatric Nursing,* 5(1), 10-16.

Watson, M. J., Emerson, S. (1988). Facilitate learning with humor. *Journal of Nursing Education,* 27(2), 89-90.

Webster's Third New International Dictionary (Unabridged). (1981). Chicago: G. & C. Merriam, 1102.

White, L. A., & Lewis, D. J. (1990, March-April). Humor: a teaching strategy to promote learning. *Journal of Nursing Staff Development*, 60-64.

Yovetich, V. A., Dale, A., & Hudak, M. A. (1990). Benefits of humor in reduction of threat-induced anxiety. *Psychological Reports*, 66, 51-58.

Yura-Petro, H. (1991). Humor: A research and practice tool for nurse scholar-supervisors, practitioners, and educators. *Health Care Supervisor*, 9(4), 1-8.

CHAPTER VII

HUMOR IN QUALITY IMPROVEMENT

by Julia W. Balzer Riley, RN, MN

Hospitals are beginning to follow industry's lead in the implementation of interdepartmental quality teams. Nurses are being appointed to teams as members, leaders, and facilitators. Humor is a useful strategy to build teams and teach quality improvement tools. Turf issues make team-building a challenge. Data-driven problem solving involves working with new tools such as flow charts and cause-and-effect diagrams. This process need not be tedious. This chapter provides guidelines for the appropriate use of humor in quality improvement teams and grew from a need identified by the author from her experience as a quality improvement facilitator and team trainer. Humor builds trust in teams, fosters creativity, and energizes team members in their interdisciplinary approach to improved patient care.

Appropriate Use Of Humor in Quality Improvement

For humor to be effective, it is important to consider the kind of humor, how it is useful, and when it is useful. Humor may be positive or negative in content. Positive humor makes people feel good. It contributes to a working environment where it is safe to voice a different opinion. It creates an expectancy of positive interaction. Team members do not have to dread meetings. Humor adds a joyful, playful quality to the most dreary environment. Negative humor puts people down, ridicules, humiliates, and alienates, and often invites retaliation (Balzer, 1991). Inappropriate humor wastes valuable team time which is costly to an organization. Intentional positive humor is both a strategy and a perspective. This chapter presents techniques to use humor and creativity to lighten the process of problem-solving and to encourage a humorous perspective along the journey. The leader who can laugh at personal foibles establishes an environment where it is safe to try new approaches and to fail.

From my own work with humor, I have found it to be useful in the following three ways:

1. *Prevention*: As a facilitator of a team, I routinely used humorous ice-breakers or props which set a positive tone for the demanding work of solving chronic organizational problems. Team members seemed more committed to their role as team member than

concerned with protecting their department's turf. When team members knew they could expect a lighthearted beginning to a meeting, it prevented the grumbling that often precedes committee meetings.

2. *Perception*: Team members who have been through other hospital-wide programs often begin with a "here-we-go-again" attitude. When a nurse is charged with the responsibility of leading or facilitating a team and takes the time to add humorous and creative touches to illustrate the importance of the work of quality improvement, team members may take a fresh look. I give facilitators a magic wand during their team training. It can be used to illustrate confidence that people working together can create new solutions by the magic of team work.

3. *Perspective*: It is not always easy to see the big picture in the midst of the painstaking process of devising and implementing data collection instruments. I used a large valentine heart at the beginning of a meeting to remind team members that the patient is the heart of the work. This served to refocus the work, especially for the clinical team members who leave the work of patient care to attend meetings. It is easy to be discouraged about the value of the meetings when the data seem to be an end rather than a means to improve care.

To know when to use humor, nurses can use three criteria described in the work of Leiber (1986), a nurse humorist. Consider the following:

Content: Is the content in good taste? Does it make light of self rather than others? Is it offensive? Sexist or racial jokes are examples of negative humor.

Timing: Is this the right time? "Ain't-it-awful?" humor was just right after one team had re-examined its flow chart for "one-time-too-many" (see Table 1, "The Flow Chart Blues").

Receptivity: Is the other person receptive? Some people see humor as an interruption in the serious business of life.

It is important to respect differences in people. If a humorous intervention is unsuccessful, the nurse can explain it was intended to be helpful. In a team which I assessed to be less receptive to humor, I chose to use a creative activity which ended with spontaneous laughter because of the involvement of the team. To illustrate the importance of regular team attendance, I cut several pictures into jigsaw puzzle shapes and made sure there were the same number of pieces as team members. I gave each person present one piece and asked them to assemble the pieces. When one puzzle was incomplete it illustrated that the work of the team requires all its members, each of whom was selected for a unique contribution.

Table 1

The Flow Chart Blues

(Sing to the melody of "I've Been Working On The Railroad"
and sing it with FEELING)
I've been working on a flow chart
I'm going 'round the bend.
I've been working on a flow chart
Will it never end?

Can't you tell me when it's over?
How many more meetings will it take?
Can't you tell me when it's over?
I'm afraid my nerves will break?
++
But wait, it's flowing now more clearly,
I think the next step's in sight.
But wait, it's flowing now more clearly,
We're doing it just right!

The steps we take seem like such small ones.
I want to solve it right now!
The steps we take seem like such small ones,
But we can make it and how!
++
As we tidy up this flow chart
I see the end's in sight.
As we tidy up this flow chart
I think I see the light.

Can't you see us work together
All along the way?
We can do this all together
And make it seem like play!

© 1993. Julia W. Balzer, RN, MN
Used with permission.

103

Benefits of Humor in Quality Improvement

It is my experience that, as health care professionals begin to implement continuous quality improvement (CQI), the benefits of humor are amply demonstrated. Humor serves to:

1. Build communication
2. Encourage creativity
3. Promote problem solving
4. Speed the team-building process
5. Reinforce learning
6. Decrease stress
7. Add fun! Must we suffer to be productive?

My experience with the benefits of humor in CQI was confirmed after a workshop I conducted on its use. At this regional forum on quality improvement, participants experienced with quality improvement commented that if they could begin their quality improvement venture again in their setting they would use more humor. They reported too much seriousness as an impediment to team building. Representatives of those teams who had discovered the effectiveness of humor were eager to share what had worked in their teams (see Table 2, Humor and Creativity in Quality Improvement Teams).

Table 2:
Humor and Creativity in Quality Improvement Teams

1. Create a humorous team logo.
2. Create a "process parable," a story to illustrate a point; e.g., , The True Story of the Three Little Pigs, (Scieszka, 1989) which was used to illustrate that things are not always as they seem.
3. Include humor in brainstorming. Use a funny problem when teaching the tool such as all the reasons a child may give for not turning in homework.
4. Use skits in training.
5. By example, give team members permission to point out the amusing portions of the process. e.g., "With twelve sources of delay identified in the discharge process, it's a miracle anyone ever gets out of this hospital."
6. Use games; e.g., At the end of the team meeting ask trivia questions to groups on the team and award points to the winner.
7. When presenting customer service content share stories about the wrong way to treat a customer.

---

8. Create a team video or multimedia presentation which shows the members in action in their various departments.
9. Put on rubber gloves to "inspect" a problem.
10. Turn lights on and off in brain storming to help "turn on the light bulb of an idea."
11. Make a brief video to exaggerate the problem.
12. Place toys such as Koosh balls on tables in meetings to lighten the atmosphere and give something to decrease tension if necessary.
13. Use appropriate cartoons or "get well" cards for the problem.
14. Tell stories of other teams' "mistakes" to encourage the ability to laugh at ones self and to give permission to the team to take risks.

©1992. Julia W. Balzer, RN, MN. Used with permission.

Implementation

Ice-Breakers for Team Meetings

A brief ice-breaker or warm-up activity may mobilize the team and speed the communication process. It is important to remember that these activities must have a purpose which is clearly communicated to the team or the credibility of the leader or facilitator and the quality process may be compromised. The following are guidelines for such activities:

1. Choose an activity that is clearly identified as fun, an energizer; e.g., "What do you plan to do this week-end?" or "Name a favorite animal and tell why."
2. Make it brief. Richardson (1992) offers some rules for the timing of ice breakers. He suggests the following:

Length of Training:	Length of Ice Breaker:
1 hour	3-5 minutes
1/2 day	5-10 minutes
full day	10-20 minutes

3. Explain that the purpose of activity is to help members see each other as people, here to work together equally.
4. Recognize that team members' time is valuable and avoid the temptation to engage members in something "fun" at the expense of team business.

Team Name

The task of choosing a name can be a team building activity that sets the tone for the use of humor. It is helpful to provide examples. One group called themselves S.O.S., the seekers of solutions. A team dealing with delays in the discharge process called themselves the Movers and Shakers. Another team found a way to call themselves the M&Ms so they could have chocolate at each meeting. The Spartanburg Hospital System (Spartanburg, South Carolina) publishes the Total Quality Management Newsletter that highlights teams with such names as: The Crime Busters (safety and security); The Skeletal Crew (radiology); The Go Getters (transport service); Captain Calorie and the Nutrinettes (food and nutrition); and The Databyte and the Diskettes (computer services).

Refreshments at Meetings

"Breaking bread" together is a tradition than symbolizes friendship and a common purpose. Providing food is a nurturing activity that may make team members feel special. Meeting oral needs is believed to decrease anxiety, making the work easier. Consider using food occasionally as a sign of camaraderie along the journey. One team member shared home-baked cookies, dubbed "Food for Thought," at a meeting held during the holiday season. Other teams have brought "do-it-yourself" ice cream sundae ingredients or ordered pizza. Having a meal at each session may distract members from the tough work of meetings that are tightly wedged into busy schedules. The work may be slowed by concerns about drinks, etc. Food served occasionally is seen as a treat and can be part of the celebration along the way.

Music in Team Meetings

Music is a shared experience and a delightful tool to highlight the quality process. A humorous song, "The Flow Chart Blues" sung to the melody of "I've been Working on the Railroad" (see Table 1, above), was written by the author after yet another painstaking review of the flow chart. Nonverbal cues from the team confirmed the facilitator's own impatience with the process. In an attempt to acknowledge this, and yet maintain team momentum, this song was sung by the team at the beginning of the next meeting. The laughter that followed seem to re-energize the group. This was a brief, team-building event that cleared the air and got the team back on "track" (humor is everywhere). Humorous rap songs written about the process or popular songs with appropriate lyrics have been used. One vice president of a hospital wrote an amusing rap song about the CQI process and performed it in a cheerleader's outfit at a team celebration party.

Meeting Agenda

A written agenda can organize the CQI team meeting and help avoid tangents. An agenda can include an objective, items of business, times for each item, and member responsibilities in the meeting. To capture team members' attention, add an appropriate cartoon or clip art, a scrambled word, a puzzle, or a Sniglet. When I intended to distribute toy kaleidoscopes at the meeting to illustrate team members have different ways to view the problem, the word kaleidoscope was scrambled on the agenda with a note, "Can you unscramble this word?" The team's member from transportation entered the meeting saying, "It was kaleidoscope!" A would-be poet lurks in many health care professionals. Who could resist a meeting announced with this on the agenda?

Roses are red
Violets are blue
Here is another
MEETING for you!

Toys to Teach the Process

A small toy, one which symbolizes the current step of the CQI process or issues of a group process, can be distributed at the meeting or attached to the agenda sent prior to the meeting as a teaser. For example, a small magnifying glass symbolizes the re-examination of the flow chart. A toy car with pull-back action denotes delays in the problem-solving process, or the frustration at what seems like having to move backward to collect more data before moving forward toward a solution. A small superball demonstrates the more energy you put into the process, the higher you soar. A small paper bag or container with the team name can be distributed to store the toys and in anticipation of more toys at future meetings. I found team members appreciated the toys as a demonstration that the facilitator and team leader wanted to relieve the tedium of tough work and make learning fun. This activity has been duplicated by team members for meetings in their own department. I am called for ideas and sources for toys. This illustrates the perceived benefit of humor and creativity in teams.

Props To Help Facilitate Group Process

A picture is worth a thousand words. A collection of props can be useful in group facilitation and training. Clown props, available at clown supply stores, are large versions of common items. A huge pencil with a big eraser gives permission for mistakes which seem inevitable in the process of data collection. It may be difficult to construct an instrument to collect the right kind and amount of data the first time a team proceeds with data collection. Large scissors demonstrate cutting the bureaucratic red tape to implement breakthrough solutions. Cross-functional teams "cut" through the excuse,

107

"We've always done it this way." A construction hard-hat was worn by one facilitator to enter a meeting after much dissention in the previous meeting. She explained she had "come prepared" this time. In team training, when I distributed magic wands to new facilitators, they were instructed to use them when necessary, signifying "Abracadabra, we're moving right along in this process." The wand also lessened the tension experienced by staff who were being asked to complete what seemed an impossible mission, to learn the CQI process complete with tools, to facilitate a interdisciplinary team, and guide it to an innovative solution to a chronic problem. Team facilitators might be staff members assigned a team with managers and directors. A little humor served to illustrate that "we're all in this together."

Comic Relief

Humor can change the perspective and interrupt the expectation that everything must be perfect and serious. Humor can unfreeze a group when people seem stuck with only one solution. A group of six vice presidents in a hospital donned huge sunglasses as an important, no doubt "dazzling" presentation was to be delivered. The presenters could relax knowing that administrators were people with a sense of humor who were anticipating positive results. A whistle or funny noise-maker can convene a meeting or call members back from a break. A clown nose applied in a timely fashion can lesson tension by introducing the unexpected. A Koosh ball can be tossed to members in a brainstorming session.

Team members can be encouraged to wear buttons that fit the mood. A favorite is a "No whining" button. Another, slightly irreverent button states, "We, the unwilling, led by the unknowing, are doing the impossible for the ungrateful." Humor can be used to acknowledge unspoken opinions or attitudes. By bringing these barriers out in the open in a light way, people learn that it is acceptable to be skeptical and part of the process. Denying such resistance leads to a "group think" mentality where it is only safe to express opinions of administration. This inhibits creativity and the tough questions that often need to be asked if innovative solutions are to be discovered and implemented. (Changing a corporate culture in not easy!)

Magic Tricks In Meetings

Simple magic tricks amaze team members and can be used to illustrate a point or concept. A break-away fan can symbolize what happens when staff do not work together to provide customer service. Service recovery "magically" restores the fan. A magic coloring book illustrates all are needed to solve the problem. The pages are blank at first. When the team is asked to raise imaginary pencils to draw pictures, they "magically" appear. Then, with the help of the group, the pictures are "magically" colored. A local magic shop can provide ideas and instructions. Remember the magic is to illustrate a concept. Use only one illusion at a time for full impact and explain the purpose of the illusion, that is, what it illustrates. Team members saw the facilitators efforts to lighten meetings as a demonstration of commitment to the team as people who although having the best of intentions, experienced boredom or frustration with the process.

Team Celebrations

From my experience in a consortium of hospitals, although celebration or reward for teams is valued, administrators are struggling with how best to provide it. One concern expressed in a regional quality professional association was that the intrinsic reward of satisfaction with a job well-done might not be enough to sustain commitment. A rebuttal was the concern that if the extrinsic rewards, especially monetary, were substantial competition might have a negative effect on the integrity of the process. At a workshop I conducted, representatives from a number of hospitals shared ways they had used humor and creativity to devise celebrations (see Table 3).

Table 3:
Quality Improvement Celebrations

Recognition luncheons or dinners with many balloons and decorations
Small awards
Annual plaques
Highlights of team progress in hospital newsletter
A movie with popcorn at the hospital
A picnic with dunking booths using administrators as targets
A birthday celebration of CQI
Official sharing party where teams present projects in booths/displays
Administrators sing CQI songs
"Pat on the Back" bulletin boards for recognition
Door prizes at celebrations
Smiley face stickers for those participating in teams
Cake and ice cream party in team meeting

At the end of a pilot team I facilitated, before an official method of celebration had been devised, we served lunch and distributed "Outstanding in the Field" buttons to members (with a picture of a cow grazing in a field).

Inside Humor

The most meaningful team building humor may be the humor that evolves from the group as it works together, or "inside humor." One team that works on customer service issues identified "fussified" customers who, without proper service recovery, pitched a "hissy-fit." Whenever a lull occurred in a meeting, a team members had only to evoke these phrases to get a good laugh which served to refocus and energize the group. Team members come up with one-liners such a "I won't think about that today. I'll think about it tomorrow at Tara," or "Toto, I don't think we are in Kansas anymore." The facilitator can encourage members to share those "under-the-breath" comments to sanction "inside humor."

Caveats

The following are lessons learned that are useful when considering the use of humor and creativity in quality improvement.

1. Humor is not for everyone. Try these techniques and evaluate them in your setting. Humor may be a selected, intentional intervention, not necessarily a natural occurrence.

2. Recruit willing participants. If someone hesitates to be in a skit, honor this. If humor is not comfortable, it causes embarrassment.

3. Some team members report hesitation about using humor with upper management in corporate quality councils meetings. At another facility, reports are routinely delivered in a humorous and creative format. Corporate cultures vary, but they are all made of real people. Humor is a risk. Personal comfort may be one predictor of success as it means confidence in presentation and the expectation of success.

4. Avoid put-downs, sarcasm, and other negative humor.

Summary

Humor and creativity delight the team members. To be willing and able to brighten the lives of colleagues whose personal and professional lives are not always smooth is a wonderful gift. With cost containment driving health care delivery and reimbursement, this is not an easy time for staff. CQI can be feared as a way to cut positions, another belt-tightening measure. It may be seen as just another of management's "bandwagons" that will go away if ignored. Team leaders and facilitators can model the healthy behavior of taking your work seriously, but yourself lightly. An example of this kind of event occurred when team members were offered a variety of beautiful or funny hats to choose as "thinking caps" for brainstorming. To see the increased interest, to feel the energy of the team, delighted the group and the facilitator.

During CQI meetings, team members from a variety of departments with varying amounts of education come together with an equal voice. Laughter is a shared human experience that connects people who may only seem different. The pride at being valued and heard may have a ripple effect throughout the organization. One transporter whose initiative and energy were noted has become touted as the "CQI guru" and serves as a reminder that involvement energizes staff.

Yes, this is serious business, but it can also be funny business . . . just like life!

Bibliography

Balzer, J.W. (1991). *Humor in the Workplace*. Jacksonville, FL: A.K.H.

Basso, B., & Klosek, J. D. (1991). *This job should be fun! The new profit strategy for managing people in tough times*. Holbrook, MA: Adams.

Iapoce, M. (1988). *A funny thing happened on the way to the boardroom: Using humor in business speaking*. New York: Wiley.

Juran, J. M. (1989). *Juran on leadership for quality: An executive handbook*. New York: Free Press.

Leiber, D. B. (1986). Laughter and humor in critical care. *Dimensions in Critical Care* 5(3), 163-170.

Richardson, T. (1992). Creative teaching strategies (workshop), Jacksonville, FL.

True, H., & Mang, A. (1980). *Humor power: How to get it, give it, and gain.* Garden City, NY: Doubleday.

Scieszka, J. (1989) *The true story of the three little pigs.* New York: Viking.

CHAPTER VIII

COMEDY CARTS, BASKETS, AND HUMOR ROOMS

by Leslie Gibson, RN, BS

Who would ever imagine that a hospital or health care environment would encourage our patients' families and staff members to laugh? Health care is a very serious business, and it is a very stressful business. We are finding, with modern technology and research, that laughter and humor are wonderful stress relievers. There is probably no more stressful place in the world than the hospital setting where patients have lost control of their environment and what people are going to do, and they don't know how they will respond to various treatments.

In this chapter, I will explore the benefits of creating a humor program for the patient, family members, hospital staff, and the medical staff. I will examine how to start such a program and how to apply humor in health care settings. I will discuss some of the obstacles to avoid. I will provide a sample budget and show how to develop creative funding ideas. I will also discuss how to train volunteers, and how to manage supplies once you have started a program. Finally, I will share humor programs that are already in place.

First let's start with the patient. When patients come into the health care setting, we have already identified some of the stress, some of the fear, and frequently pain that they are experiencing. When a patient is allowed to play, to laugh, the first benefit of a humor program is the distraction from that physical pain, even if it is just for a few moments, while watching a movie, playing a game, playing cards, or watching a clown provide a close-up magic. First, it is a distraction as well as a form of relaxation. Patients start to feel a sense of control and participation with the volunteer or the person who is working with them to get them to laugh and relax just a little. For some patients who have been in the hospital for quite a while, the diversion is a respite from the monotony that they face on a daily basis.

Current research reveals that there are many healing powers in the physiology of laughter (Fry, 1992). Dr. Fry discusses the findings of research which he acknowledges is a very young science. The first researchers actually started studying humor in the 1930s. Their findings were that the initial effect of laughter is stimulatory; the pulse and respiratory rate are elevated and, after the laughter subsides, a relatively brief relaxation phase ensues. Fry says that muscles not participating in the laughter behavior are generally flaccid, while the involved muscles undergo a light workout. With a very hearty, boisterous laugh, a large mass of muscle tissue participates, creating a total body response that is clinically beneficial because it provides bedridden or wheelchair-bound patients with some conditioning or exercise. Postoperative patients physiologically benefit from exercising the lungs and the pulmonary toilet effects are highlighted in this research (Fry, 1992). We have taught our patients to cough and deep-breathe while bracing the new incision to exercise the lung to prevent pneumonia. We have a patient take a deep breath, brace the incision, and go "ha-ha-ha" three times in order to exercise the lungs.

Cousins (1979) has become a classical clinical model in the positive healing effects of laughter as a therapy. His detailed experiences are available in the bestseller, Anatomy of An Illness, where he records how he cured his own collagen-related degenerative spinal disease by using large doses of vitamin C and a regular diet of Candid Camera episodes and humor-provoking movies. He would provoke himself into ten minutes of genuine belly laughter, which acted as an anesthetic and provided at least two hours of pain-free sleep. When the pain returned, he would turn on the humor stimulus again. He wanted to prove scientifically that laughter and the effects of positive emotions could improve the body chemistry. His physician took blood samples for sedimentation rate readings just before, as well as a few hours after, the laughter episodes. Each time there was a drop of at least five points. This drop by itself was not substantial but it held and was cumulative. This has been one of the few documented cases available to prove the physiological value of laughter as good medicine. Cousins also describes how laughter interrupts the panic cycle of an illness. Anyone who is a parent or has taken care of a small child knows that after a small child has fallen, skinned a knee or an elbow and sees the sight of blood, the child begins to panic and cry. The caring person, whether it be a babysitter or parent, picks up that child and usually puts the child on the hip and distracts the child by singing a nursery rhyme, pointing to a bird or a squirrel in a tree to distract the child from the painful or bloody type of experience. This is a simple yet classic example of some of the psychological benefit of using humor in the health care setting.

The Patient's Family

If the family is in a waiting room or an emergency area, family members are usually frightened so their stress levels are high; a humor program might provide relief from that emotional pain (Buxman, 1991; Cousins, 1978). If they can be watching a two-hour funny movie, it might distract them for the hours that they may have to wait during surgery. A humor program doesn't eliminate that source of fear and frustration, but it gives them a form of relief. It can also help family members share some positive

114

communication as they visit with their loved ones at bedside. If there are some joke books on the bedside table, they can pick up the joke books and start sharing some funny stories and start laughing together, creating a win-win situation when the family and the patient can interact.

As they leave their loved one to return to their home responsibilities, family members also find a sense of relief that the relative in the hospital or health care setting can watch a movie or read a good book. Relatives feel less guilty as they leave and go on to other tasks.

Hospital Employees

The next benefits of a Humor Program that I would like to discuss are those that effect hospital employees, such as nurses and doctors. I find that nurses are often the ones who order the comedy carts or the baskets to be delivered to a patient's room. These items will distract the patient , and allow the nurse more time to be with other patients, get the charting done, and possibly lessen the need to medicate the patient for discomfort.

It is quite interesting to see the positive reactions of hospital personnel. Nurses occasionally play a few tricks on the doctors, and vice versa, if there is a basket or cart nearby with props such as a pair of Groucho glasses. (We have seen excellent examples of this in the television series, M*A*S*H, as enacted by Alan Alda.) Creativity starts to flow and it helps communication between staff members when they are able to have a little laughter or a little fun at the nursing station, which is normally a stressful area. Staff members can use their own unique sense of humor and have some fun with their co-workers. Humor can be a reminder that the patient is a person; it helps the doctor, the nurse, the social worker, and health professionals in general to avoid looking at a person as a number or disease. For instance one might hear, "the gallbladder in room three" instead of "Mr. John Smith with the gallbladder problem." As healthcare becomes more specialized and technical, it is important to balance the high technology with a high sense of personalization.

The Administration

From the administrative point of view, quality is a key word in health care today, and the administration at Morton Plant Hospital (Clearwater, FL) is delighted to have a humor program that prompts favorable responses from patients. One patient wrote, "This is the first time I have ever enjoyed a hospital stay," after having used a comedy cart during hospitalization. It is good business for health care facilities to learn of the positive psychological benefits that a humor program can provide (Strombach, 1992).

115

Getting a Humor Program Started

When starting a humor program of any kind, it is important that you assign some key people to work as a small group. It is important that you try to include people from the volunteer program, someone from Pastoral Care, a representative from the nursing department, someone from the physical therapy or occupational therapy departments, a person from social services, and someone from administration. Your starting committee should contain less than ten people to determine what kind of program would work best for your facility.

As with any new program, the very first question that will be asked is, "How much will this cost?" So the committee needs to prepare a budget. You need to ask the committee some specific questions such as, "Do we want to serve the patients with baskets or bags that will be readily available at nursing stations, or do we want to have portable carts that can be wheeled to patient's rooms?" "Can we afford multiple carts or do we want to set up a sample humor room or a library where the patients and staff members can check out materials?" There are a variety of ideas already in practice, and as you start to feel the excitement of the group you will find a lot of creative suggestions for your own settings. Although this project seems simple and it would be easy to want to serve everybody at one time, it is better to go slowly. I recommend that you start on one floor and get the patients and staff members motivated. To help you in your brainstorming efforts, examine the following ten steps in developing a low-cost, effective humor program (see Table 1).

Table 1.
Ten Steps for an Effective Humor Program

1. **Designate Area**
   A. Waiting Room
   B. Media Center
   C. Book Shelves
   D. Filing Cabinets
   E. Humor Room
2. **Decorate and Label Area**
   A. Signs
   B. Cartoons
   C. Posters

---

3. **Resource Library**
   A. Collect reading materials, books, comics, magazines
   B. Seek out used bookstores for humorous books
   C. Encourage staff and patients to bring in favorite humorous material
   D. Keep puzzles and crossword books available
4. **Surprise Box**
   A. Keep a box or basket filled with funny glasses, animal noses, masks, puppets, gags, card games, etc.
   B. Check garage sales for these items
   C. Change these materials regularly
5. **Audio-Visual Resources**
   A. Arrange an exchange with your local libraries
   B. Consider all the media available (tapes, albums, cassettes, etc.
   C. Catalog the available humor material
   D. Provide headsets for the hearing impaired
   E. Place ratings on the video tapes for patient reference
6. **Bulletin Boards**
   A. Display patient's best jokes, pictures, or cartoons
   B. Change this material weekly
   C. Encourage employees or family members to participate
7. **TV and Cable Programs**
   A. Scan program schedules and highlight humorous entertainment
   B. Post the schedules of presentations
   C. Use closed-circuit humor programs when able
   D. Purchase a video contract to show humorous movies
8. **Advertising Your Humor Program**
   A. Encourage group involvement through your hospital newsletter
   B. Promote contests and awards
   C. Keep flyers in waiting rooms and nursing stations
9. **Assign Jesters**
   A. Use volunteer groups to help
   B. Plan social events
   C. Enhance team spirit with volunteers
   D. Promote creative ideas such as theme days at the institutions
10. **Evaluate**
   A. Request patient responses
   B. List favorite material available
   C. Change material regularly to met the needs of individual departments
   D. Be sensitive to minors, ethnic groups, and avoid sexual humor

The most popular and common items to stock humor rooms, comedy carts, or baskets include video tapes, audio cassettes, cartoon albums, humorous books, games, gags, bulletin boards, and a costume corner or costume selection (Buxman, 1991; Gibson, 1990; Johnson, 1991; Wooten, 1992).

The overall budget will determine the extent of your costs to start a program. I have worked with some hospitals that have been given a grant for over $20,000. They were able to create a room from scratch and could offer both room and carts for the patients. This was in Canada, where the cancer patient could go to a humor room or have a cart stocked with a variety of items and baskets that could be delivered to rooms with wigs and games provided. As you look at your needs and what your facility would like to have, keep these ideas in mind and let the creativity flow.

Financing

Morton Plant Hospital's Comedy Connection has been providing humor therapy since 1989. We started after receiving a grant from the Humor Project founded by Dr. Joel Goodman. We started on one floor and our growth has expanded from 1989 with one cart to twelve carts. We now average over one-thousand requests monthly. We also have had time to train nearly seventy volunteers. In our experience, we have found that there are many hurdles to climb to develop a humor program. Our first hurdle was that of funding. We used many creative resources in order to get our program off the ground. There are many local clubs that seek non-profit projects. I would recommend that the committee explore local service clubs such as Rotary, Kiwanis, Women's Leagues, and ask them to sponsor a program in your facility. There are also grants that are available under research ideas. A sample budget is included as a guideline (see Table 2).

Table 2

Sample Budget

Talking Books	$ 500.00	Practical joke and gag items	200.00
		Portable games	225.00
Portable Cassette Players	300.00	Photo albums for cartoon journals	150.00
VHS VCR (1/2 inch) w/remote	500.00	Printing charges	300.00
VCR cabinet with wheels		Decorating	200.00
and locking doors	800.00	Arts and Crafts Supplies	500.00
Humor videotape selections	1,000.00	Advertising	300.00
Clown Makeup Kits	75.00	Miscellaneous	200.00
Costumes	125.00		
Humor Library	200.00	EXPENSES TOTAL....................$5,575.00

118

This sample budget is designed to be used as a tool to talk with administration, the auxiliary or, service organization, to serve as a guideline of what you will need to start a humor program. It should be flexible. Depending on your needs, if you limit your program to a basket you can remove the VCR and portable cabinet from the list. You will then customize your budget to have sufficient funding for the items you do want to obtain.

You can expand the program to include additional carts or wagons or additional video tapes. In the mid-1990s, an average cart and VCR costs around $1,300 for a combination. As you continue to grow, which will happen with this program, additions will not be as expensive as your initial start-up cost. Many of the departments within the health care facility can also start planning their budgets around a humor program. Administration, in many cases, often starts this kind of program. Many hospitals have a foundation and have donors who would like to donate funds to a worthy cause. Once you get the word out, you may not even have to ask people for help. Sometimes opportunities arise in unexpected places. In Virginia, a video store was going out of business. They donated 2,000 videotapes and all of their recorders to the hospital cancer center for the patients' use. A hospital in Pennsylvania put a request for donations of humorous items in the newspaper. They received thousands of items. So don't think funding is an obstacle for your organization.

Communication

Communication is a major problem in almost every organization. We often wonder if the right hand knows what the left hand is doing. The better communication that your committee can promote and share with the patients, the staff, and the volunteers, the more successful your program will be. It is important that you get the word out about this program by using flyers, posters, or any kind of publication that your facility has on a weekly or monthly basis. Some programs have failed because they did not get the word out to the staff and the patients. They had beautiful rooms and supplies available, and no one used them. What a waste! Get creative, call in the press, have parties around the event, balloons, festivities, and clowns. Try to kick off the program with a party atmosphere. Then people will pick up on the excitement for such a program.

Space

Space shortage seems to be another obstacle for most institutions. Hospitals are very limited on space. Every department wants more space, and they may view a program such as a humor program being definitely low on the totem pole for square footage. This reinforces the need to start your program on one floor where you have a designated area. You could start with a portable cart that holds everything and that can be locked, but kept at the end of a hallway as a decorative piece. Have specific hours for use and keep a sign posted on it so people won't just walk by and say, "Gee, what is this?"

After your program begins to expand and the popularity of the programs grows, then a natural need will emerge: a storage room for all your supplies. We have gone from being in a janitor's closet to having two patient rooms set aside for our program. This program has been growing for over five years, so don't think it happened overnight. There are solutions to space wars and one of those is to be patient, to go gently, and to be grateful for any space that your facility will allot you for this program.

Managing Supplies

As you get the supplies, management of all of the equipment is your next hurdle. Table 3 represents a sign-out sheet.

COMEDY CART

Auxilian Name: _____

Room	Patient	VCR's/Audio Machines	DATE Out	In	Tapes, Books, Games	DATE Out	In	Comments

Daily Location of VCR's:	Volunteer General Comments:	Joke of the Day:
1.		
2.		
3.		
4.		
5.		
6.		

This is a system that has worked extremely well for our program. In the beginning, we did not encourage people to sign things out, feeling that they would be excited about

120

our program and return the materials. This did not happen. Unfortunately, we lost many valuable supplies and books because they were popular and everyone could enjoy them. It would be embarrassing and legally binding to accuse a patient or staff member of removing these items from the program. It is, therefore, important to develop a system so that the participants who want to use your materials can fill out the date, the department or the room number, and the resource they have taken, whether it be a magazine, game, or videotape. When they return the item, they could use a column to fill in the return date and comments about the material that they have had. Keep a check on where the carts were left, so that volunteers can pick them up in certain locations and replace them in the appropriate spots.

In managing the supplies, it is important to have an inventory of all your materials. This can be done by having one group of volunteers inventory all the books and label them. Put a number on them so that you can catalog them. Bookkeeping is a lot easier if your books, cassette tapes, and videotapes are labeled with number systems so that you don't have to write out the full names each time. As you receive donations of tapes and supplies, it makes everything better organized if they are well managed and documented. This cataloging will also serve as a wonderful tool to let patients know what you have available. Putting together a simple catalog of your inventory for patients, staff members, or nursing stations serves as a tool for communication, as well as a management of supplies, to let people know what is available.

The last and most important item for the success of your humor program is to train volunteers and to have in-service programs to train and educate staff members, including programs for physicians. Many people think a humor program won't involve much training. In reality, training is important particularly if you are using volunteers from the community who have never had hospital exposure. They must know some of your hospital policies. We recommend that you have volunteers go through your organizational orientation program to learn the protocols for basics. It is often difficult for people to find their way around the many corridors and constructions, and they will get frustrated.

It is vital that your volunteers and the people who work on the program know their roles. It is important that you set up guidelines regarding what's expected of them. Are they going to have the time and want to play a game of checkers or sit with a patient and enjoy their company? Early in your program, your volunteers will need extra projects like this to keep busy until word of the program starts to spread. It is important to keep your volunteers busy because if they are not, they may become discouraged and drop out of the program.

We have steps to begin actual work on our comedy connection. A new person comes in and receives training with the hospital orientation program, as well as on-the-job training for at least two weeks with the individuals on the comedy connection. A typical

121

day begins by looking through the daily needs, then checking messages-whether on an answering machine or phone mail system, and keeping a message book with a dated notebook for each day. Then comes picking up the machines and the equipment logged out the previous day and returning them to storage. Next is answering the requests that have come in from the messages on a first-come first-served basis. The amount of time that a patient can keep a unit or a cart in the room should be limited to twenty-four hours if there are many requests.

As the videotapes and audiotapes come back to your program, it may be necessary to rewind tapes after checking them in. Sometimes tapes are returned in different boxes, and need to be placed in the correct containers after rewinding. If a form to sign out the supplies is used in your orientation of volunteers, it is important that you teach them how to complete the form. It is just like preparing anyone for a new job; however, this is an exciting job because the goal of participation is to cheer the patients and family members. The goal is also to have fun and enjoy your outreach as well as helping those in need.

Volunteers need to know not to touch patients and not to be loud, especially if they are clowns, in a hospital. We also strive not to force ourselves on anyone, and we encourage children and adults to join us. We are not performers, we just want to smile and promote good cheer. A good piece of advice for your volunteers is to caution them to avoid asking the patient, "How are you today?" because we want to divert them from the "poor me" angle. It is better to ask, "What can we offer you today?"

It is important to first ask patients if they would like to have their photo taken, especially in the case of a photo with a clown. Confidentiality is important as you review hospital policies with your volunteers. Most volunteers should go to the nursing stations prior to going around on the floors to ask if there are any isolation rooms or any particular areas that they should stay away from so they can avoid problem situations.

It is sometimes a good idea if you have a sticker or card with a "smiling face" that you can leave with patients if you want them to leave the hospital remembering the good cheer that you brought. It helps them to remember a positive experience. Whenever your volunteer is in doubt about a given situation, it is better to avoid going into the room. Let me emphasize that it is more important for a patient to come out to the cart or up to the clown for the stimulation than for volunteers to appear to force themselves upon them by entering their room. Many people are in the hospital grieving the loss of a loved one or are visiting a patient who has received tragic news. There is a time and a place for everything, and we are there as adjuncts to medical treatment-not deterrents.

Recruiting volunteers to work on the program is made fairly easy by the many people who are retired and are looking for ways to feel useful and needed. Your committee may want to send out a notice to local churches or civic organizations who may be interested in publishing the need for volunteers. After you decide how many volunteers you need, gather them together for a get-acquainted party. They will tend to be enthusiastic and devoted to the success of your program. Most important, it should be fun for your volunteers as well as an opportunity for them to reach out to the community and work with your health care facility.

The Administrative Head of the program is usually a staff member but may be a volunteer. This leader helps with program development, management of supplies, and training of volunteers. The program will need three or four volunteers in the initial stages; as the snowball grows into a snowman, you will get more volunteers, more requests, and in time it will grow together beautifully. Keep in mind, Victor Borge's phrase "Laughter is the shortest distance between two people."

Reactions of patients and staff members to these programs are the best part of reaching out to start such a program. At Riverside Methodist Hospital (Columbus, Ohio), they have a cart called Tickle Me Pink and the program is centered around a big pink cart stocked with laughter-inducing samples — chattering teeth, fake noses, coloring books, toy spiders, games, and other amusements. One of their cancer patients, a 31-year-old man, was asked about this program and his comment was, "I would rather laugh than walk around and be gloomy."

We have had several tragic cases at Morton Plant Hospital. In the summer of 1991, a 35-year-old man became a quadriplegic as a result of a diving accident. He signed out Groucho glasses from the comedy cart and, when the volunteers went in to see him the following day, he was wearing the glasses. He told our volunteer that he learned that if you can't be good in bed, at least be funny. We found in cases like this young man's that gag items such as funny glasses or clown noses are valuable resources for the patients to express themselves. We leave these gifts with them if it is therapeutic during the recovery period.

A funny thing happened with two of our volunteers who had just completed orientation and were eager to take the cart around. While making rounds, they noticed a police officer sitting outside one of the rooms; they ignored him, not realizing his reason for being posted in front of a patient's room. They went in and asked the patient if he would like to have something from the comedy cart, that it was a free program for the patients. He responded, "Yes, I would like to have a movie. What do you have?" Innocently, one of our volunteers suggested Cool Hand Luke. The patient broke out laughing, raised his hands which were in chains, and said, "I don't think I'd like to see that since I'm chained to the bed." The embarrassed volunteer was sincere, and felt embarrassed that she had suggested this movie. However, when he was given the selection list, she grinned when she saw that this large adult male wanted to watch the Disney movie, "The Little Mermaid."

There are two hospitals in England that have started comedy programs. In

Saskatchewan, Canada, a hospital started a program called Jokes on Spokes. Northern Maine Medical Center (Fort Kent, ME) has started a humor wagon. Duke University has had a laugh-mobile since 1989. We do not have a complete list of all of the humor programs that have been created throughout the world; however, we have discovered that the term "laughter" is contagious and is epidemic. We hope that this book will help convince you to be an infectious carrier.

Bibliography

Buxman, K. (1991). Make room for laughter. *American Journal of Nursing.* 91(12), 46-51

Cousins, N. (1978). *Anatomy of an illness.* New York: Norton, 1979.

Fry, W. F. (1992) The physiologic effects of humor, mirth, and laughter. *Journal of the American Medical Association,* 267(13), 1857-1858.

Gibson, L. (1990). *Laughter: The universal language.* Ozona, Fl: Pegasus Expressions.

Goodman, J. (1992). Laughing matters: Taking your job seriously and yourself lightly. *Journal of the American Medical Association,* 267(13), 1858

Jaworski, M. (1992, November). Circle this: Take two laughs. *Family Circle,* p. 11

Klein, A. (1989). *The healing power of humor.* Los Angeles: Jeremy Tarcher

Lloyd, E. L (1938). The respiratory mechanism in laughter. *Journal of General Psychology,* 10, 179-189.

Paskind, H. A. (1932). Effects of laughter on muscle tone. *Archives of Neuro Psychiatry,* 28, 623-628.

Wooten, P. (1991) Jest for the health of it: Creating a comedy cart. *Journal of Nursing Jocularity,* 1(4), 42-43.

Strombach, B. (1992, May-June). Selling your humor program to administration. *Laugh It Up,* p. 5

CHAPTER IX

HUMOR JOURNAL FOR NURSES

by Doug Fletcher, RN

It is now generally accepted that humor is an effective tool in nursing (Robinson, 1991). However, this was not always the case. The following is a historical perspective of the development of the first (and so far, only) humor magazine for nurses, the Journal of Nursing Jocularity.

Conception of the Idea

Through all of my nursing school courses, only one of my instructors gave my class any resources related to the use of humor as a therapeutic modality. The one reference she made wasn't even from a nurse. She made brief mention of Norman Cousins' (1971) book, Anatomy of an Illness, in which he used, among other things, laughter therapy to combat ankylosing spondylitis, a very painful chronic inflammatory disease that affects the spine and adjacent structures. The positive effects of humor and laughter were not mentioned once in any of my nursing textbooks. Humor was used in the classroom to calm the anxious nursing students. But information about the serious side of humor? Not much.

I did graduate from nursing school with my sense of humor intact (although a little skewed). After working for four years as a nurse in telemetry and critical care, I was vaguely aware of the need for humor in the health care setting, especially in critical care and emergency areas where death and suffering were just part of the job. Gallows humor reared its head whenever the stress of the job got to us. After seeing a copy of the Journal of Polymorphous Perversity, a psychology journal parody, it dawned on me just how important the use of this type of humor really is for our mental health. Being able to laugh at the horrible stress-inducing situations that nurses see and participate in gives them a new perspective to situations that add hypertension, ulcers, heart disease, digestive disorders, mental illness, and burnout to our already busy schedule. With all that in mind, I decided to publish a humor magazine for nurses.

Development of the Idea

My research began at two university libraries. I found a couple books and a handful of journal articles about the use of humor in the health care setting, but almost nothing that actually poked fun at, or allowed nurses to laugh at this bizarre profession of ours. I was intrigued and baffled by this. A day seldom went by that I didn't see nurses using gallows humor in their jobs, and something funny was always posted on the nursing lounge bulletin board having some fun with our stressors. I telephoned a couple of the major nursing journals and told them (well, I lied) that I was a nurse cartoonist, and wanted to know if they would be interested in my work. In general, their response was, "That type of humor is inappropriate in a nursing magazine." I was even more baffled. If humor was such an important coping mechanism for nurses who are actually doing the nursing care, why did the major publications ignore it or refuse to acknowledge it? I was soon to find out.

Implementation

In October 1989, I placed a classified ad in four of the major nursing journals stating "Nurses with a sense of humor needed as writers, artists, and contributing editors for a humor magazine for nurses." Much to my surprise, I received over 400 responses from nurses with an interest in the idea. I was able to put together a volunteer staff of 18 contributing editors and many more artists and writers (all nurses) to begin the process of developing a humor magazine for nurses. I put together a draft copy of the first issue of the Journal of Nursing Jocularity and mailed it to the editor of every nursing journal I could find an address for. In my naive excitement at the publication of the first humor magazine for nurses, I expected rave reviews and letters of announcement in the other nursing journals. Was I in for a shock! From working nurses who received a draft copy of our first magazine, the response was over 90% positive, but I did get some negative letters, one from a nurse who had only seen the ad but not the magazine.

> I am appalled at the prospect of this trash. This is a crucial time for nursing. When many professionals are working diligently at demonstrating to the public the seriousness and importance of nursing. Now, you people are going to help our profession take several steps back by making fun of it. There is a time and place for laughing with one another, but publishing it is not the place. This will only serve to detract from the seriousness, critical analysis, and professionalism of nursing. My vote is against this absurdity! (Grant, 1991, p. 3).

And another letter sent to the Journal of Nursing Jocularity: "Your magazine stinks. I hope I drop dead before the Jello-brained people of your generation are in charge of everything " (Walker, 1992, p. 5).

From the editors of the nursing journals who did reply (only about 20%), I got an interesting response. Most of them were very cautious, with comments such as "Very interesting, best of luck," "Be cautious, a few nurses will be offended by caricatures of themselves," and "Very funny, please do not print my response."

But what happened next really shocked me. Because the Journal of Nursing Jocularity was being sold by subscription only, I decided to advertise for subscribers in the other journals. Was I surprised when the American Journal of Nursing REFUSED my ad. Especially since they did run my classified ad when I was looking for "Writer and artists for a nursing humor magazine." I got a brief letter from someone in the advertising department informing me that my ad was inappropriate for their magazine. Were the nurses at this magazine completely without a sense of humor? Were they afraid that a humor magazine for nurses would be perceived as unprofessional? Did they lack the capacity to see the funny side of this bizarre and stressful profession? I really wanted to find out, so I called American Journal of Nursing and asked to speak to the person who made the decisions about what was appropriate for nurses to read in advertisement. I was never able to actually speak with anyone that knew anything. I was informed by an advertising rep that those decisions were made by committee, but nobody on the committee was available. I requested a return phone call from anyone on "The Committee," but after numerous calls to different departments, without a response, or even a reasonable explanation, I just gave up. So why are the nurses who are editing the current nursing literature afraid to allow us a brief reprieve from the endless pages of gallbladder dressings and chest tube updates? Probably because of the misunderstanding and misconception of humor's value.

The following is an excerpt from the letters to the editor section of Critical Care Nurse, the publication for American Association of Critical Care Nurses (Bockwoldt, 1992). It is an excellent example of a nurse who perceives the use of humor or fun, completely inappropriate.

"I just received my second issue of Critical Care Nurse and I am quite displeased. The magazine does not look like it is being published by a professional organization. Specifically, the excessive use of color and multiple font styles and sizes throughout the articles is very distracting . . . ."

"I was shocked at the inclusion of the cartoon-like illustrations sprinkled throughout. They are unnecessary, look foolish and further stereotype nurses as young, smiling, Caucasian females in crisp white dresses. I'm surprised you didn't paint caps on them "as well . . . ." Frankly, if the magazine were not a member benefit, I would cancel my subscription immediately. The new

127

format detracts considerably from the credibility of the journal, and I will seriously reconsider whether to reference it in my papers in the future"(Bockwoldt, p.18).

Have we become so professional that we are unable to enjoy our work? The author insinuates that there is something wrong with young and smiling. Could the young and smiling be nurses with high ideals, enthusiasm, and the ability to remember why they went into nursing, or have they been trampled down by our rampant "terminal professionalism?" It sounds as if the writer believes that nurses should not be able to express their work in a creative fashion with the use of colors or decorative fonts. She insinuates that drab and uncreative is a sign of professionalism.

As a publisher, I know that eye appeal has a tremendous effect on how we respond to the printed word. It used to be that professional journals were printed in black and white with very limited graphics. But this is not professionalism, it's lack of budget. These journals serve a very useful purpose as an avenue for the publication of research. They printed articles with funds provided by advertisers, or from paid subscriptions. But it is difficult to attract advertisers to a periodical that does not have visual appeal. Colors and decorative fonts are perceived values, and advertisers want to be associated with value, whether real or perceived. Keeping a magazine financially viable on subscription sales alone is virtually impossible. Only a handful of the over 10,000 periodicals in the U.S. have been able to do it.

Does nursing, research, and academia have to be dull and boring to be professional? Can't it be fun? It can, and it should be fun. If you watch someone working, who is also having fun, you will also see enthusiasm. And caring. Why can't we show our enthusiasm for our work by dressing the story up?

Humor is a touchy subject, especially gallows humor. Gallows humor which might poke fun at the patient or customer is only appropriate when used within the confines of the health care provider group. Once that gallows humor has gone beyond the group, it will be perceived as spiteful and uncaring by the patient, and rightly so. For the patient is unable to empathize with the stress of caring for the sick and dying on a daily basis.

As the first humor magazine for health care professionals, we took some big risks trying to determine what should and should not be included in the magazine. When black or gallows humor is used within the confines of a small group of health professionals, it can easily be forgotten, or passed off as an attempt to deal with the stressors of the moment. But once black humor is printed, it takes on a whole new perspective. It is permanent. It cannot be taken back.

An observation that I have previously mentioned in my Editor's Note (Fletcher, 1991) "The closer our work is to pain and death, the darker our humor is. ER and ICU nurses are some of the sickest people I know when it comes to humor" (p. 3). That dark sense of humor created a small scandal in one issue of the Journal of Nursing Jocularity. Each issue of the magazine has a contest in which readers send in their funniest caption for a captionless cartoon. The journal uses an impartial judging committee of nurses to choose the winner. In one instance, the judging committee happened to be comprised of critical care nurses. The cartoon illustrated a patient in bed, and another patient in a wheelchair, with a large head dressing, being brought into the room by a nurse. Much to my surprise, the critical care nurses chose the caption "I ordered a steak, not a vegetable!" as the winner. I knew this caption was beyond the realm of good taste, but because the impartial judges chose it, I felt it was my responsibility to publish it. Much to my surprise, we only received two letters objecting to the caption .

Your winning caption contest where a person in a wheelchair is referred to as "a vegetable" is offensive. It's one thing to poke fun at ourselves or situations but not to label another in such an offensive manner. Since I strongly support the use of humor therapy in nursing, this issue was a disappointment. Nursing should be above denigrating others — it is against the basic credo of our profession (Zlock, 1993, p. 4).

And

I had the opportunity to see your magazine at work and was totally disgusted at what was printed. In this day and age when nurses are trying so hard to be respected and seen as a professional, your magazine only deters from this achievement. Your efforts to bring humor to our everyday situations has only brought embarrassment. How could you reward the cartoon caption "I thought I ordered a steak, not a vegetable." How could you find humor in this? Your publication is a disgrace to the bedside professional (Mush, 1993, p. 4).

And this is how I responded:

When I published that caption, I knew it would get a few negative responses. I use a panel of nurses who are not associated with the Journal of Nursing Jocularity to help determine which caption is the funniest, and that caption was the winner. Their initial response was "that's sick." But they laughed because it's real, and because they deal with it. Their laughter was a very healthy coping mechanism. I'm not trying to avoid responsibility for that caption. I set up the judging system, and I carried through with accepting the caption that was chosen. I knew that caption was gallows humor that maybe was a little over the line of good taste and political correctness, but I will always defend the use of gallows humor for medical professionals. In a profession that deals daily with death and dying, or even worse, dealing with the brain dead patient that is not allowed to die, gallows humor can be a very appropriate as long as it is used exclusively within members of the profession.

129

It would NOT be appropriate to share that cartoon with a patient or family member but this magazine is subscribed to by health professionals, not lay persons (Fletcher, 1993, p. 4).

Did these letters change our editorial content? No, not really. We were always cautious about what we published. And we have rejected many manuscripts that would have been totally offensive to the general public and a large percentage of health care professionals. We only hope that future winning cartoon caption in our contest is within good taste (relative to the readership, of course).

As the Journal of Nursing Jocularity has grown, so has the number of manuscripts received, allowing us to be a little choosier about what we publish, thus improving the quality of stories used. In general, quality writing doesn't have to rely on shock value to get its laughs. But we do walk a fine line, publishing a humor magazine for a profession that is stressed by its daily activities. We want to provide the humorous release that stressed-out nurses need. As I said in one of my editor's notes:

> Cute stories about a flower arrangement shaped like a heart for a recovering CABG patient are nice, but they don't help us relieve the anxiety of watching a 32-year-old man with two young children die of a massive coronary. Sometimes we need to degrade a little; kick the "Professional Pedestal" out from under our feet, so that when we pick ourselves up, we get a little different perspective (Fletcher, 1991, p. 3).

At the time of this writing, the journal has over 30,000 subscribers and continues to grow. Over 95% of the letters we receive are in a positive vein. We continue to receive constructive criticism from nurses who feel strongly about the use of humor as a therapeutic tool, and see the journal as an insightful periodical necessary for the well-being of nurses. Since the winter 1993 issue, the journal has been indexed in Cumulative Index to Nursing and Allied Health Literature. The journal's annual "Humor Skills for the Health Professional" conference is attended by over 800 health care humor enthusiasts. These events reinforce the validity of humor in the health professions.

Conclusion

Nurses need to differentiate between being the butt of the joke and being a part of the joke. Publishing nursing humor will always be a delicate undertaking. If we publish a squeaky-clean magazine that only tells cute stories, we would lose subscribers who are most in need of gallows humor due to their work environment. If we publish only the blackest of humor, we would lose subscribers who only need to brighten their profession, because it would remind them just how oppressive the profession can be. Nurses should be able to enjoy their profession. The Journal of Nursing Jocularity was intended to look at the lighthearted side of our profession, and avoid the "terminal professionalism" that creeps in and squelches the ideals we once held as new grads. Because nursing is such a high-stress profession, we have to publish humor that reflects the atmosphere prevalent in the nursing setting today. It is a legitimate concern that the black humor of nursing will fall into the hands of the layman and the humor be misconstrued as the work of a heartless, cynical profession. But because humor is one of our most powerful coping mechanisms, I feel that publishing gallows humor for health professionals is a risk we need to take. A humorless, burned-out nurse will be viewed as a heartless, cynical professional-maybe even the proverbial battle-axe.

Bibliography

Cousins, N. (1979). *Anatomy of an illness.* New York: Norton.
Bockwoldt, D. (1992). Letter to the editor. *Critical Care Nurse,* 10(12), 18.
Fletcher, D. (1991). Editor's note. *Journal of Nursing Jocularity,* 1(4), 3.
Fletcher, D. (1993). Editor's note. *Journal of Nursing Jocularity,* 3(1), 4.
Grant, S. K. (1991). Letters to the editor. *Journal of Nursing Jocularity,* 1(1), 3.
Mush, K. (1993). Letters to the editor. *Journal of Nursing Jocularity,* 3(1), 4.
Walker, N. (1992). Letters to the editor. *Journal of Nursing Jocularity,* 2(2), 5.
Zlock, T. (1993). Letters to the editor. *Journal of Nursing Jocularity,* 3(1), 4.

CHAPTER X

CARING THROUGH HUMOR: ETHICAL CONSIDERATIONS

by
Sandra E. Ritz, RN, MSN, MPH
and
Ute Goldkuhle, RN-ANP, MS, MPH

"We nurses use humor jest for the health of it, but make sure the jest is just, and not for just us!" Sandy Ritz.

Nursing is a moral art which emphasizes a commitment to care for as well as to give care to other human beings (Curtin, 1990). That commitment underlines the value of the nursing profession to the patient's or client's quality of life. The nurse is the only one among health care professionals who spends twenty-four hours with institutionalized patients or has sustained contacts over time with clients in the community. This places the nurse in a unique position to assess and/or affect the patient's quality of life. Facts cannot be changed; i.e., irreversible morbidity, a child born with a severely handicapping condition, a quadriplegic person as a result of trauma or disease. However, the conditions under which people live out these facts can be changed: "It is nursing's responsibility to create the opportunities and the atmosphere in which patients or clients can actualize their potentials and live their lives as fully as possible" (Curtin, 1990, p. 284).

Humor can be realized as a therapeutic value to enhance quality of life. Although not proven to cure disease, humor can help patients cope with the stress of illness and feel better. Humor may not cure the cause of pain, but it can alleviate suffering. So, when is the use of humor appropriate and beneficial in the fragile and highly charged arena of health care?

Professional Values and Principles

Professional values and principles described in the code of ethics (American Nurses Association, Code for Nurses, 1985) provide guidance for conduct and decision-making in carrying out professional responsibilities. Hippocrates, who identified the need for a proper balance of body "humors" to maintain health, also stated the first rule of medicine: *Primum Non Nocere, or First, Do No Harm*. It stands to reason, then, that the use of

133

humor in health care must be of benefit and not harm. Beneficence (doing good or not doing harm) and nonmaleficence (avoiding harm) have remained the universal moral principles guiding the health care professions. They both imply a fundamental principle, respect for persons, which justifies nursing actions (American Nurses Association, 1985).

Whether a health educator, nurse, physician, or other health professional, the principles of beneficence and nonmaleficence obligate the provider to care for the client above and beyond what might otherwise be in the best interest of other parties. Nurses, in their decision to use humor in communication and the choice of what type of humor to use, must always consider the patient's or client's needs first. The professionals must determine whether the humor they choose to use is for the benefit of the patient's needs or their own coping needs. In practice, nurses engage in a therapeutic partnership with the patient or client. For this partnership to be effective, it is essential to build mutual trust and confidence in each other's role. A fiduciary relationship exists, as the patient is dependent on the nurse. The patient is in dire need of care, while the nurse is held accountable to a standard of performance to provide the care needed and to promote well-being in the best interest of the patient. As a patient advocate, the nurse has a responsibility to respect and protect the patient's right to self-determination. When applied within the context of this nurse-patient relationship, humor can be therapeutic for both the patient and the nurse. As such, the use of humor in health care is an issue of professionalism and calls for adherence to a code of ethics. Caring through humor requires skills, strategies and assessment techniques for it to be beneficial to the patient or client and to be certain to not do harm.

> I don't know what humor is. Anything that's funny-tragedy or anything, it don't make no difference so [long as] you happen to hit it just right. But there's one thing I'm proud of — I ain't got it in for anybody. I don't like to make jokes that hurt anybody (Will Rogers, cited in Peter & Dana, 1982, p. 207).

Therapeutic Use of Humor in Nursing Care

Nursing practice is highly rewarding, yet it is also highly stressful and tension-laden. In general, health care professionals often feel overwhelmed and inferior when faced with today's problematic health care settings. By the very nature of their intimate contact with patients over extended periods of time, nurses are at high risk to release tension through inappropriate humor expressions. Although this anxiety-releasing humor may benefit the nurse, it may violate the principles of beneficence or nonmaleficence. The care for the ill, dealing with complex family dynamics and crises, attending to physician directives, meeting the obligations of institutions and/or considerations of complex psychosocial and economic factors-all may lead to inappropriate use of humor as tension release without concern for the well-being of the patient or client.

Robinson (1991) questions whether the gallows type of humor used by staff with their peers is appropriate to be cultivated to use in interaction with patients. Carlyon and Carlyon (1987) believe that health providers should keep professional gallows humor in the "in-group" as patients would be devastated by such apparent callousness and indifference to their suffering. Humor used unintentionally by health professionals for their own needs can be at the expense of the recipient and violate the principles of the therapeutic partnership. It can instill shame or a feeling of loss of power, causing injury to self-esteem in patients and/or loss of self-respect in some co-workers. For instance, health care situations such as operating rooms or intensive care units are highly stressful. Patients are in extreme compromised and/or dependent positions. As a way of coping, health professionals often see them from a "detached view." This detachment may be expressed through humor as a relief from tension, anxiety, frustration or the release from the harsh realities of life (Robinson, 1991).

It is essential to consider the context of humorous interactions, as from the patient's perspective it is easy to assume that joking and laughter is occurring at the patient's expense (Leiber, 1986). Patients who are unable to share in the laughter with the nurses may be harmed by feeling that the nurses are laughing at them and/or do not care about them. A commitment to caring for patients and their needs can be maintained while nurses use humor for their own coping needs. For example, self-control and delayed gratification can be utilized by nurses to delay the laughter until there is a safe distance to assure that the patient will not be harmed (Warner, 1991).

Purtilo (1990), a professor of Medical Ethics, points out that joking and teasing between the patient and the health professional can be used constructively to allow people to express hostility, covert exhibitionism, and anxiety. It can permit exploration of the humor and irony of the condition in which the patient is placed by illness or injury and can reduce tension when it unnecessarily exists. Joking, however, can also be an attempt to sidestep an issue that needs to be addressed directly. Jokes used as put-downs or continual verbal fencing or humor applied to boost low self-worth as a control mechanism should be discouraged as they violate the therapeutic relationship with the patient or client.

"The real wit tells jokes to make others feels superior, while the half-wit tells them to make others feel small" (Wheeler, cited in Peter & Dana, 1982, p. 112). Salameh (1983) emphasized that therapeutic humor may question or amplify specific maladaptive behaviors, but does not question the essential worth of a person. However, harmful humor questions a person's sense of personal worth, such as in racist or ethnic jokes.

Therapeutic humor is concerned with the impact of humorous feedback on others as a sign of acceptance while harmful humor brings out signals of rejection and has a callous, bitter aftertaste. Tasteless humor restricts, stigmatizes, and retaliates while tasteful humor strengthens, brightens, and alleviates discomforts.

From a sociological and anthropological perspective, humor used as a method of social control can actually undermine one's self-esteem. Ethnic or "sick" jokes, satire, ridicule, or teasing can thus be harmful to the patient, as it can instill feelings of shame, failure and self-doubt. This negative humor makes fun of the perceived behavior, customs, personality, or any other traits of a group or its members by virtue of their specific sociocultural identity (Apte, 1987). The culture of the butts of ethnic jokes is subordinate to and derivative from that of the joke tellers, and "the butts of the jokes may be liked or disliked, but they are not esteemed" (Davies, 1990, p. 322).

The objective of any therapeutic humorous intervention is to laugh with another, not at another. There is a balanced sense of humor among those laughing together (Leiber, 1986). Carlyon and Carlyon (1987) recommend that if one must initiate humor, it is best to be of the self-deprecating type. If health professionals poke fun at themselves, it indicates to the patient that there is humor in all of us and our situations.

It dawned on me then that as long as I could laugh, I was safe from the world; and I have learned since that laughter keeps me safe from myself, too. All of us have schnozzles-are ridiculous in one way or another, if not in our faces, then in our characters, minds or habits. When we admit our schnozzles, instead of defending them, we begin to laugh, and the world laughs with us (Jimmy Durante, cited in Peter & Dana, 1982, p. 44).

Humor can also be seen as one tool in health education to forestall negative emotions, especially fear and panic (Carlyon & Carlyon, 1987). Beyond the use of humor to help a person cope, it may be even more valuable if therapeutic humor is used to help one hope. "Coping humor is a valid and essential use of the sense of humor . . . . [Humor] is a generator of energy, allowing one to 'hang in there.' By itself it cannot sustain the human spirit. If our humor is limited to laughing at the hopeless, in time, it will become, sarcastic, cynical and destructive" (Eberhart, 1986, cited in Fry, 1987, p. 61). Carlyon and Carlyon (1987) suggest that the best humor in patient care happens spontaneously to meet the needs of the moment as perceived by the patient. However, contrived cheerfulness and trying to be funny might be resented. Instead, it can be very therapeutic and effective to create a warm, friendly and reassuring atmosphere by genuinely smiling a lot.

Another consideration of caring through humor in respect to the patient's right to autonomy is to evaluate whether the patient or client prefers to use humorous interaction. Such preference is influenced by the individual's own value system, culture and mores, personalities and attitudes. For example, in some persons of Japanese descent, their

136

laughter may not be a sign of humor; it may actually be a culture-specific physiological response to feelings of embarrassment or shame.

"In matters of humor, what is appealing to one person is appalling to another" (Melvin Helitzer, Comedy Writing Secrets, 1987). As indicated earlier, a therapeutic partnership with the patient or client implies the principle of respecting the patient's right to self-determination. Health professionals have a duty to honor the self-respect and dignity of each individual as an autonomous, free actor (Hiller, 1987). Haig (1988) warned that humor should only be introduced to a patient who is known in some depth by the therapist in order to facilitate therapy. He also recommends that all humor be implemented only at appropriate times for the patient and that it be preceded by a "play signal" so that the patient can understand the context. Fry (1987) identified the powerful significance of paradox in humor and that the "self validating/invalidating paradox, 'I am joking'" establishes the "play-frame" that is essential for humor to be experienced "as humorous, rather than peculiar, or assaultive, or eccentric" (p. 57).

With certain patients it may be inappropriate to attempt any use of humor. For instance, it has been shown that patients with certain types of mental illness, (schizophrenia, obsessive/compulsive disorder, hysteria) prefer nonhumorous interventions (Rosenheim, Tecucianu, & Dimitrovsky, 1989). Leiber (1986) believes that humor has no place at the height of a crisis. However, after the acute crisis subsides, humor may assist with adjustment to the crisis and may decrease tension (Bellert, 1989; Leiber, 1986). Of note is that sometimes humor at the height of crisis may occur and may be appropriate only if generated by the person actually experiencing the crisis. This ability to produce spontaneous humor is an effective coping mechanism during stress (Bizi, Keinan, & Beit-Hallahmi, 1988; Rosenberg, 1991).

"Dying is not difficult. But comedy. . . . that is difficult" (Actor Edmund Keene on his deathbed, cited in Harrison, 1991, p. 241). Norman Cousins' positive influence on literature devoted to the idea that people can control their immune systems with their minds can also have negative implications (Cousins, 1979, 1989). As Angell (1989) points out, it can result in an approach that ultimately leads to "blaming the victim" (p. 249). If the patient is not amused by a health professional's attempts at humor, and if there is a subsequent worsening of his or her medical condition, it could be seen as the patient's fault. Angell (1989) stressed that "at a time when patients are already burdened by disease, they should not be further burdened by having to accept responsibility for the outcome" (p. 253). Another aspect of the principle of autonomy in a therapeutic partnership is the case where a health care provider may be opposed to a form of treatment and the patient requests the treatment despite the opposition of the health care provider (Brody & Engelhart, 1987). For instance, Norman Cousins (1979) was fortunate to have a physician who was willing to permit his self-directed care and choice of humor

137

treatment in the course of his disease. Other patients may not be as fortunate. In any case, the patient has the right to seek out another health care provider who is willing to provide the preferred form of treatment (i.e., laughter therapy) and must be free to do so. But the patient has no right to impose a servitude on the health care provider (Brody & Engelhart, 1987); in this case, to directly provide humor. As a patient advocate, the nurse might inquire about and facilitate humor therapy or provide information to the patient on available options.

Humor Assessment

To gain an appreciation of the patient's sense of humor, the nurse can make a humor assessment. The situational context, the nature of the nurse-patient relationship, the patient's receptivity (i.e., level of consciousness) and timing must all be incorporated into a humor assessment. Examples of questions when interviewing the patient include whether the patient values the use of humor; what types of humor and jokes the patient prefers; what are the patient's favorite comedians, movies and sitcoms; what would the patient give as an example of a humorous event; what are the patient's likes and dislikes about humor, etc. This will help the nurse to better understand and respect the patient's autonomy, while demonstrating a fine sense of caring for another individual's well-being. In addition, before implementing humor, the patient has a right to be informed of the harms and benefits of humor. Nurses can share what their intentions are in trying to uplift the patient and create a humorous atmosphere.

Conclusion

The essence of caring through humor is having an impact on the quality of life of the patient or client. Quality of life relevant to clinical medical ethics is defined as "the subjective satisfaction expressed or experienced by an individual in his or her physical, mental, and social situation;" or "the subjective evaluation by an onlooker of another's subjective experiences of personal life" (Jonsen, Siegler, & Winslade, 1986, p. 102). To advocate for a quality of life of patients involves therapeutic approaches that may not actually cure a patient's condition, although it could alleviate suffering and enhance comfort. Through a professional code of ethics, nurses are obligated and empowered within the context of the nurse-patient relationship to use any means of nursing interventions that may strengthen, enhance, and secure the patient's quality of life. Humor can be a powerful and effective therapeutic approach to improve a patient's perceived quality of life.

Caring through humor requires knowledge of the ethical principles and professional obligations underlying a therapeutic partnership. Principles of beneficence and nonmaleficence stand out to not harm the well-being of the patient or client. Respect for the patient's autonomous rights requires an assessment of the patient's sense of humor, humor preferences and objections, sociocultural background, particular situation, and contributory contextual factors (i.e., ability to communicate, etc.). Caring through humor requires keen sensitivity to know when and how it is appropriate to use humor or joking in the best interest of the patient.

"There is a striving among health caregivers for a connectedness with others, for a culture of caring in organizational structures, for the high touch with the high technology. There is indeed a call to consciousness, a call to get in touch, a call to caring for the compassionate healer" (Gaut & Leininger, 1991, p. ix). Having fun while caring for the sick is not a paradox but a heightened level of professional conduct. Caring through humor strengthens and elevates both the patient and the nurse in their therapeutic partnership when they can laugh and smile together.

According to Victor Borge, "Laughter is the shortest distance between two people."

Bibliography

American Nurses Association. (1985). *Code for nurses with interpretive statements.* Kansas City, MO: Author.

Angell, M. (1989). Mind over disease is a myth. In B. Szumski (Ed.), *The health crisis: Opposing viewpoints* (pp. 249-253). San Diego: Greenhaven.

Apte, M. L. (1987). Ethnic humor versus "sense of humor." *American Behavioral Scientist*, 30(1), 27-41.

Bellert, J. L. (1989). Humor: A therapeutic approach in oncology nursing. *Cancer Nursing*, 12 (2), 65-70.

Bizi, S., Keinan, G., & Beit-Hallahmi, B. (1988). Humor and coping with stress: A test under real-life conditions. *Personality and Individual Differences*, 9(6), 951-956.

Brody, B. A., & Engelhardt, H. T. (1987). *Bioethics: Readings and cases.* Englewood Cliffs, NJ: Prentice-Hall.

Carlyon, W., & Carlyon, P. (1987). Humor as a health education tool. In P. M. Lazes, L. H. Kaplan, & K. A. Gordon (Eds.), *The handbook of health education, 2nd edition,* (pp.111-121). Rockville, MD: Aspen.

Cousins, N. (1979). *Anatomy of an illness:* Reflections on healing and regeneration. New York: Norton.

Cousins, N. (1989). *Head first: The biology of hope.* New York: Dutton.

Curtin, L. (1990). The commitment of nursing. In T. Pence & J. Cantrall (Eds.), *Ethics*

139

in *Nursing: An anthology* (pp. 283-286). New York: National League for Nursing (Pub. No. 20-2294).

Davies, C. (1990). *Ethnic humor around the world*. Bloomington: Indiana University Press.

Fry, W. F. (1987). Humor and paradox. *American Behavioral Scientist, 30*(1), 42-71.

Gaut, D. A., & Leininger, M. M. (Eds). (1991). *Caring: The compassionate healer*. New York: National League for Nursing (Pub. No. 15-2401).

Haig, R. A. (1988). *The anatomy of humor*. Springfield, IL: Thomas.

Harrison, R. (1991). *A damned serious business: My life in comedy*. New York: Bantam.

Helitzer, M. (1987). *Comedy writing secrets*. Cincinnati, OH: Writer's Digest Books.

Hiller, M. D. (1987). Ethics and health education: Issues in theory and practice. In P. M. Lazes, L. H. Kaplan, & K. A. Gordon (Eds.), *The handbook of health education*, 2nd edition (pp. 87-107). Rockville, MD: Aspen.

Jonsen, A. R., Siegler, M., & Winslade, W.J. (1986). *Clinical ethics, 2nd edition*. New York: Macmillan.

Leiber, D. B. (1986). Laughter and humor in critical care. *Dimensions of Critical Care Nursing, 5* (3), 162-170.

Peter, L. J., & Dana, B. (1982). *The laughter prescription: The tools of humor and how to use them*. New York: Ballantine.

Purtilo, R. (1990). *Health professional and patient interaction*, 4th edition. Philadelphia: Saunders.

Robinson, V. M. (1991). *Humor and the health professions,* 2nd edition. Thorofare, NJ: Slack.

Rosenberg, L. (1991). A qualitative investigation of the use of humor by emergency personnel as a strategy for coping with stress. *Journal of Emergency Nursing, 17*(4), 197-203.

Rosenheim, E., Tecucianu, F., & Dimitrovsky, L. (1989). Schizophrenics' appreciation of humorous therapeutic interventions. *Humor, 2*(2), 141-152.

Salameh, W. A. (1983). Humor in psychotherapy: Past outlooks, present status, and future frontiers. In P. E. McGhee and J. H. Goldstein (Eds.) *Handbook of Humor Research*, vol. II (pp. 61-88). New York; Springer.

Warner, S. L. (1991). Humor: A coping response for student nurses. *Archives of Psychiatric Nursing, 5*(1), 10-16.

Unit 2:
Focus: Patient

CHAPTER XI

HUMOR IN THE HA-HA HOSPITAL

by Patty Wooten, BSN, RN

The acute care hospital setting can present many challenges and threats for the patient and the nurse. Humor and laughter can be effective coping tools for them both. This chapter will examine the beneficial effects of humor for the patient during recovery from the acute stages of illness as well as for nurses during delivery of care.

Illness, either acute onset or exacerbation of a chronic illness, can be a stressful event for the patient. Hospitalization, separation from family, invasive procedures, complex technology, or unfamiliar caregivers all can create feelings of anxiety, loneliness, discomfort, anger, panic, or depression. These emotions are known to produce physiological changes that are harmful to the body. The patient's emotional response can also affect compliance with treatment and their ability to cope with fear, pain, and loss.

Nurses as well as patients are vulnerable to the impact of stress in the hospital. Because of our sympathetic tendencies, we may feel the same emotions that our patients feel such as fear, anger, helplessness, and depression. We can experience feelings of failure when our efforts are ineffective. We feel anger and frustration when a patient rejects our care or does not comply with instructions. We may feel grief when patients die or families mourn. Most nurses are compassionate people who choose to work in a profession that places them at risk for their physical, emotional, and spiritual well-being.

Patient Response to Humor

During the last twenty years, I have been active in the profession of nursing. Most of those years have been spent at the bedside in intensive care units. I have also worked in home care, hospice, and cardiac rehabilitation. I can remember many situations where humor and laughter made a significant difference in a patient's response to care, but none as profound as this story:

Fred was 60 years old and recovering from a mitral valve replacement. During his immediate postoperative recovery, Fred experienced mild psychosis and severe depres-

141

sion. The acute psychotic episode resolved prior to discharge, but the profound depression continued for many weeks. Fred lacked enthusiasm for anything. He refused to eat, to walk, and even refused to wear anything but pajamas. His surgeon referred him to our outpatient cardiac rehabilitation program. Upon entry into our program, Fred walked with a shuffling gait, responded to questions with one or two words, and was unable to make eye contact. His wife was exhausted and discouraged. For several weeks we saw little improvement in his depression, in spite of antidepressant drugs and psychological counseling. One day, about a month after beginning rehab, he was walking on the treadmill, his 25-pound weight loss noticeable as his sweat pants hung loosely over his hips. After about six minutes of walking, his sweat pants suddenly fell down around his ankles, revealing bright red boxer shorts. We hit the emergency stop button in time to prevent his falling and went to assist him. He was looking down at his dropped drawers and when he lifted his head we could see a big grin and he began to laugh. We smiled and joined him in the laughter, grateful for the permission to respond by laughing at the ridiculous situation. Our mutual embarrassment and tension were released through laughter. From that moment on, Fred's depression continued to resolve, he became involved in his recovery process and was able to regain his strength. He eventually returned to active involvement in his church and community. Recalling this story reminds me of this popular folk saying: "It's easy enough to smile when the world goes round and round, but the man worthwhile is the man who can smile when his pants are falling down" (Anonymous). How, then, may laughing be therapeutic for both patient and nurse? Laughter is a pleasurable experience; it momentarily banishes feelings of anger and fear; it gives us a feeling of power and control; we feel carefree, light-hearted, and hopeful during the moments of laughter. These feelings seem to have therapeutic benefits by reversing the immunosuppressive effects of the emotions of anger, fear, and loneliness that often accompany hospitalization and recovery from illness (Cousins, 1989).

Physiological Response

Humor physiology is undergoing an expansion in exploration and understanding. Laboratory study has demonstrated that mirth and its physical expression have impact on most of the major physiologic systems of the human body. This does not mean that the changes occurring with laughter provide a solution for all the problems associated with illness. Laughter does not make the physical problems disappear; however, it can modify the impact of the disease process.

Fry (1986) has reviewed the physiological research and correlated the data to possible effects on the aging process. Physical response to mirth is characterized by a

142

pattern of stimulation followed by a period of relaxation. The musculoskeletal system is profoundly affected by laughter. The deep belly laugh activates the diaphragm, abdominal, intercostal, and facial muscles. These in turn stimulate the circulation, strengthen the heart, and may increase plasminogen activator preventing thrombosis. For those elderly who are bed-bound or unable to exercise due to muscle deterioration, arthritis, or paralysis, laughter offers an alternative to vigorous physical activity. The muscle relaxation which occurs after laughing can break up the spasm-pain cycle that is a part of joint and limb discomfort.

The cardiovascular system is also significantly impacted during the physical response to humor. Heart rate and arterial blood pressure (both systolic and diastolic) increase and are directly proportional to the intensity and duration of laughter. This increase in cardiac output serves to enhance peripheral blood flow enhancing the delivery of oxygen, cellular nutrients, and immune components to tissues. Many patients suffer degrees of immobility, and laughter can effectively stimulate the cardiovascular system to ease the impact of lack of activity (Fry, 1986). Another important part of humor physiology is the participation of the respiratory system. During laughter, the regular cyclic nature of respiration is disturbed and expiration becomes slightly greater than inspiration. This serves to diminish the residual volume of air in the lungs which offers little oxygen supply for the body tissues and contains high concentrations of carbon dioxide and water vapor. Carbon dioxide contributes to development of acidotic conditions and excess water vapor provides increased potential for overgrowth of bacterial flora and pulmonary infection. Vigorous laughter resembles respiratory therapy and chest physical therapy in that deep inspiration and expiration are accompanied by chest vibrations and occasional coughing (Fry, 1986). Research has also confirmed that epinephrine, norepinephrine, and dopamine levels are also increased during laughter and have been shown to stimulate alertness and enhance ability to focus attention and learning (Levi, 1965).

Some of the most exciting research exploring the potential healing value of laughter is in the area of psychoneuroimmunology (also referred to as neuroendocrinology or neuroimmunology). Psychoneuroimmunology is an area of research which explores the connections between the nervous system (the seat of thought, memory, and emotion), the endocrine system (which secretes powerful hormones), and the immune system (which defends the body from microbial invasions). Loma Linda University Medical Center has recently completed research showing that the neuroendocrine system is affected during the experience of mirthful laughter. This work by Berk and Tan (1989) has shown that serum cortisol levels decreased with laughter. Also, the experimental group demonstrated a lower baseline epinephrine level than the control group (possibly due to their relaxed status in anticipation of the laughter experience). Levels of cortisol and

143

epinephrine (known to be immunosuppressive) are elevated during the stress response. Therefore, Berk and Tan conclude that, by decreasing these levels, we can diminish the suppression of the respective immune components. Other research (Berk, 1989) has demonstrated that mirthful laughter increases the spontaneous lymphocyte blastogenesis and the natural killer cell activity. Natural killer cells (NK) are a type of lymphocyte that have a spontaneous cytolytic activity against tumor cells.

Frequency of stressful life changes, severity of depression, and coping styles have all been shown to affect the immune response. Steven Locke (1984) of Harvard has shown that the activity of natural killer cells is decreased during periods of increased life change accompanied by severe emotional disturbances, whereas subjects with similar patterns of life change and less emotional disturbances had more normal levels of NK cell activity. Similar findings were confirmed by Michael Irwin (Irwin, Daniels, Bloom, Smith & Weiner, 1987) at the San Diego VA Medical Center, noting that NK cell activity decreased during depressive reaction to life changes. Janice and Ronald Glaser (1985) of Ohio State University School of Medicine studied the cellular immunity response patterns of medical students prior to exams. Their work showed a reduction in the number of helper T-cells and a lowered activity of the NK cell just prior to the exam. In 1985, Marvin Stein at Mt. Sinai School of Medicine in New York looked at the effect of conjugal bereavement by studying men whose wives had advanced breast cancer (Stein, Keller, & Schleifer, 1985). His work showed that the lymphocyte response pattern in his subjects dropped significantly within one month after the death of their wives. This finding was also confirmed by the research of Steven Schleifer and Robert Bartrop (Schleicher, Keller, Camerino, 1983).

Research by Arthur Stone (Stone, Cox, Neale, Valdimarsdottir & Jandorf, 1987) at State University of New York has revealed that salivary immunoglobulin A (our first line defense against the entry of infectious organisms through the respiratory tract) response was lower on days of negative mood and higher on days with positive mood. This finding was duplicated by Kathleen Dillon (Dillon & Baker, 1985) at Western New England College showing an increased concentration of salivary IgA after viewing a humorous video. The research in the field of psychoneuroimmunology continues to prove that the mind (emotions) and the body (immune system) are interrelated. Positive emotions seem to enhance the immune response while negative emotions suppress it (Martin & Dobbin, 1988; Stone et al., 1987). Current research seems to be confirming what Sir William Osler, a physician and pioneer of modern medicine, stated years ago: "It is more important to know what sort of patient has the disease than what sort of disease the patient has" (Osler, as quoted in Cushing, 1940).

Psychological Impact of Humor

Humor and laughter affect how we perceive and respond to change. Herbert Lefcourt, a noted psychologist from the University of Waterloo in Canada has explored the possibility that a sense of humor and its use can change our emotional response to stress (Lefcourt & Martin, 1986). In this study, subjects were asked to review the frequency and severity of stressful life changes occurring to them over the previous six months, and their recent negative mood disturbances were evaluated. Lefcourt then administered tests to evaluate use of humor, perception of humor, appreciation of laughter, and efforts to include opportunities for humor and laughter into each subject's lifestyle. Results of this study have shown that the ability to sense and appreciate humor can buffer the mood disturbances which occur in response to negative life events (Lefcourt & Martin, 1986; Lefcourt, Davidson-Katz, & Kueneman, 1990).

Humor gives us a change of perspective on our problems and with an attitude of detachment, we feel a sense of self-protection and control in our environment. Freud noted the powerful psychological influence of humor stating: "Like wit and the comic, humor has a liberating element. It is the triumph of narcissism, the ego's victorious assertion of its own invulnerability. It refuses to suffer the slings and arrows of reality" (Freud, 1905).

Some of the best humor about illness and recovery has been written by former patients. My favorites are Surviving the Cure by Janet Henry, They Tore Out My Heart and Stomped the Sucker Flat by Lewis Grizzard, Patients at Large by cartoonist Tom Jackson, Please Don't Stand on My Catheter by T. Duncan Stewart, and Have a Heart by Wilford Nehmer, Jr. Each of these authors reveals some of the absurdity, irony and incongruity of being a patient under care. When we choose to laugh at or about a situation, we give ourselves the subtle message, "This is not so threatening; look, it's amusing and absurd sometimes. I can't take it too seriously."

Humor can also influence the mind by enhancing the ability to learn. Health professionals spend considerable time educating the patient and family about drugs, diet, lifestyle change, and treatment benefits. Delivering the information with humor will improve the communication in three ways: it will capture the attention of the learner, it will enhance retention of the material, and it will help to release the tension that blocks learning. The use of cartoons or funny stories can be an effective way to add humor (Kelly, 1988; Parfitt, 1990; Parkins, 1989). Shown in Figure 1 are four cartoons, drawn by Tom Jackson, based on real-life situations (Jackson, 1984).

Because you have a "Group Medical Plan."

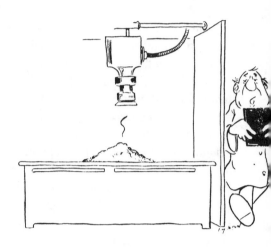

"You can put your clothes on now; we have enough x-rays."

"Well you wouldn't let us catheterize you."

"I don't think the patient is fully anesthetized yet, doctor!"

Caregivers work in a stress-filled environment and are prone to professional burnout. A major causative factor in burnout is powerlessness. Hans Selye, MD, a pioneer in the field of stress research, noted in 1954, "Stress is not the event, it's our perception of it" (Selye, 1956). Susan Kobassa (Kobassa & Puccetti, 1983) clarifies this concept even further with her research into personal hardiness factors. She found that some personality types seem resilient to the harmful effects of stress because they possess three traits: (a) commitment to self and work; (b) a sense of control within their environment; and (c) a feeling of challenge rather than threat when events change. Kobassa discusses the importance of "cognitive control." Control of events in our external world may not be possible, but we all have the ability to control how we view events and the emotional response we choose to have to them (Kobassa & Puccetti, 1983).

Humor gives us perceptual flexibility and thus can increase our cognitive control. A nurse used her perceptual flexibility to help her cope with a demanding patient who frequently interrupted the nurse's busy schedule with minor complaints and requests. The nurse's patience and tolerance were wearing thin. It was lunchtime and the patients were eating when again the nurse was called to this patient's room. Upon entering, the patient indignantly pointed to her tray and told the nurse, "This is a bad potato!" The nurse then picked up the potato and began spanking it, saying "Bad potato! Bad potato!" The patient and nurse both laughed and the tension of the moment was dissolved.

Any thorough discussion of caregivers' use of humor must include a style called "gallows humor." Freud (1905) named it when he reported an incident of joking which occurred on the gallows by a man about to be hung. It refers to the style of humor which laughs directly at tragedy or death, as if it were amusing. Gallows humor is found in professions which deal directly with the gruesome reality of pain, suffering, and death. Police, social workers, news reporters, psychologists, all areas of the health professions use this style of humor to help them cope with the sympathetic tendencies they feel when working with those who suffer.

This type of humor is most often misunderstood or unappreciated by those who do not work closely with the suffering client or who are perhaps new to the profession. One often develops an appreciation for this humor when the tension is so great that one must release it or begin to feel crushed from the pressure. Freud (1905) describes the use of this humor as the caregiver's self-care technique that attempts to convert unpleasant feelings into pleasant ones. A group of intensive care unit (ICU) nurses attempted to explain this phenomenon to the patients' visitors by posting a sign in the waiting room:

Laughter in ICU
If you are waiting....
You may possibly see us laughing;

147

or even take note of some jest;
Know that we are giving your loved one
our care at its very best!
There are times when tension is highest;
There are times when our systems are stressed;
We've discovered humor a factor,
in keeping our sanity blessed.
So, if you're a patient in waiting,
or a relative or friend of one seeing,
Don't hold our smiling against us,
it's a way that we keep from screaming.

Some of the best collections of "gallows humor" for the health professions can be found in books like A Chance to Cut is a Chance to Cure by Rip Pfeiffer and Tales from the Bedside by John Wise; or in the Journal of Nursing Jocularity (see list of "Humor Resources" at end of chapter).   Samuel Shem's book House of God gives classic examples of gallows humor (1978). One of my favorites is the "Gomer Assessment Scale-How do you know someone is a G.O.M.E.R.?" (a definition from Shem's book which stands for 'Get Out of My Emergency Room').

1.   Old chart weighs more than 5 pounds
2.   Ties foley catheter into pajama strings
3.   Has seizure and never drops his cigarette
4.   Asks for cigarette during pulmonary function test
5.   BUN is higher than IQ.
6.   PO2 is less than respiratory rate

Perhaps one of the most accurate, poignant, and personal discussions of the importance of gallows humor for the caregiver was written by a nurse anesthetist working in an emergency room in Illinois. Johnston (1985) shares his personal experience and viewpoint in "To the Ones Left Behind":

You saw me laugh after your father died . . . to you I must have appeared callused and uncaring . . . .Please understand, much of the stress health care workers suffer comes about because we do care . . . .Sooner or later we will all laugh at the wrong time, I hope your father would understand, my laugh meant no disrespect, it was a grab at balance. I knew there was another patient who needed my full care and attention. . . . my laugh was no less cleansing for me than your tears were for you (p. 936).

Caregivers can express their understanding and appreciation of the patient's struggle through the use of humor. For example, when a patient complains about the inadequate length or coverage of their gown, we could respond with, "Well, now you know your doctor admitted you for observation!" or " It's a designer creation by Seymor Butts." Humor can also help to reframe a situation by creating a context suggesting a more pleasant environment. As you instruct in the use of the call light, "Now I'm going to place your room service button right here." Or after completing an uncomfortable procedure, smile and say, "I bet it's hard for you to believe I'm on your side right now." When you've completed a ventilator check, blood gas analysis, or vital sign check, smile and say, "Well, you look good on paper. How does it feel on the inside?" Each of these statements, while not profoundly funny, will communicate a gentle awareness of the patient's dilemma or discomfort and express a relaxed and lighthearted attitude by the caregiver — giving the subtle message that the caregiver is confident and in control of the situation.

It is extremely important that the patient first be convinced of the health professional's competence and ability to deliver expert clinical care. A carefree, joking demeanor can be used to cover up inept skills or to deflect and ignore the importance of a patient's feelings. The appreciation of humor is highly individual and there are no guarantees that your attempts will be successful; thus, observe the patient's response. Sometimes it may be subtle, a glistening of the eyes or flushing of the cheeks. Of course, we all hope for the big smile, chuckle, or playful retort; but if you suspect that the patient felt insulted or misunderstood your intention, it is helpful to say something like, "Gee, I sure hope you weren't offended by that. I was just trying to lighten up the situation and help you to relax. I didn't mean to upset you, sorry." If the humorous attempts aren't working with that patient, then quit. Always remember, never use sexual, ethnic, or racial material with patients or their families. It is unprofessional, and you risk offending them and losing rapport and respect (Robinson, 1991).

Using Humor as a Nursing Intervention

Before using humor in a particular situation, the nurse should attempt to assess that patient's appreciation, preference, and previous use of humor. Raines (1991) has developed useful guidelines for nursing assessment. Assessment questions could include:
1. Can you think of a time when humor has made you feel better?
2. Since you've been ill (growing older) do you find yourself using humor more, less or about the same?
3. Do you like telling funny jokes or stories?
4. What activities do you find amusing or enjoyable?
    Nurses must also incorporate their own observations of the patient before deciding to use a humorous intervention.

149

5. What cues has the patient given indicating he/she is receptive to humor?
6. What cues have been given that the patient would not be receptive to certain kinds of humor or is sensitive in certain areas?
7. Is the patient's physical or emotional state such that humor might be annoying or indicate a lack of caring?

Before using humor, nurses should establish rapport with the patient and family and ensure trust in their professional competency. Special consideration should be given to the patient's developmental level, physical condition, sensory awareness and psychological status. Of course, humorous incidents may occur before the nurse has the opportunity to do any of this. Response would then be spontaneous, with observation and notation of the patient and family reaction made for future reference. As a general guideline, ethnic, sexual, and religious topics are not appropriate for humorous interpretation by the professional because the risk of being offensive is greatest in these areas. Humor interventions can take many forms. Listed here are some ideas and contact information to assist with implementation.

1. Keep a lending library of humorous audio- or videotapes.
   National Library Services for the Blind & Physically Handicapped - A government service which provides audiotapes.
   Postings. Mail order catalogue distribution of video- and audiotapes of comedy (current to classic).
2. Post or share cartoons with patients and their families. Use cartoons in teaching materials.
   A good source of medical/family humor is contained in Jim Unger's Herman Treasury, vols. 1-7, and in Tom Jackson's Patient's at Large.
3. Wear funny costumes, noses, and hats for visual impact.
   Clown Supplies. Mail order catalogue for props, costume accessories, and gags.
4. Tell funny jokes or stories.
   Whole Mirth Catalog. Mail order catalogue for funny joke books and humorous items.
   Laughing Matters. Quarterly journal with ideas on how to build humor into your life.
5. Invite a local clown or storyteller to visit the facility.
   Clowns of America International. A national organization of clowns; provides information about clown training or clown groups in your area.
   Clown Camp - Clown training, week long intensive experience. Tel. (608) 785-6505
   University of Wisconsin at La Crosse, 1725 State St, La Crosse, WI 54601.

150

Summary

I have attempted to provide information, qualifications, and inspiration for the possibility that laughter and humor can be a source of therapy for both the patient and the caregiver. My intent was to answer the questions: Why are humor and laughter important? What happens to the body, mind, and spirit when we laugh?

You are now probably wondering, How can I get myself and others to laugh more? When is humor appropriate to use? Who is most likely to laugh? For help in finding answers to these questions, consult the following bibliography and resources. Begin to explore your own style and appreciation of humor. Find what works for you and your patients. Remember, the shortest distance between two people is a shared laugh.

Bibliography

Bartrop, R. W., Lazarus, L., Luckhurst, E., Kiloh, L. G., & Penny, R. (1977). Depressed lymphocyte function after bereavement. *Lancet*, 1, 834-836.

Berk, L., Tan, S., Fry, N., Napier, B., Lee, J., Hubbard, R., Lewis, J., & Eby, W. (1989). Neuroendocrine and stress hormone changes during mirthful laughter. *American Journal of Medical Sciences*, 298, 390-396.

Berk, L. (1989). Eustress of mirthful laughter modifies natural killer cell activity. *Clinical Research*, 37(115) A.

Cousins, N. (1979). *Anatomy of an illness*. New York: Norton.

Cousins, N. (1989). *Head first: The biology of hope*. New York: Dutton.

Cushing, J. (1940). *The life of Sir William Osler*. New York: Oxford University Press.

Dillon, K., & Baker, K. (1985). Positive emotional states and enhancement of the immune system. *International Journal of Psychiatry in Medicine*, 15(1), 13-18.

Freud, S. (1905). *Jokes and their relation to the unconscious*. (James Strachey, Trans. and Ed., 1960). New York: Norton.

Fry, W. (1986). *Humor, physiology, and the aging process* (pp. 81-98). In L. Nahemow, K. McCluskey-Fawcett, & P. McGhee (Eds), Humor and aging. Orlando, FL: Academic Press.

Fry, W. (1979). Mirth and the human cardiovascular system. In H. Mindess & J. Turek (Eds.), *The study of humor* (pp. 55-61). Los Angeles, CA: Antioch University Press.

Glaser, J. K. (1987). Psychosocial moderators of immune function. *Journal of Behavioral Medicine*, 9, 16-20.

Glaser, R. (1985). Stress-related impairments in cellular immunity. *Psychiatry*

151

Resident, 6, 233-239.

Grizzard, L. (1982). *They tore out my heart and stomped that sucker flat.* New York: Warner.

Guillemin, R. (1985). *Neural modulation of immunity.* New York: Raven.

Irwin, M., Daniels, M., Bloom, E., Smith, T., & Weiner, H. (1987). Life events, depressive symptoms, and immune function. *American Journal of Psychiatry,* 144(4), 437-441.

Johnston, W. (1985). To the ones left behind. *American Journal of Nursing,* 85(8), 936.

Kelly, W. (1988). *Laughter and learning: Humor in the classroom.* Portland, ME: Weston Walsh.

Klein, A. (1989). *Healing power of humor.* Los Angeles, CA: Tarcher.

Kobasa, S. C., & Puccetti, M. (1983). Personality and social resources in stress resistance. *Journal of Personality and Social Psychology,* 45, 839-850.

Lefcourt, H., & Martin, R. A. (1986). *Humor and life stress.* New York: Springer.

Lefcourt, H., Davidson-Katz, K., & Kueneman, K. (1990). Humor and immune system functioning. *International Journal of Humor Research,* 3(3), 305-321.

Levi, L. (1965). The urinary output of adrenalin and noradrenalin during pleasant and unpleasant emotional states. *Psychosomatic Medicine,* 27, 80-85.

Locke, S. E. (1984). Life change stress, psychiatric symptoms, and natural killer cell activity. *Psychosomatic Medicine,* 46(5), 441-453.

Martin, R. A., & Dobbin, J. P. (1988). Sense of humor, hassles, and immunoglobulin A: Evidence for a stress-moderating effect of humor. *International Journal of Psychiatry in Medicine,* 18(2), 93-105.

McGhee, P. (Ed). (1983). *The handbook of humor research, vols I-II.* New York: Springer.

Parfitt, J. M. (1990). Humorous preoperative teaching: Effect on recall of postoperative exercise routines. *AORN Journal,* 52 (1), 114-120.

Parkins, C. (1989). Humor, health, and higher education: Laughing matters. *Journal of Nursing Education,* 28, 229-230.

Raines, C. F. (1991). Humor. In J. L. Creasia & B Parker (Eds.) *Conceptual foundations of professional nursing practice* (pp. 541-555). St. Louis MO: Mosby-Year Book.

Robinson, V. M. (1991). *Humor and the health professions,* 2nd edition. Thorofare, NJ: Slack.

Schleifer, S. J., Keller, S., Camerino, M., Thornton, J., & Stein, M. (1983). Suppression of lymphocyte stimulation following bereavement. *Journal of the American Medical Association,* 250 (3), 374-377.

Selye, H. (1956). *The stress of life.* New York: McGraw-Hill.

Shem, S. (1978). *The house of God.* New York: Dell.

Stein, M., Keller, S., & Schleifer, S. J. (1985). Stress and immunomodulation: The role of depression and neuroendocrine function. *Journal of Immunology*, 135, 827s-833s.

Stewart, D. (1982). *Please don't stand on my catheter.* Fullerton, CA: Sultana Press.

Stone, A. A., Cox, D. S., Neale, J. M., Valdimarsdottir, H., & Jandorf, L. (1987). Evidence that secretory IgA antibody is associated with daily mood. *Journal of Personality and Social Psychology*, 52(5), 988-993.

Unger, J. (1979-1989). *Herman Treasury*, vols. 1-7, Kansas City MO: Andrews, McMeel, & Parker.

Resources

American Association for Therapeutic Humor. Produces a quarterly newsletter and is a networking source for humor authors, researchers, etc. $ 35/yr. 222 Meramec, Suite 303, St. Louis, MO 63105. (314) 863-6232.

Clown Camp: Clown training, week long intensives, travelling camp. c/o University of Wisconsin at La Crosse, 1725 State St., La Crosse, WI 54601. (608) 785-6505.

Clown Supplies: Catalogue sales of a wide variety of clown supplies, costumes, props, gags, make-up, balloons, etc. Catalogue $1.00. M. E.-Persson, 17 Chesley Dr., Barrington NH 03825. (603) 664-5111.

Henry, J. (1984). Surviving the Cure. Cleveland, OH: Cope Inc. To order call (216) 663-0855.

Humor Project. Sponsors "Humor and Creativity" conference biannually. Also excellent humor book catalogue. Publishes Laughing Matters a quarterly journal with ideas on how to bring humor into your life. Order: 110 Spring St., Saratoga Springs, NY 12866. (518) 587-8770.

In the Hospital. Tape & guidebook for nurses & parents of hospitalized children. Order from: Peter Alsop & Bill Harley, Moose School Records, P.O. Box 960, Topanga, CA 90290.

In Your Face Cards: Hilarious greeting cards, many with hospital themes, created by an anesthesiologist. For information call (800) 377-8878 ($5/catalog) or write: Dr. Brian Moench, 4091 Splendor Way, Salt Lake City, UT 84124.

Jackson, T. (1984). Patient's at Large. To order write to: Jackson's Corner, P.O. Box 504, Pacifica, CA 94044.

Jest for the Health of It Services: Presentations about humor and laughter for health professionals. Consultation for creating humor rooms, clown training in hospitals.

Patty Wooten, BSN, RN (a.k.a. "Nancy Nurse"), P.O. Box 4040, Davis CA 95617-4040. (916) 758-3826.

Journal of Nursing Jocularity. A hilarious quarterly publication, written for nurses, by nurses, about nurses. Annual subscription rate: $14.95 to: JNJ 5615 W. Cermak Rd. Cicero, IL 60650-2290. Send contributions for publication to: Doug Fletcher, RN-publisher, P.O. Box 40416, Mesa, AZ 85274.

Laughter Therapy. Candid Camera Video films for free rental to use for stimulating laughter for recovery from illness. Send letter explaining plans for use to: P.O. Box 827, Monterey, CA 93942.

Laughter Works. A quarterly newsletter full of helpful tips, articles, funny items, jokes, book reviews, and upcoming humor events. Also has extensive catalogue of humor books and supplies. $ 18/ yr. P.O. Box 1076, Fair Oaks, CA 95628. (916) 863-1592.

Medical Antics. "No Code" T-shirts, hats, mugs,.and much more. (201) 391-1901. P.O. Box 309 Park Ridge, NJ 07656-0309; Fax orders to 201-391-1342

National Library Services for the Blind, and Physically Handicapped.

Provides a list of libraries in your area where you can borrow "Talking Books" audio tapes and equipment for patient use. Large catalogue on "Humor." 1291 Taylor St. NW, Washington, DC 20542. (202) 707-5100.

Nehmer, W. (1988). *Have a Heart.* Cudahy, WI: Reminder Enterprise Printing. To order write to author at: 5362 Cedardale Dr, West Bend, WI 53095.

Pfeiffer, R. (1983). *A Chance to Cut is a Chance to Cure.* A funny book about medicine, surgery, hospitals, and patients; written by a cardiovascular surgeon. To order, send $5 check to: Rip Pfeiffer, MD, 171 Louiselle St., Mobile, AL 36607.

Postings. Mail order catalogue for video/audiotapes of comedy classics. P.O. Box 8001, Hilliard, OH 43026-8001. (800) 262-6604.

United Ad Label Co., Inc. Large variety of fun & whimsical labels and stickers with health themes. P.O. Box 2216, Brea, CA 92622 (800) 423-4643

Whole Mirth Catalog. Access to many humorous items, toys, gags, books. Order: 1034 Page St, San Francisco, CA 94117.

Wise, J. Tales From the Bedside (vol. 1, 1991; vol. 2, 1994). ($14.95) Order from: John Wise, P.O. Box 5104, Clearwater, FL 34618

CHAPTER XII

HUMOR IN THE AGING SOCIETY

by Carolyn H. Aust, RN, MS

All nurses recognize that America is facing an age wave. We can expect the United States to experience steady growth of the elderly population from 1990 to 2010. After 2010, growth of the elderly population will be more dramatic as the Baby Boom generation (born 1946-1964) becomes the Grandparent Boom. More Americans are surviving to their elder years, and a significant minority will also see their 85th birthday. Three million Americans were 85 years or older in 1990. One million were 90 years or older. People aged 100 or older numbered almost 36,000 in 1990. As a result, we can expect the four-generation family to become more common. Because more people are living to oldest ages, people in their fifties and sixties are likely to have surviving relatives who need assistance. Nurses will most likely find themselves playing two roles, that of professional caregiver and that of lay or family caregiver. How will they cope? As caregivers, in either role, nurses may find the valve of using humor as their "saving grace." The fact that laughter makes people feel better can be verified by many nurses, and humor as therapy is rapidly growing.

Humor Theories

Humor as a therapeutic intervention has received increasing attention in recent years. Three major functions of humor (physiological, psychological, and sociological) related to positive adaption and health have been identified (Goldstein, Harmon, McGhee, & Karasik, 1975). Fry is credited with extensive research on the physiological effects of humor and laughter. Findings identified that a pattern of stimulation followed by relaxation of the various body symptoms occurs in response to laughter (Fry, 1986). Norman Cousin's remarkable recovery from a serious collagen disease demonstrated what laughter and positive emotions can do to help overcome illness (Cousins, 1979). Moreover, mirth and laughter can be specifically employed to reduce stress and hypertension and to improve respiratory and cardiovascular function.

Laughter is a means of releasing excessive amounts of psychic energy (Freud, 1928). According to Mindness (1971), the most fundamental and most important function of humor is its power to release us from many inhibitions and restrictions under which we live our daily lives. It is because of this cathartic effect that people feel as if excess energy and tension have been drained away following laughter. It is not too far-fetched to aver that laughter is related in several ways to longevity, mainly through the reduction of stress (Goldstein, 1975). According to Robinson (1970) humor can be used appropriately in the health professions both as a therapeutic intervention for patients and as a stress reduction technique for staff. For patients, humor has been used successfully to diminish discomfort, manage sensitive situations, and enhance communication. It may also be used as a mechanism for establishing relationships, relieving anxiety, and releasing negative emotions (Robinson, 1970, 1977). Humor helps patients adjust to hospitalization and the sick role, to cope with depression (Leiber, 1986) and to negotiate the acceptability of potentially difficult topics of discussion (Warner, 1984).

Lay or Family Caregiver

Family caregivers face a crisis at home. They provide the majority of care for America's chronically ill. By 2040, the Census Bureau estimates there will be more than 66.9 million people 65 and over and the 85 and over group is expected to increase 490% (Spencer, 1989). Older people also are more likely to have chronic conditions such as arthritis and Alzheimer's Disease. Because of the long-term nature of these diseases, their victims need continual assistance or care. Only 5% of people 65 and over live in nursing homes. It is estimated that working family members provide 80% of the care needed by older relatives. The majority of caregivers are women and, to add fuel to the fire, more women work outside the home; society is now also more transient, and the average family size is declining, providing fewer people as caregivers (Meyer & Rood, 1987).

With the advent in 1984 of Diagnostic Related Groups (DRGs) and Prospective Payment came decreased lengths of hospital stays, decreases in hospital admissions, increases in one-day surgery, as well as increases in outpatient health care services and home care. In today's American health care system, it is to everyone's advantage (except perhaps the family caregiver) to maintain the client at home.

The impact on the family caregiver is immense. Numerous descriptions of the problems include the concepts of role strain, role overload, and role conflicts. The concept of role is well developed in social psychology theories, and is a major component of the adaption theory of nursing known as the Roy Adaptation Model (Roy, 1984). Based on developmental theory, roles may be described as primary, secondary, and tertiary (Nuivayid, 1984). An elderly woman caring for an invalid husband could be described as having a primary role of elderly woman, a secondary role of wife, and a tertiary role of caregiver.

In a study motivated by Bowers (1987), all the women caregivers had at least one

156

chronic disease. Some even died during the caregiver process. George and Gwyther (1986) labeled the spouses of disabled elderly men as "hidden patients," warning gerontologists to take heed. To further muddy the waters, more women work outside the home, altering the traditional role of women caring for aging family. Such women are in middle age, in the middle generation, and in the middle of demands of various roles that compete for time and energy (Bowers, 1987), sometimes referred to as the "sandwich generation."

The caregiver's mental health risk is great. Stresses placed on the adult child as caregiver are numerous. These include role reversal, losing autonomy, reopening unresolved wounds, loss of freedom, the weight of decision-making responsibilities, shared living arrangements, possible declining physical health, financial stresses, and intrapsychic and intra-family stresses (Dunn & Gallaway, 1986).

In general, depression and isolation are major consequences the caregiver must deal with. Symptoms documented in the literature comprise feelings of hopelessness, despair, worthlessness, irritability, anger, flat affect, painful sadness, frequent crying spells, loss of appetite, weight loss or gain, sleep disturbances, physical complaints, poor personal hygiene, confusion, poor problem-solving ability, drug/alcohol use to escape, loss of energy, and loss of interest or pleasure in usual activities (Ekberg, Griffith, & Foxall, 1986; Haley, Levine, Brown, Berry & Hughes, 1987; Silliman, Fletcher, Earp, & Wagner, 1986).

The literature further suggests that caring for the dementia patient affects the caregiver even more profoundly. Specific behavior patterns associated with this care are related to prolonged grief evolving into major depressive episodes. Difficult behaviors dealt with include sleep disturbances; confusional states; argumentative, uncooperative and apathetic behavior; physical violence; memory loss, and incontinence (Deimling & Bass, 1986; Drinka, Smith, & Drinka, 1987). A survey of 117 caregivers by Snyder and Keefe (1985) found that the majority reported physical and emotional problems ranging from hypertension and back problems to depression and mental exhaustion.

Support Group Response to Humor

Three years ago, I started a support group for caregivers in our community. I recognized a great need for people to come together and share experiences and to learn to cope as they care for their frail and ill loved ones. The group is called "You're Not Alone" and is sponsored by the Senior Life Center at St. Mary's Hospital & Medical center in Western Colorado. The group meets monthly and there is no charge. An average of eight to ten people are usually in attendance. Typical techniques for guiding a support group are used. People of all ages, both sexes, and all walks of life learn that it is a safe

157

place to express their range of emotions. They come to listen, share, and learn about all the aspects of what it means to be a caregiver. Most importantly they are all on common ground. Also, each month a speaker of their choice joins the group to discuss community resources, respite care, medications, legal issues, stress, and any other subject they might choose.

As a speaker, over the years I have learned to spice up most topics with a bit of humor. One evening the problem arose of finding a physician who truly understands Alzheimer's Disease and all the dilemmas the caregiver faces. I talked about searching for the "right doctor" and that, after all, "It's your body (or your loved one's), your money, and your mental sanity, and it sometimes takes some looking around." I reiterated that doctors have different specialties, interests, and beliefs. Like the joke about the old guy having a problem with his knee. The doctor said, "Well, my friend, age catches up with all of us. You're just getting old and worn out." The old guy said, "Yeah, but funny thing, my other knee is the same age and it's just fine."

After a good laugh by all, I grabbed the opportunity to discuss the power of humor and how it can change our daily lives. I covered the basic physiological and psychological advantages, and suggested the group might want to incorporate some humor in their next meeting. They mostly agreed and decided to bring something they thought was funny to the next support group.

At the beginning of the next meeting, I discussed and handed out some important guidelines.
1. People are heterogenous-not everyone enjoys the same thing.
2. Humor should be appropriate.
3. Humor should be timely.
4. Humor should be tasteful.
5. It's OK to have forgotten how to laugh.
6. It's OK to not "get the joke."
7. Humor can be risky.
8. Everyone has good and bad days — it's OK.
9. Humor is economical.
10. Everyone has a funny story.
11. It can be fun to feel silly.
12. It's OK to talk to yourself and then answer — it gets funny.
13. Laugh together: no put downs (including self), no sarcasm, no attacks. Be sensitive.
14. Humor is a choice — so is misery.
15. Practicing humor can be as important as practicing the "Caregiver's Bill of Rights."

Most of the meeting focused on humor, and most of the group had come prepared with at least one thing that was funny to them. The most skeptical person was a highly

158

educated, quiet, elderly gentleman caring for a wife with Huntington's Disease, but even he cracked a smile or two, although he did not have anything to share. People shared that they really had to search for one funny thing, and asked for ideas in re-learning and remembering how to find some humor.

At the next meeting they put together a list as they explored how to add some humor into their daily routines:

1. Watch funny videos and movies (George Burns, Jack Benny, Charlie Chaplin, Marx Brothers, "Lucy").
2. Only watch funny television shows.
3. Listen to the radio show — Prairie Home Companion.
4. Collect jokes and one-liners.
5. Scan the daily papers for cartoons and make a scrapbook.
6. Make a list of books on humor and buy one.
7. Buy a wind-up toy.
8. Collect funny family stories.
9. Make it a challenge to find daily humor in the local TV newscast.
10. Share bloopers.
11. Collect funny photographs.
12. Choose to laugh instead of cry when your husband brushes his hair with a toothbrush.
13. Remember your grandmother's folk wisdom.

After that, humor and laughter became part of the monthly meeting. I have witnessed people choosing to live with laughter and the restored emotional balance in their worlds of guilt, fear, isolation, loneliness, pain, and grief. Humor draws the group together, lessens tension, creates energy, and empowers them to go home and cope one more time in their 36-hour days.

In fact, one evening the gentleman with the wife suffering from Huntington's said, "I'm as old as my tongue and a little older than my teeth." He got great laughs and cheers as he and all the others realized he had "turned the corner and chosen humor." Then a lady dealing with her husband's advancing Alzheimer's Disease said, "I found one advantage to having Alzheimer's. My husband hid the grandchildren's Easter eggs and then had equally as much fun finding them!"

The book, The Healing Power of Humor by Allen Klein, is always recommended to newcomers as well as the lists of ways to add humor back into one's life. Allen Klein (1989) has written wonderful chapters entitled "Learning to Laugh," "When You Feel Like Crying" and "The Last Laugh." It is very humorous and enlightening. I often use a quote found in his book: "Laughter and tears are both responses to frustration and exhaustion . . . I myself prefer to laugh, since there is less cleaning up to do afterward" (Kurt Vonnegut, as quoted by Klein on p. 19).

159

Summary

Are nurses ready to help care for an aging society? Awesome responsibilities lie ahead. Humor has been shown to have an important psychological effect on people as witnessed by a caregiver's support group. It has been found that a well-developed sense of humor eases the difficult daily tasks, and in general makes life for a caregiver more bearable.

As the nation faces increasingly difficult times dealing with Health Care Reform and an aging population, all nurses, in various roles, will do well in body, mind, and spirit by choosing humor and making it a part of daily life.

Bibliography

Bowers, B. (1987). Intergenerational caregiving: Adult caregivers and their aging parents. *Advances In Nursing Science*, 9(2), 20-31.

Cousins, N. (1979). *Anatomy of an illness.* New York: Norton.

Deimling, G., & Bass, D. (1986). Symptoms of mental impairment among elderly adults and their effects on family caregivers. *Journal of Gerontology*, 41(6), 778-784.

Drinka, T., Smith, J., & Drinka, P. (1987). Correlates of depression and burden for informal caregivers of patients in a geriatric referral clinic. *The American Geriatrics Society*, 35, 522-525.

Dunn, C., & Gallaway, C. (1986, July). Mental health of the caregiver. *Caring*, 36-42.

Ekberg, J., Griffith, N., & Foxall, M. (1986). Spouse burnout syndrome. *Journal of Advanced Nursing*, 11, 161-165.

Freud, S. (1928). Original papers: Humor. *International Journal of Psychoanalysis*, 9: 1-6.

Fry, W. (1986). Humor, physiology, and the aging process. In L. Nahemow, K. McClusky-Fawcett, & P. McGhee (Eds.). *Humor and aging* (pp. 81-98). Orlando, FL: Academic Press.

George, L., & Gwyther, L. (1986). Caregiver well-being: A multidimensional examination of family caregivers of demented adults. *The Gerontologist*, 26(3), 253-259.

Goldstein, J. H., Harmon, J., McGhee, P. E., & Karasik, R. (1975). Test of an information processing model of humor: Physiological response changes during problem and riddle-solving. *Journal of General Psychology*, 92, 59-68.

Haley, W., Levine, E., Brown, S., Berry, I., & Hughes, G. (1987). Psychological, social, and health consequences of caring for a relative with senile dementia. *American*

160

Geriatrics Society, 35, 405-411.

Klein, A. (1989). *The healing power of humor.* Los Angeles: Tarcher.

Leiber, D. B. (1986). Laughter and humor in critical care. *Dimensions of Critical Care Nursing*, 5(3), 162-170.

Meyer, M., & Rood, S. (1987). Caregivers: New challenge for health care executives. *Health Care Executive*, 2(2), 39-42.

Mindness, H. (1971). *Laughter and liberation.* Los Angeles: Nash.

Nuivayid, K. A. (1984). Role function: Theory and development. In S. C. Roy (Ed.). *Introduction to nursing: An adaptation model.* Englewood Cliffs, NJ: Prentice-Hall.

Public Policy Agenda. (1993, January-March). *Diversity and growth: Four perspectives on aging.* Washington, DC: National Council on Aging.

Robinson, V. M. (1970). Behavioral concepts and nursing interventions. In C. E. Carlson & B. Blackwell (Eds.). *Behavioral concepts and nursing interventions* (pp. 191-210). Philadelphia: Lippincott.

Robinson, V. M. (1991). *Humor and the health professions,* 2nd edition. Thorofare, NJ: Slack.

Roy, S. C. (Ed.) (1984). *Introduction to nursing: An adaptive model.* Englewood Cliffs, NJ: Prentice-Hall.

Silliman, R., Fletcher, R., Earp, J., & Wagner, E. (1986). Families of elderly stroke patients: Effects of home care. *American Geriatrics Society*, 34, 643-648.

Snyder, B., & Keefe, K. (1985). The unmet needs of family caregivers for frail and disabled adults. *Social Work In Health Care*, 10, 1-13.

Spencer, S. (1989). *Projections of the population of the United States by age, sex, and race: 1988 to 2080.* Washington, DC: U.S. Bureau of the Census, Current Population Reports, Series P-25 No. 1018.

Warner, U. (1984). The serious impact of humor in health visiting. *Journal of Advanced Nursing,* 9, 83-87.

CHAPTER XIII

HUMOR FOR MENTALLY ILL PATIENTS

by Elaine Anne Pasquali, RN, PhD

The psychiatric literature suggests that humor is an effective strategy in psycho-therapy. Because humor can benefit clients and promote wellness, the nursing literature has increasingly described ways in which humor may facilitate the accomplishment of client-centered goals. The nature of long-term mental illness often generates self-defeating feelings and behaviors in both clients and nurses. Within a framework that looks not only at the nature of chronic mental illness but also at the nature and functions of humor, this chapter explores the appropriateness of humor therapy for chronically mentally ill patients. The benefits of humor are explored, as are uses of humor that may be considered inappropriate. Ways that nurses may assess clients' humor potential are discussed, and strategies for implementing humor programs for chronically mentally ill clients are suggested.

For many individuals, mental illness may be a long-term disorder that poses multiple challenges to their quality of life. These challenges involve not only having a disorder whose etiology is largely unclear, but also experiencing the social isolation that seems nearly inevitable with long-term mental illness. Although symptom control may be of primary importance to both the individual and the family, helping clients to maintain equilibrium and prevent or deal with social isolation and crises are also areas that need attention.

The relapsing/episodic nature of long-term mental illness and the high rate of recidivism may engender a sense of hopelessness, helplessness, and/or frustration in some nurses; other nurses, however, may view it as a challenge to develop strategies to improve the quality of life of these clients. Humor may offer just such therapeutic strategies. When nurses use humor therapy with long-term mentally ill clients, they may not only enhance the quality of life for their clients but may also provide a model for functioning in the world. As a bonus, humor may help prevent burnout in nurses who work with such patients; in fact, Keller (1984) advocates humor as a way for nurses to energize and replenish themselves.

163

Characteristics of Long-Term Mental Illness

In their review of the literature, Harris and Bergman (1987) described many of the behaviors that characterize the subjective experience of being chronically or long-term mentally ill (CMI). Of primary importance is the inability to establish a secure identity and sense of self. This impaired core identity along with cognitive impairment, intrapsychic fragmentation, and/or organic impairment, often related to substance abuse, contribute to feelings of confusion, disorganization, easy distractibility, and overburdening when faced with even minor changes in the external environment. Dealing with activities of daily living may be so energy-depleting that little energy is left to plan for even the next month or week. A further complication is the individual's vulnerability to stress and poor problem-solving skills. CMI individuals often respond with impractical or unrealistic strategies or passive dependency when faced with a problem that calls for a plan of action.

Orem (1985) views the ability to balance social interaction and solitude as essential in establishing social relationships and adjusting to society. However, maintaining a balance between social interaction and solitude may be difficult for CMI individuals and may contribute to their high use of inpatient treatment settings as a major source of care (Aiken, 1987; Bachrach, 1988; Talbott, 1981). Because CMI individuals may appear and act differently from others in the community, it may be difficult for them to establish social relationships and they may experience chronic loneliness. Solitude may become a lifestyle and social isolation a common theme for them (Drew, 1991; Manderino & Bzdek, 1987).

Physical Illness

Long-term mental illness does not protect an individual from physical health problems. In fact, the incidence of physical illness among CMI clients appears to be higher than for the general public. Korany's (1979) study of a psychiatric clinic population found that approximately 43% of the clients had a major medical problem, while 62% of them had multiple medical problems. In a more recent study of a group of severely impaired, low socioeconomic psychiatric clients, 80% evidenced medical problems (Hall, 1980). Similar results were supported by a study (McCarrick, Manderschied, Bertolluci, Goldman & Tessler., 1986) that specifically investigated the physical health risks of CMI patients. Based upon the reports of case managers, over 42% of the subjects experienced at least one chronic medical problem severe enough to limit their functioning.

While these studies suggest that CMI individuals are at high risk for physical illness, other studies suggest that they are also less apt to avail themselves of medical health care. Several studies indicate that they underutilize health care services even when medical problems exist (Karasu, Waltzman, & Lindenmayer, 1980; Klienman, Gold, & Makuc, 1981; Roca, Breakey, & Fischer, 1987). Many factors appear to contribute to the underutilization of health care services. Because CMI individuals may experience social withdrawal, depression, passivity, and periods of exacerbation or remission, as well as somatic hallucinations and paranoid delusional systems, they may be resistant to seeking out and following treatment regimens (Worley, Drago, & Hadley, 1990). Medical health care workers also may experience fear and/or frustration when working with CMI clients, and may perceive their behavior as disruptive (Hall, Beresford, Gardner, & Popkin, 1982).

Humor Therapy

Human beings are biophysical, psychological, and sociocultural beings. By functioning on several levels, often simultaneously, humor both expresses and reinforces these dimensions of the human self.

(Biophysical Functions.) The physiological value of laughter has been recognized from as far back as 1860 when Spencer described how excess nervous tension could be physiologically released through laughter. Many years later, Koestler (1964) expanded on the physiological value of laughter. Comparing laughter to tears, Koestler pointed out that both are physiological responses that facilitate the release of tension, and that intense mirthful laughter may move some people to tears. In fact, the tears shed in both laughter and crying secrete hormones, steroids, and toxins that have built up during periods of stress (Mazer, 1982).

Laughter also produces other physiological responses. When people laugh (a sound produced by the vocal cords), they open their mouth to expose teeth, raise their cheeks and upper lip and corners of their mouth, crinkle their eyes, and move other body parts such as their eyebrows, arms, hands, torso, and head (Apte, 1985). In addition, they experience rapid, shallow breathing along with an increase in heart rate and blood pressure. Because laughter evokes a stimulus-response pattern, for a brief period of time after people stop laughing, respiratory and cardiovascular responses fall below baseline. The combined musculoskeletal, respiratory, and cardiovascular effects of humor are similar to those effected through physical exercise (Fry, 1982, 1986). This is the reason why laughter is sometimes referred to as internal jogging. Stimulation of catecholamine production and endorphin release may not only result in people feeling good after a "good laugh" but research also indicates that they may experience an increase in memory, learning, and creative thinking (Goodman, 1988; Martin & Lefcourt, 1983; McGhee, 1982; Siegel, 1986; Ziv, 1982). As mentioned before, because CMI clients may experience confusion, disorganization, easy distractability, and overburdening, they may

165

especially profit from the catecholamine/endorphin effects of mirthful laughter.

Although relieving tension and experiencing a sense of physical well-being are certainly important, laughter also has another function: to strengthen the immune system. By stimulating the contraction of the zygomaticus major facial muscle, the thymus gland (referred to as the master gland of the immune system because it regulates the production of T-cell lymphocytes) is stimulated to secrete thymosin. Thus, the immune system, which is compromised during periods of depression and stress, may be strengthened by mirthful laughter (Abeles, 1982; Goldstein, 1982; Locke, 1980). In light of the previously mentioned studies that suggest that long-term mentally ill individuals are at high risk for physical illness, stimulating the immune system through mirthful laughter may be very important to the health of CMI individuals.

Psychological Functions

Humor can function as a viable coping behavior. Freud (1928) pioneered in the psychological study of humor as a relief-release mechanism. Through humor, aggressive and sexual impulses may be expressed in a socially acceptable manner. Freud described two types of humor: harmless and purposeful. Harmless humor evokes a sense of joy at no one's expense. Purposeful humor — as illustrated by sexual, blasphemous, and aggressive jokes — unconsciously meets one's psychic needs. Gallows humor, a type of purposeful humor, jokes about death and tragedy in an attempt to cope with the emotional pain that the situations engender (Peschel & Peschel, 1985). By releasing tension, humor is thought to allow people to cognitively reframe situations, thereby liberating them from habitual ways of perceiving and thinking (Ruxton, 1988; Siegel, 1986).

Kubie (1971) cautions about the injudicious use of humor in psychotherapeutic situations. Humor that is used as an escape mechanism (e.g., to avoid the seriousness of problems, to mask feelings) by either client or therapist, or humor that is introduced too early in the therapeutic relationship, may block the process of working through client problems. In addition, there are some clients whose mental illness may make them poor candidates for humor therapy (e.g., those with severe depression and clients with severe conceptual disorganization).

It has been noted that clients with schizophrenia may evidence specific patterns of humor. Some clients with chronic schizophrenia may have an impaired sense of humor, while others may evidence a sharp psychotic wit. On the other hand, during an acute episode of schizophrenia, clients may have severe conceptual disorganization which impedes their ability to "get a joke." The use of humor may increase schizophrenic ideation with these clients. Ironically, the looseness of association that characterizes

166

thought patterns during acute schizophrenic episodes may be interpreted by an uninformed observer as a bizarre sense of humor (Haig, 1988).

Because of preoccupation or frozen affect, clients with affective disorders may have an impaired appreciation of humor, and a sense of humor may be obliterated in clients with major depressive disorders (Nussbaum & Michaux, 1963). Conversely, clients with mania or hypomania may evidence an excess of joking and laughing that is consistent with their symptoms of mood elevation, witty self-confidence, grandiosity, and flight of ideas (Haig, 1988).

While Mindess (1981) agrees that humor should be used judiciously in the psychotherapeutic relationship, he also contends that, just because clients are experiencing emotional pain, it does not follow that they cannot participate in humor: "People can laugh through their tears, thus achieving a broader perspective on themselves. They are then in a position to see the comedy of their tragedy, rather than experiencing their dilemmas as unrelievedly tragic" (p. 12).

The documentation of pathological laughter related to psychiatric conditions was first mentioned by Bleuler (1950), who described the compulsive laughter often manifested in schizophrenia, but it has since been expanded to include mania, personality disorders, and hysteria (Askenasy, 1987). Debate continues over whether the pathological laughter manifested by these psychiatric conditions is organic or psychogenic in origin.

Sociocultural Functions

Humor decreases tension, hostility, and conflict; it also acts as a leveling mechanism. Therefore, humor facilitates perspective, communication, social solidarity, and group harmony (Apte, 1985; O'Connell, 1981). For example, by laughing at a shared joke, people engage in consensual validation and bonding. If the joke deals with issues of social conflict (e.g., socioeconomic conditions, people in power), then feelings and attitudes that might otherwise be socially unacceptable are expressed in a socially acceptable manner. If the joke should poke fun at God or religion, then people are able to laugh at the existential paradox of God-mortal, while good news/bad news jokes enable people to laugh at the sad/glad paradox. Samra (1986) believes that mirthful humor, like prayer, helps people cope with adversity and grow spiritually.

How Does Humor Therapy Work?

Harris and Bergman (1987) suggest that the process of internalization can facilitate the personal growth of CMI individuals. Internalization refers to the process of

167

incorporating some aspect of the external world and making it part of oneself. While Freud (1940) described internalization in the formation of the superego, Schafer (1968) later explored how both real and imagined environmental characteristics may become internalized. More recently, Meissner (1981) described how mimicry may be the first step in identification and eventual internalization. This process of internalization may account for the importance that many CMI individuals place on a humorous story being a "true story." A humorous story based on real-life experiences (as seen in Levenson's book, Everything but Money) may provide a humorous perspective on every-day irritations, trials, and tribulations (Pasquali, 1990a).

Bibliotherapy, the psychotherapeutic use of reading material, can serve several healing functions in humor therapy. Identification with a real-life character who has been able to cope with problems and still smile or laugh, may contribute to CMI clients' realization that it is possible to gain mastery over external events and may help them develop a more positive sense of self. Reading about a similar situation experienced by a real-life character who is unknown to them may also be validating for them. In addition, Goldstein (1990) suggests that interactive bibliotherapy, which incorporates guided discussion about reading material and client response, by focusing on therapeutic interaction, facilitates the psychotherapeutic process. Such reading material needs to be selected with care. The therapist should be thoroughly familiar with the material and be mindful of why it was selected. Goldstein cautions that adult clients are especially apt to view reading material as reflecting the beliefs of the therapist. Such clients may regard the material as more significant than the therapist had intended.

Appropriateness of Humor

Nurses need to assess both the situation and the client in order to determine whether it is appropriate or inappropriate to use humor as a psychotherapeutic strategy. Fry (1979) cautions that humor should only be introduced into a therapeutic relationship after rapport has been established and the caregiver can determine whether it will be well received by the client. Timing, style, and context of humor are all factors in assessing its appropriateness. The following criteria may assist nurses to determine when and how to use humor (Apte, 1985; Leiber, 1986; Reynes & Allen, 1987; Robinson, 1991).

Timing. The timing of humor is just as crucial for CMI clients as for any other clients. Because humor may help to broaden client perspective, focus on the lighter side of a problem, and enhance learning, humor is an appropriate approach for clients who have mild to moderate anxiety. However, when they are in the midst of a crisis or when their anxiety ranges from severe to panic level, attempts at humor may be experienced as distracting and offensive. The use of humor to mask feelings, avoid problem-solving, or derogate others is also inappropriate.

Style. It is important to assess the receptivity of CMI clients to humor in general and to types of humor in particular. There are many styles of humor — joke telling, puns, slapstick, gallows, funny stories. When the psychopathology of CMI clients makes it difficult for them to understand or appreciate a particular style of humor, they may find it offensive, boring, or ludicrous. For example, clients with chronic paranoid schizophrenia may misinterpret or personalize a joke, while depressed clients may regard humor as an affront to their feelings. One depressed client who had been assigned to a humor program complained that it was "the cruelest thing that ever was done to me."

Context. The environment in which humor occurs is another factor in determining its appropriateness for CMI clients. For example, it may be inappropriate when discussing the ramifications of an angry outburst. To make a joke at such a time might be confusing to the client, because it could be interpreted as not taking the incident seriously or as derogating (laughing at) the client. To laugh when a client discusses suicidal ideation probably indicates the nurse's discomfort with the situation, but the client will probably feel devalued and angry. "Laughing at" humor erodes trust, heightens tension and hostility, and undermines self-esteem. Laughing at client behavior or symptoms is inappropriate. On the other hand, "laughing with" clients tends to be reassuring and relaxing; it fosters empathy and comraderie. In the proper situation, "laughing with" humor is an appropriate treatment strategy. "Laughing at" and "laughing with" humor serves very different functions. The former is not therapeutic. Differentiating between the two is one of the most important determinations nurses must make when using humor with CMI clients.

Caution. Humor should be used cautiously with CMI clients. If used inappropriately, it can block communication and the expression of feelings, and confuse clients about the seriousness of the therapeutic process. However, when used judiciously, humor can decrease stress, promote effective coping and problem-solving, and facilitate rapport in the nurse-client relationship. An assessment guide has been developed in order to assist nurses to better understand what makes clients laugh, and to use humor therapeutically with CMI clients (see Table 1).

Table 1.
Assessment guide: Humor profile.

Reminiscent humor style:
1. What are the client's childhood memories of humorous exchanges among family members, childhood friends?

169

2. What type of childhood humor was engaged in (jokes, funny stories, practical jokes, teasing, sarcasm)?
3. What were the client's feelings and reactions to that childhood humor?
4. What was the client's role in that childhood humor (comedian, audience, butt)?

Current humor style:
5. What kind of humor does the client now enjoy?
6. With whom does the client participate in humorous exchanges?
7. What is the client's role in these humorous exchanges (comedian, audience, butt)?
8. What are the client's feelings after these humorous exchanges?
9. How often does the client laugh (daily, every few days, once a week, once in a while)?
10. When is the last time the client laughed?
11. What occasions for laughter does the client build into the daily routine (watch situation comedies on TV, go to funny movies, read humorous books or comic strips)? Have the client give examples of favorites.
12. What is the client's favorite joke? (This provides an experiential example of the client's humor style.)
13. What type of humorist(s) does the client find funny? Check off as many types as are appropriate:

satirist	clown	practical joker
kidder	joke teller	gag man (one-liners)
tease	slapstick comedian	punster

Other (describe):
14. What type of humor does the client find funny? Check off as many types as are appropriate.

in-jokes	sarcasm	slapstick comedy
putdowns of self	putdowns of others	ethnic humor
sexual humor	scatological humor	gallows humor

Other (describe):

Developmental stage:
15. What is the client's level of humor activity? Check off as many items as are appropriate.
Sensorimotor: tactile stimulation, auditory games, visual stimulation, symbolic play

170

Preoperational: nonsense words, incorrect naming, repetitious rhyming
Intuitive: incongruous pictures, simple riddles, others' mishaps
Concrete operations: language absurdities, complex riddles
Formal operations: complex jokes, gallows humor

16. In which of the following ways does the client use humor? Check
    off as many items as are appropriate.
    To learn more easily and enjoyably.
    To put situations in perspective.
    To avoid dealing with problems.
    To mask feelings.
    To feel more comfortable with people.
    To put people down.

Sources: Goodman (1981, 1988), McGhee (1979),
Pasquali (1990b), Robinson (1991).

Humor Program and CMI Clients

Long-term mental illness knows no age barrier. Cognitive dysfunction often results
in diminished abstract thinking and resultant concrete thinking. Therefore, it is important
for nurses to understand the role that cognitive functioning plays in the appreciation of
humor. Using Piaget's equilibration concept, McGhee (1979), Jalongo (1985), and
Schaeffer and Hopkins (1988) have explored types of humor activities associated with
specific developmental stages (see Table 2).

Table 2.   **Cognitive development and humor appreciation.**

Cognitive stage	Developmental Activity	Humor Activity
Sensorimotor (infant to toddler)	Recognizes change and adjusts accordingly; begins to vocalize at about 4 months; begins to use symbolic actions	At 2 months smiles, at 3 months laughs when being tickled or playing auditory games (peek-a-boo). At 9 months laughs when presented with funny visual effects (making funny faces). At 18 months to 2 years, laughs when engaged in funny pretend play (using potato for pretend doll).

171

Table 2 Continued

Cognitive stage	Developmental Activity	Humor Activity
Preoperational (early childhood- preschool)	Increases language skills. Recognizes that words represent objects. Classifies objects by only one attribute. Increases language skills, enabling repetitious rhyming. Functions completely egocentrically.	Uses nonsense words to make jokes (Mommy is an oogly-googly) or distorts words (poe for toe). Makes jokes by incorrectly naming objects (calls a girl a boy, or points to nose and calls it Mr. Ear). Laughs at scatological, sexual, or taboo words and at socially unacceptable behavior; at actual or unacceptable behavior; at nonsense words that are repetitious or rhyming (mitsy, bitsy, fitsy, or flew, stew, shoe).
Intuitive (early childhood/primary grades)	Understands rules. Classifies objects by more than one attribute. Recognizes degrees of incongruity.	Laughs at incongruous appearance of funny pictures (giraffe with trunk of elephant); at insults, practical jokes, and hostile humor (accidents that happen to others). Children 5-7 years laugh at multiple meanings of words (simple riddles, begin to memorize riddles and jokes).
Concrete operations (middle childhood)	Starts to use logic and objectivity. Uses reason when dealing with real, concrete events. Hierarchically orders objects. Breaks a whole into parts, then reassembles it differently.	Laughs at hidden meanings (riddles based on homonyms, I vs. eye); at complex, reality-oriented riddles that appeal to the child's understanding of the workings of the world. Older children laugh at absurdity riddles that reflect the idea that absurd answers follow acceptance of absurd premise (elephant riddles). Enjoys sequential cartoons
Formal operations (adolescence)	Thinks abstractly. Engages in active problem-solving, develops realistic solutions. Evidences imagination.	Laughs at intricate jokes that require abstract thinking; at gallows humor, and thereby makes tragic situation seem temporary, less frightening (misery jokes).

Sources: Jalongo (1985); McGhee (1979); Piaget (1973); Schaeffer & Hopkins (1988).

Equilibration refers to balancing and integrating new experiences with those of the past as one progresses developmentally (Piaget, 1973). The principles underlying Piaget's equilibration theory can be applied to adult CMI clients. Clients will best respond to humor that matches their cognitive ability to understand the humorous material. If a joke is too abstract for a client who uses concrete thinking, then the client will not get the joke. If the joke is too immature for a client's level of cognitive functioning, then it will not appear funny. Although humor activities should be synchronous with a client's developmental level, bear in mind that humor activities that appeal to the child within are always appropriate (see Table 2).

Incorporating Humor into Client Care

Whether humor is in the form of an ongoing program or a spontaneous joke or situation, when working with CMI clients nurses need to be mindful of the following principles (adapted from Peter & Dana, 1982):
1. Recognize that clients may use humor to make an ominous situation seem less fearful, to create a friendly relationship with the nurse, or to decrease anxiety.
2. Tune into the amount of smiling and laughing that clients engage in. An atmosphere of security and ease may allow for more spontaneous humor.
3. Open yourself to silly and playful thoughts.
4. Look for the silliness in situations by recognizing the absurdities and incongruities of the situations.
5. Laugh at incongruities in situations or behaviors, never at client symptoms. Then you will be laughing with and never at clients.
6. Start by laughing at the absurdities in your own behavior. This involves laughing at your own mistakes while taking your responsibilities to self and others seriously.
7. Prime yourself for opportunities to make people laugh. When you bring laughter to others, you are rewarded with laughter and a sense of accomplishment.
8. Realize that you do not have to be a comedian in order to exercise your sense of humor. Learning to look for the funny side of life develops a sense of humor. When people learn that you are interested in humor, they will come to you with their humorous sides showing and share with you the fun in their lives.

Humor Strategies for CMI Clients

Humor in a therapeutic milieu not only provides pleasure, but laughter also permits clients to acquire a sense of mastery over problems (Warner, 1984). Humor programs and humor rooms may use humor bulletin boards to display cartoons, comic strips, jokes, and funny anecdotes. Humor carts stocked with humorous stories, joke books, comic books, and comedy audio/visual materials may be circulated throughout the unit. Humor programs may also utilize such noncompetitive games as those found in Weinstein and Goodman's Playfair:Everybody's Guide to Noncompetitive Play (1980). As long as the games are not competitive, nurses can use them as ice-breakers and facilitators of fun and mirthful laughter.

CMI clients can be helped to recall incidents of laughter, whether they occurred as embarrassing moments or pleasant events. For instance, Keller (1984) suggests sharing oneself experiencing an event; this can be facilitated by such questions as: "Remember back to a time when you were embarrassed/happy. Tell me what was funny or amusing about it." The nurse should encourage the client to recall as many sensory details as possible. However, since psychotic clients need to stay in touch with reality and remain centered in the here-and-now, it is important not to use visualization with them.

With most people, telling jokes is a skill that needs to be practiced, but it is not an impossible skill to acquire. For example, nurses and clients who repeatedly forget punch lines often are trying to remember the entire joke verbatim. If they can learn to remember the punch line and skeleton outline of a joke, it can then be fleshed out when it is told. Over time, some clients become adept at joke-telling and may even begin to write their own material and spontaneously make puns. McNary (1979) believes that joke-telling "can be just as revealing as other forms of communication, such as eye contact, silence, touch, and verbalization" (p. 228). This is especially true of favorite jokes or when people repeatedly tell the same types of jokes (misery jokes, fat jokes, sexist jokes).

Comic strips and cartoons can also be used to elicit humorous responses. Clients can cut out and share their favorites with the group. Some clients may even make an album of favorite cartoons to enjoy at their leisure. Poorly functioning clients may be assisted by the nurse to select a cartoon. If they are reluctant to read it to the group, then the nurse may read it. Such an activity can be followed by a discussion focusing on what was funny about the cartoon, how it related to daily life, and/or how it reflected their situation.

The use of comedic audio/visual tapes is another humor strategy. Clients can be involved in deciding which audio- or videotapes to use, both in the actual rental/purchase of the item and in setting up the equipment. The program can conclude with a discussion of the mirthful feelings evoked.

Reading aloud from humorous books enables clients to identify with or vicariously experience some of the pranks of the literary characters. When the book is based on real events, it helps clients to see how humor can be found in even every-day predicaments. Discussion can center around similar events in clients' lives. Sometimes, spontaneous streams of genial and often funny reminiscing may occur. If the book is illustrated, it offers yet another dimension-that of sight-to engage clients in humor.

The aim of these programs, rooms, and exercises is the implementation of the following goals:
1. Facilitate communication and socialization.
2. Develop a sense of belonging.
3. Encourage decision-making.
4. Decrease anxiety and tension.
5. Identify feelings of mirth and joy.
6. Temporarily divert attention from problems and onto the joy and fun of life.
7. Promote the healthful benefits of humor physiology.

Summary and Future Research

Therapeutic humorous nursing intervention is predicated on thorough assessment of client humor profiles as well as on the creativity and initiative of nurses. They need to be open to the fun and joy in life in order to help CMI clients experience those same qualities in their own lives.

Humor is a complex phenomenon encompassing biophysical, psychological, and sociocultural functioning. Psychologically, humor releases tension and anxiety, and it helps clients gain a sense of perspective. Socioculturally, humor facilitates group cohesiveness and conflict resolution. Although it should be used judiciously, it offers a creative means of intervening with CMI clients and improving the quality of their lives. Humorous nursing intervention is based on thorough assessment of client coping patterns, developmental stage, and humor style.

Therapeutic use of humor with CMI clients poses many questions. Guides to assess client humor need to be tested for validity, reliability, ease of use, balance, and scope. Nursing research designed to study the role and value of humor in the care of CMI clients needs to be undertaken. Specific areas for investigation might include: (1) factors that facilitate the use of humor with CMI clients, (2) factors that impede the use of humor with CMI clients, and (3) the relationship between specific humor modalities, client functioning, and cognitive ability. Research into these areas will add to the body of knowledge about humor therapy and the care of CMI clients.

Bibliography

Abeles, H. (1982). Letters. *The Sciences*, 22(9), 3.
Aiken, L. (1987). Unmet needs of the chronically mentally ill: Will nursing respond? *Image*, 19(3), 121-125.

Apte, M. L. (1985). *Humor and laughter: An anthropological approach*. Ithaca, NY: Cornell.

Askenasy, J. (1987). The functions and dysfunctions of laughter. *Journal of General Psychology*, 114(4), 317-334.

Bachrach, L. L. (1988). Defining chronic mental illness: A concept paper. *Hospital and Community Psychiatry*, 39(4), 383-388.

Bleuler, E. (1950). *Dementia praecox*. New York: International Universities.

Drew, N. (1991). Combating the social isolation of chronic mental illness. *Journal of Psychosocial Nursing*, 29(6), 14-17.

Freud, S. (1928). Humor. *International Journal of Psychoanalysis*, 9, 1-6.

Freud, S. (1940/49). *An outline of psychoanalysis* (J. Strachey, Trans. and Ed.). New York: Norton.

Fry, W. F. (1982). The psychobiology of humor. Paper presented at the Psychobiology of Health and Healing Conference, sponsored by Brigham Young University, Salt Lake City, UT.

Fry, W. F. (1986). Humor, physiology, and the aging process. In L. Nahemow, K. A. McCluskey-Fawcett, & P. E. McGhee (Eds.). *Humor and aging* (pp. 81-98). Orlando, FL: Academic Press.

Goldstein, H. (1982). A laugh a day — Can mirth keep disease at bay? *The Sciences*, 2(6), 21-25.

Goldstein, S. V. (1990). You are what you read: The use of bibliotherapy to facilitate psychotherapy. *Journal of Psychosocial Nursing*, 28(9), 7-10.

Goodman, J. (1981). The magic of humor: Laughing all the way to the learning bank. *Laughing Matters*, 1(1), 5-15.

Goodman, J. (1988, Sept.). *The humor project newsletter*. Saratoga Springs, NY: Saratoga Institute.

Haig, R. A. (1988). *The anatomy of humor*. Springfield, IL: Thomas.

Hall, R. (Ed.). (1980). *Psychiatric presentations of medical illness: Somatopsychic disorders*. Jamaica, NY: Spectrum.

Hall, R. C., Beresford, T. P., Gardner, E. R., & Popkin, M. K. (1982). The medical care of psychiatric patients. *Hospital and Community Psychiatry*, 33(1), 25-34.

Harris, M., & Bergman, H. C. (1987). Case management with the chronically mentally ill: A clinical perspective. *American Journal of Orthopsychiatry*, 57(2), 296-302.

Jalongo, M. R. (1985). Children's literature: There's some sense to its humor. *Childhood Education*, 62(2), 109-114.

Karasu, T., Waltzman, S., & Lindenmayer, J. (1980). The medical care of patients with psychiatric illness. *Hospital and Community Psychiatry*, 31(7), 463-472.

Keller, D. (1984). *Humor as therapy*. Wauwatosa, WI: Med-Psych.

176

Klienman, J., Gold, M., & Makuc, D. (1981). Use of ambulatory medical care by the poor: Another look at equity. *Medical Care*, 19(10), 1011-1021.

Koestler, A. (1964). *The art of creation*. New York: Macmillan.

Korany, E. K. (1979). Morbidity and rate of undiagnosed physical illnesses in a psychiatric clinic population. *Archives of General Psychiatry*, 36(4), 414-419.

Kubie, L. S. (1971). The destructive potential of humor in psychotherapy. *American Journal of Psychiatry*, 127(1), 37-42.

Levenson, S. (1966). *Everything but money*. New York: Watts.

Lieber, D. (1986). Laughter and humor in critical care. *Dimensions of Critical Care Nursing*, 5(3), 162-170.

Locke, S. (1980). Stress, adaptation and immunity: Studies in humans. *General Hospital Psychiatry*, 4(1), 49-58.

Manderino, M. A., & Bzdek, V. M. (1987). Social skills building with chronic patients. *Journal of Psychosocial Nursing and Mental Health Services*, 25(9), 18-23.

Martin, R. A., & Lefcourt, H. M. (1983). Sense of humor as a modulator of the relation between stressors and moods. *Journal of Perspectives in Social Psychology*, 45, 1313-1324.

Mazer, E. (1982). Ten sure-fire stress releasers. *Prevention*, 34, 104-106.

McCarrick, A., Manderschied, R., Bertolluci, D., Goldman, H., & Tessler, R. (1986). Chronic medical problems in the chronically mentally ill. *Hospital and Community Psychiatry*, 37(3), 289-291.

McGhee, P. E. (1979). *Humor: Its origin and development*. San Francisco: Freeman.

McGhee, P. E. (1982, Aug.). Children's humor and humor in education. Paper presented at the Third International Conference on Humor and Laughter, Washington, DC.

McNary, L. H. (1979). The use of humor in group therapy. *Perspectives in Psychiatric Care*, 17(5), 228-231.

Meissner, W. (1981). *Internalization in psychoanalysis*. New York: International Universities Press.

Mindess, H. (1981). Pies in the face and similar matters: A round table discussion. Voices: *The Art and Science of Psychotherapy*, 16(4), 10-23.

Nussbaum, K., & Michaux, W. W. (1963). Response to humor in depression: A predictor and evaluator of patient change. *Psychiatric Quarterly*, 37:527-539.

O'Connell, W. (1981). The natural high therapist: God's favorite monkey. Voices: *The Art and Science of Psychotherapy*, 16(4), 37-44.

Orem, D. E. (1985). *Nursing concepts of practice*, 3rd edition. New York: McGraw-Hill.

Pasquali, E. A. (1990a). Learning to laugh: Humor as therapy. *Journal of Psychosocial Nursing*, 28(3), 31-35.

177

Pasquali, E. A. (1990b). Humor: A holistic nursing intervention. *Journal of Holistic Nursing*, 8(1), 5-14.

Peschel, R. E., & Peschel, E. R. (1985). Aberrant medical humor: Case histories. *Pharos*, 48(1), 17-22.

Peter, L. J., & Dana, B. (1982). The laughter prescription. *Laughing Matters*, 2(4), 154-157.

Piaget, J. (1973). *The child and reality: Problems of genetic psychology.* New York: Grossman.

Reynes, R., & Allen, A. (1987). Humor in psychotherapy: A view. *American Journal of Psychotherapy*, 41(2), 260-270.

Robinson, V. M. (1991). *Humor and the health professions*, 2nd edition. Thorofare, NJ: Slack.

Roca, R., Breakey, W., & Fischer, P. (1987). Medical care of psychiatric outpatients. *Hospital and Community Psychiatry*, 8(7), 741-745.

Ruxton, J. P. (1988). Humor deserves our attention. *Holistic Nursing Practice*, 2(3), 45-62.

Samra, C. (1986). *The joyful Christ: The healing power of humor.* San Francisco: Harper & Row.

Schafer, R. (1968). *Aspects of internalization.* New York: International Universities Press.

Schaeffer, M. B., & Hopkins, D. (1988). Miss Nelson, knock-knocks, and nonsense: Connecting through humor. *Childhood Education*, 65(2), 88-93.

Siegel, B. S. (1986). *Love, medicine, and miracles.* New York: Harper & Row.

Spencer, H. (1860). Physiology of laughter. *Macmillan's Magazine*, 1, 395-402.

Talbott, J. A. (1981). *The chronic mentally ill: Treatment, programs, systems.* New York: Human Science Press.

Warner, U. (1984). The serious import of humour in health visiting. *Journal of Advanced Nursing*, 9(1), 83-87.

Weinstein, M., & Goodman, J. (1980). *Playfair: Everybody's guide to noncompetitive play.* San Luis Obispo, CA: Impact.

Worley, N. K., Drago, L., & Hadley, T. (1990). Improving the physical health-mental health interface for the chronically mentally ill: Could nurse case managers make a difference? *Archives of Psychiatric Nursing*, 4(2), 108-113.

Young, W. (1982, Aug.). The effect of humor on memory. Paper presented at the Third International Conference on Humor and Laughter, Washington, DC.

Ziv, A. (1982, Aug.). Cognitive results of using humor in teaching. Paper presented at the Third International Conference on Humor and Laughter, Washington, DC.

CHAPTER XIV

HO-HO-LISTICS-THE ROLE OF CULTURE AND HUMOR

by Josepha Campinha-Bacote, PhD, RN, CS, CTN

The proportion of minorities in the United States population is expected to increase greatly in the last decade of the twentieth century (Harris, 1992, p.43). The greatest challenge to nurses is to provide culturally relevant services for these culturally diverse patients. The use of humor can be considered a culturally responsive approach when rendering nursing care to patients from culturally diverse backgrounds. This chapter will begin by giving the reader a brief overview concerning the role of humor and culture. Transcultural Nursing Theory and the Africentric World View Model will serve as the conceptual frameworks for conducting humor groups with African American psychiatric patients. The chapter will conclude by citing techniques used when conducting a culturally specific humor group with African American psychiatric patients.

Robinson (1977) asks many questions when exploring the relationship between culture and humor:

1. Is there a difference in the kind of humor which emanates from a particular culture or ethnic group?
2. Does culture or ethnicity make a difference in the kind of humor which is appreciated?
3. Are there similarities or are there universal topics for humor?
4. Is there a relationship between a specific culture and its use of humor in times of stress like illness?
5. If so, what is it?
6. Would the culture of the patient make a difference in the health professional's use of humor if the professional were a nonmember of the culture? (pp. 102-103)

These questions are critical for nurses to explore if humor is to be used therapeutically with culturally diverse populations. Humor has often been described as a universal language. Yura and Walsh (1988) identified humor as a basic human need of every individual. Ziv (1988) further concluded that there is no society in which humor has not been reported (p. iv). Although humor and the physiological responses to it are universal, humor serves different functions in each culture.

The greatest difference among cultures is found in the content of humor and in the

179

situations in which humor is used and considered appropriate. Feinberg (1971) asserted that in every culture there is an unwritten agreement not to express aloud certain unpleasant or embarrassing truths (p. 10). Hughes (1966) stated that "humor is what you wish in your secret heart were not funny, but it is, and you must laugh. Humor is your own unconscious therapy" (p. vii). Therefore, many cultures use humor as a tool to express their conflicts of hostility, as well as their aspirations.

Grotjahn (1957) reported that the "Jewish joke constitutes victory by defeat" (p. 22). The persecuted Jew deflects his dangerous hostility away from the persecutors onto himself by making himself the butt of the joke. The result is not defeat or surrender but victory and greatness (p. 22). The use of humor to release feelings of hostility and anger are seen in other minority groups. Robinson (1977) stated that some African American comedians use wit and humor as a force in easing racial tension (p. 106). This type of humor transcends the seriousness of the individual's or group's past experience. However, the role and type of humor that is expressed within an ethnic group cannot be duplicated by individuals outside that specific ethnic group. When individuals outside a specific ethnic group attempt to duplicate this humor, it is referred to as ethnic humor. Ethnic humor, or "ethnic put-down," is based on racial, religious, national, regional, local, social, and sexual issues. This type of humor involves stereotyped thinking, bias and prejudice and condescending remarks (MacHovec, 1988, p. 116). It is obvious that this type of humor is not therapeutic, for humor that is therapeutic does not use ridicule.

Therapeutically, humor can be used to create a cohesive force between individuals. However, when people are from different cultural backgrounds, humor must be used in well-thought-out situations (Giger & Davidhizar, 1991, p. 22). Therefore, it is critical to conduct a humor assessment prior to using humor as a therapeutic tool with patients from diverse ethnic backgrounds.

Conceptual Frameworks

Transcultural Nursing Theory and the Africentric World View Model can be used as conceptual frameworks for conducting culturally specific humor groups with African American psychiatric patients. Leininger (1978) defines transcultural nursing as:

[The] learned subfield of nursing which focuses upon the comparative study and analysis of different cultures and subcultures with respect to nursing and health-illness caring practices, beliefs, and values with the goal of generating scientific and humanistic knowledge and of using this knowledge to provide culture-specific and culture universal nursing (p. 493).

The goal of transcultural nursing is to provide culturally relevant nursing care. Transcultural nursing is based on the premise that cultures should be able to determine

180

the extent and type of care they receive from professional caregivers, and that the culture's viewpoint, knowledge and experience are crucial factors to consider in assessing, planning and implementing nursing care (Leininger, 1978). Leininger (1983) further asserts that no individual can survive without culturally based care.

To provide effective therapy to African American patients it is necessary to take an "emic view" (or native view) of that individual. The emic view of African American patients is expressed within the Africentric World View Model. Affective epistemology is one component of the Africentric World View. Affective epistemology is the process and belief of a people discovering knowledge and truth through feeling or emotion (Phillips, 1988). Humor therapy can be an effective culturally relevant intervention, for humor is considered a human emotion. Within the Africentric World View, spirituality is a basic value. "African American people come to awareness and process reality through a feeling experience which can also be spiritually-intuitive" (Phillips, 1988, p. 2). This value is consistent with the use of humor therapy with African American patients. There is a growing interest in the use of humor from a spiritual perspective. The Fellowship of Merry Christians is one professional organization which is meeting this new challenge. The Bible clearly documents the spiritual aspects of humor. Proverbs 17:22 states, "A merry heart doest good like medicine: but a broken spirit drieth the bones." Child-Clarke and Sharpe (1991), as well as Samra (1985), document several other cases of the spiritual healing power of humor.

In summary, the Transcultural Nursing Theory and the Africentric World View Model provide nuses with a culturally specific framework in which to consider the use of humor therapy with African American patients.

Humor Groups for African American Psychiatric Patients

A humor assessment is the first step in initiating a humor group. It can be said that "there are different jokes for different folks." Specifically, if you are a nurse from a different cultural group than that of the African American patient, you may be unaware of the role that humor serves in this ethnic group. There are several available humor assessment tools. The author has developed a semi-structured, opened-ended assessment tool entitled, "How's Your Laugh Life?" The following eight questions allows the nurse to assess humor from an emic perspective:
1. Tell me what you consider is a good sense of humor.
2. Tell me the last thing you laughed about.
3. What type of humor do you enjoy? (films, cartoons, jokes, games)
4. What type of humor offends you?
5. Are there times when you shouldn't use humor? Tell me about those situations.

6.   How do you use humor in your life?
7.   What does the phrase "laughter is the best medicine" mean to you?
8.   Are you aware of the effects of humor and laughter in maintaining a healthy
     lifestyle?

These eight questions allow the nurse to assess humor from two cultural perspectives: (a) the culture of mental illness; and (b) the cultural/ethnic background of the African American patient. This humor assessment tool also addresses the questions that Robinson (1977) stated were critical factors to explore when interacting with patients from culturally diverse backgrounds.

Once the humor assessment is completed, the nurse can utilize the information to structure a culturally specific humor group. The author, an African American nurse, utilized the information obtained by conducting a humor assessment on seven African American psychiatric patients to structure weekly humor groups. One technique used in the humor group was the "humor walk." With this technique, the group leader had the patients take a note pad and walk about a specific area to notice things that made them happy, smile, or laugh. The specific assignment was to tour several outpatient clinics with the author (group leader), and write down thoughts or things that they saw which made them smile. Our original goal was to look for the positive, in what might appear to be depressing environment. The seven African American patients had a dual diagnosis of substance abuse and mental illness (predominantly schizophrenia and cocaine abuse). They appeared at one clinic, looking around to see what positive or pleasant things they could write about, when a white nurse confronted them and asked, "What are you people doing here?" I immediately came from behind the patients and replied, "My name is Dr. Josepha Campinha-Bacote and we're on a humor walk!" The nurse replied, "That's not funny!" With that comment we proceeded to return to our own clinic. We all laughed at the nurse's response. One patient laughed and stated, "Dr. Josie, they thought we were crazy, and we are!" Another patient laughed and remarked, "They were afraid of us all being Black!" Still another patient laughed and commented, "Dr. Josie, I bet they didn't even think you were a professional." It was obvious that our laughter was in response to the stigma of being mentally ill, as well as being a minority in a European American, private clinic. After this laughter we were able to talk seriously about our feelings of rejection. This humor group session served as an outlet to vent feelings regarding prejudices.

Another technique used in this culturally specific humor group was the use of culturally sensitive audiovisuals. The author used Bill Cosby videos to discuss specific issues in the group. Bill Cosby tapes were selected because during the humor assessment some members expressed that they did not like humor that was verbally offensive. Bill Cosby uses humor that is not verbally offensive and exemplifies everyday life situations.

182

Since Bill Cosby is an African American, the group's members were able to relate to him.

The singing of humorous songs was still another technique used in this culturally specific humor group. The author used Ellis' (1987) "rational humorous song" approach as the foundation of the this group technique. The rational humorous song approach is based on Ellis' rational-emotive therapy (RET), which states that emotional problems are based on man's irrational thinking. Ellis contends that:

1. Humor helps clients laugh at their failings and train themselves to refuse to take anything too seriously.
2. Humor exaggerates and counter attacks the overly serious exaggerations that lead to disturbances.
3. Humor interrupts and tends to break up old ingrained and rigid habits of thinking.
4. Humor activates a philosophy of joy and happiness that constitutes the basis for sane living, including a philosophy of striving for long-range as well as short-range pleasure.
5. Humor tends to help clients gain objective distance with respect to their self-defeating behaviors and makes it easier for them to acknowledge and attack their self-sabotaging (pp.280-281).

The author modified Ellis' (1987) rational humorous song approach to incorporate the Africentric world views of culturally specific music and spirituality. Specifically, the songs were sung in a "blues" style. Goines (1973) stated that "the blues" can be used as a simple and inexpensive form of psychotherapy for African Americans. The blues music was combined with humorous lyrics that also reflected spiritually. In one example, the author had the members sing the following lyrics to the tune of "On Top of Old Smokey":

> If God can love turkeys, then God can love you,
> for you are a turkey, and I am one, too.
> So when you get lonely, remember it's true,
> If God can love turkeys, then God can love you.

The author asked each group member to point to one another as they sang the phrase, "for you are a turkey . . ." We all began to laugh as we reflected on this song. The group was then able to discuss the role that God and religion had played in their lives, and how it was the actual "backbone of the Black family."

Conclusion

In order to provide effective health care to individuals from different ethnic/cultural backgrounds, it is necessary to take an emic, or native, view of the individual's values, beliefs, lifeways, and practices. Incorporating the individual's world view into the treatment plan is an important component in rendering culturally relevant nursing care. Humor is one intervention that is congruent with the world view of African Americans. Humor is also an effective therapeutic tool used with psychiatric patients. The key to conducting an effective therapeutic humor group with any cultural group is to first assess the role that humor serves in that culture. A humor assessment tool that captures the emic perspective of the patient's culture can assist the nurse in this process. If the nurse shares the same ethnic/cultural identity as the group members (as the author did) he/she has the potential to discuss topics that deal more directly with that culture's frustrations and anger. However, regardless of the ethnic background of the nurse, the goal of a culturally specific humor group is to incorporate the culture's world view of humor when conducting the group.

Bibliography

Childs-Clarke, A., & Sharpe, J. (1991). Keeping the faith: Religion in the healing of phobias anxiety. *Journal of Psychosocial Nursing*, 29, 22-24.

Ellis, A. (1987). The use of rational songs in psychotherapy. In W. Fry and W. Salameh (Eds.) *Handbook of humor and psychotherapy*. Orlando, FL: Professional Resource Exchange.

Feinberg, L. (1971). *Asian laughter*. New York: Weatherhill.

Giger, J., & Davidhizar, R. (1991). *Transcultural nursing*. St. Louis: Mosby-Year Book.

Goines, L. (1973). *The blues as black therapy*. Black World, 23(1), 28-40.

Grotjahn, M. (1957). *Beyond laughter*. New York: McGraw-Hill.

Harris, L., & Tuck, I. (1992). The role of the organization and nurse manager in integrating transcultural concepts into nursing practice. *Holistic Nursing Practice*, 6(3), 43-48.

Hughes, L. (1966). *The book of negro humor*. NY: Mead.

Leininger, M. (1978). *Transcultural nursing*. New York: Wiley.

Leininger, M. (1983). Cultural care: An essential goal for nursing and health care. *American Association of Nephrology Nurses and Technicians Journal*, 10(5), 11-17.

MacHovec, F. (1988). *Humor: Theory, history, Appalachians*. Chicago, IL: Thomas.

Phillips, F. (1988, July 8). *NTU psychotherapy: An Africentric approach*. Washington, DC: Progress Life Center, unpublished manuscript.

Robinson, V. M. (1991). *Humor and the health professions:* 2nd edition. Thorofare, NJ: Slack.

Samra, C. (1985). The joyful Christ. CA: Harper & Row.Yura, H., & Walsh, M. (1988). The nursing process. Weston, CT: Appleton & Lange.

Ziv, A. (1988). *National styles of humor*. New York: Greenwood.

CHAPTER XV

HUMOR AND RECOVERY FOR SUBSTANCE ABUSERS

by Donna Strickland, MS, RN, CS

Twenty years ago, I would have told you that people who needed to study humor were clowns joining the circus or comedians joining the night club circuit. I did not count myself among those who needed that information. I had a nursing career in mind, and was very successful in school. I thought of myself as someone who was ambitious, but who knew how to lighten up. I did not realize I was ripe to become addicted to and later find humor the most valuable component of my personal recovery. As far as I could tell, I was headed for a successful career with the right personality traits to fulfill the goals I was determined to realize.

Like most nurses, I wanted to get things right. I wanted to come up with the right answers in school, associate with the right people and live my life right. That seemed perfectly reasonable to me. It was certainly reinforced by my parents. I was raised in a Southern Baptist family which emphasized over-achievement, perfectionism, and pleasing others. Idle hands were considered to be the devil's workshop in my family. We kept busy and identified with what we did, not who we were. At the time, I believed I was being flexible to accommodate the demands placed upon me by parents, teachers, and peers. The idea that I was being rigid and too serious would not have occurred to me. I was happy to be getting excellent grades and pleasing everyone who took an interest in my academic performance.

Fueled by approval and my own expectations, I was named an Outstanding Teenager in America. I got listed in Who's Who Among College and University Students. I became Editor of the Nursing School Yearbook. I graduated Magna Cum Laude. As far as I could tell, I was doing things right. It made no sense to me that I felt empty, alone, and depressed when I slowed down for a minute. My discrepant feelings increased my need to maintain a breakneck pace. I moved on to graduate school and earned a higher grade point average. I became the quickest and youngest woman to graduate from Texas Women's University. These rip-roaring accomplishments were not extinguishing the gnawing doubts inside me. Feelings were surfacing that did not fit the picture of my commendable accomplishments.

My need to do the right thing took on an air of urgency. I had to find the right job, pay level, husband, house, and neighborhood. Otherwise those conflicting feelings would erupt into bouts of depression that I could not suppress. I could control my outward appearances, attitudes, and accomplishments. I could not control my feelings. In keeping with my previous winning streak, I spent the next ten years with the right husband, house, job, and income. All the right stuff. I had myself pretty much under control. It still would not have occurred to me that I was being extremely rigid and too serious. I was bending to pressures from all sides and keeping a lot of different people happy. I was not one of those I was keeping happy, however.

Ten years after graduate school, this smart cookie began to crumble. I went to work about as many days as I stayed home. I did not have sufficient money to pay my bills even though I made more than enough. I lost a lot of weight, didn't open my mail and got more depressed. When I was a Junior in College, I had begun to use alcohol to lighten up. I now began to use alcohol to settle down, to erase some of the pain, to take away some of my need to be so terminally serious. A drug addiction soon followed.

At this time, I began to sense that the subject of humor might offer something I needed. Humor is not something you study to get good grades or approval. I was starting to look inward for a change. I groped anxiously, pitifully, sadly for the meaning of humor. Where was it? How could one find it? Could it help me? I began to study and read. I really was searching in a different way from my old approach of confidently tackling new subject matter. About that same time, a nurse colleague friend of mine did an alcohol intervention with my parents, and I entered treatment. I am sober now and have been for a number of years. As important as it has been for me to get a spiritual life, it has been almost as important for me to learn how to laugh, how to let go, and how to lighten up; in other words, how to be a "Human Being rather than a Human Doing."

Humor comes from the Latin word "umor" which means to be like water: to flow, to be fluid, and to be flexible (Metcalf, 1992). In order to be like water, one has to be willing to be a little bit out of control. Experiences of love, laughter, joy, spontaneity, and creativity all stream into our experience by letting go of the controls. In order to get those things, one has to be willing to be in the moment with another human being. That requires being willing to risk foolishness, to risk failure and to risk embarrassment. Everything I had done for commendation was intentional. My addiction was both unintentional and out of my control. I was not laughing at myself for letting this happen to me. I was one to make things happen, not one to let things happen. I was trying to be in control of my feelings like everything else in my life. I was taking care of everyone but me.

Being humorous was the exact opposite of what I had become. Humor was the medicine I needed to become fluid, out of control and caring for myself. My experience of myself, my relationships, my ambitions and my career went through profound changes as a result. I was laughing at myself and laughing with others for a change. Little did

I know that the subject of humor would take me into a brand-new career working with other nurses, physicians, health care providers who have the disease of addiction. I did not foresee that "fluid spirit" would guide me to my suppressed grief. I did not anticipate that I would become uninhibited enough to teach others how to be silly. It has helped me with my relationships with my parents, my spouse, my friends. I speak of humor as something that has led me in its direction instead of something I took control of. It has transformed my approach to living.

I first began to use humor with clients in the early phases of their recovery and treatment of addictive disease. I was the Nurse Manager of an Inpatient, Dual-diagnosis, Addictions/Psychiatry Unit where I co-led a Cathartic Therapy Group. In early recovery, people with addictive disease take themselves very, very seriously; especially health care providers with addictive disease because they want to "get it right." The substance abuse has usually been their only resource for lightening up. Without it, they are faced with all the internalized rules and condemnations which make them rigid — serious. Humor offers a toxic-free replacement for feeling much less serious. We used laughter, humor and play skills in this group to help patients play with their tension, play with their pain and play with their stress around being an addict. Some of the techniques I will be discussing here also helped these folks deal with their humanness and their vulnerability. We helped them find ways to laugh at themselves around all kinds of issues.

We stressed to our patients that they were not alone; that there were other kindred spirits out there trying to get well, making every effort to change their lives. It is no easy feat. In order to get clean and sober, we said, one really has to be willing to not know the way. Healing comes to us like laughter comes to us. We cannot make ourselves laugh. It hits us when we quit trying so hard. The forced aliveness produced by substance abuse can be replaced by uncontrollable feelings of love, laughter, joy, spontaneity, and creativity. It occurs to people to feel humorous when they notice themselves getting too serious. It's a survival skill worth developing. By feeling powerless to control things, one's situation begins to feel less out of control. Recovery is paradoxical, not straightforward. Logic says making personal changes happens with determination. The paradox recommends taking oneself less seriously than that. We encouraged gradual surrender to a process that could strengthen immune responses, change neurochemical imbalances and help to keep them sober. The healing occurred to them as we went along, more a result of the process than our professional efforts.

Humor appears to be a powerful antidote to internalized shame. One well-accepted model for addictions regards it as a shame-based disease, meaning that a person feels embarrassed about who they are. Guilt is when you feel badly about making a mistake. Shame is when you feel you are a mistake (Bradshaw, 1988). Feeling defective as a human being kills spontaneity and risk taking. Addicts don't trust their impulses. Their

187

rigidity is an attempt to follow internalized rules to the letter so their own inclinations don't destroy them. If they yield to what they might do spontaneously, they fear they will self-destruct. Their experiences with making bad judgments under the influence is discouraging and frightening to them. They see the need to keep themselves under control.

Humor provides a contradictory experience of becoming alive by yielding to their own unreliable impulses. People find there is some good inside them when they are a little out of control. They are not as defective as they assumed. They risk being a little uninhibited and are rewarded by experiences of laughter, joy, or even tears. They feel more real and alive instead of fake and dying. Instead of making bad decisions when they let go, they find something positive comes to them from within themselves. This often has a profound effect on the hopeless outlook that accompanies the earliest phases of sobriety. Feeling defective is not something people share willingly. Laughing at oneself is out of the question. The flaws they take as fact are a well kept secret behind the mask of determined efforts to please others. The internalized shame develops a tremendous charge on it. It takes lots of energy to suppress it. People imagine they would be humiliated to death if they shared what they keep inside themselves. The deadening effect of the shame leads people to abuse substances to feel alive again. They experience their condition as a "flawed human being" as no laughing matter. Any laughter would be at them for being defective.

When people share with a support group what they think is totally disgusting, disgraceful, or contemptible about themselves, they survive the disclosure. That comes as a shock to someone who has kept the secret for years. They are amazed that people did not taunt, jeer, tease, and embarrass them. They imagined they would die if they told anyone. They have condemned themselves for it when it has crossed their own minds. They easily imagine others would disgrace them as well for their defects.

The tremendous energy to keep their flaws a secret is released by laughter and tears. In Alcoholics Anonymous, we say "secrets keep you sick." To keep a secret requires that one use up a lot of energy to maintain that secret, energy which isn't available for loving, laughing, and being in the moment. A wave of aliveness sweeps over people when they disclose their internalized shame. They have less need to abuse substances to help forget what they thought was so terribly wrong with them. The chances of relapse are reduced by their catharsis and working through of those issues that created tension to begin with. Sometimes, issues cannot be fully resolved. Then, the role of humor is to help shift patients' perspective long enough so that they can insert a coping tool that will help maintain this perspective. It is a process, a journey, that requires patience, perseverance, and a willingness to "not know the way." They can suddenly laugh at themselves for having been so serious and self-critical. Their faces are beaming in such moments. They feel as fluid as the water from which humor derives its original meaning.

The process of releasing shame through self-disclosure benefits the recovery process in another way. People reveal information about personal issues based on how they communicate their anxiety through their humor (Freud, 1905/1961). What people laugh about can tell you what they are having other feelings about, perhaps where the caregiver needs to help the patient in dealing with those issues (Freud). For example, patients who are experiencing fear often has a high-pitched "jittery"-sounding laugh, their skin temperature is cool, and there is an increased urinary output. When someone is discharging anger and tension, their laughter sounds more throaty and low, and skin temperature is warmer. More of a patient's past history and current concerns are worked through once they have surfaced through catharsis.

The effectiveness of teaching humor skills depends on the patient being sober, and the patient's ability to tell the truth or at least acknowledge the truth. People who are facing their shame, their disease and its effects, their history of abuse, desperately need to learn humor skills to survive and thrive in recovery, to gain some perspective. It is thought that the high suicide rate with recovering folks might be related to the seriousness by which they take themselves, and the overwhelming flood of shame that is experienced especially in the first five years of sobriety. The pain and awkwardness of life without alcohol is indeed surprising when it comes time to date, be sexual, socialize, dance, make small talk, do those things that most of us take for granted. Hence, learning to make light of these awkward moments, these frailties related to learning to being a human creature in the universe. Someone said that, "Imagination was given to us to compensate for what we are not. A sense of humor was given to us to console us for what we are" (anonymous).

Being joyful or light-spirited is a developed skill we can use or lose. It's never easy. It is even more difficult for alcoholics to get a sense of lightheartedness because they have their neurochemistry to overcome (Gallant, 1987). And often they have family of origin issues to work through. If addicts do not learn to reclaim their right to be happy, joyous, and free, the consequences are far more serious than for those who do not have addictions. Addicts face the chances for relapse and lethal outcomes. They need the joy to counterbalance the intense challenges of facing sobriety.

We presented humor as a coping tool for immediate use in recovery, as well as all of life yet to come. Patients learned to use humor as a way to decrease their anxiety about what uncertainties lie ahead. Our group mixed experiential and instructional learning modes. Much of the information we conveyed about humor relieved anxiety and answered some unspoken concerns. The processes we explored often produced unexpected benefits. Catharsis is something that can occur when it is least expected and not occur when it should. Often the best "gems" of our Humor Support Groups and Cathartic Therapy Groups were in the unplanned, spontaneous moments of people, patients and therapists alike, coming together to learn, work, and move on down the road of recovery.

What follows is a review of the humor work we did in the cathartic therapy group from three different angles: information we conveyed about the physiological benefits of laughter, shifts that occurred in clients' outlooks and expectations, and particular exercises we found most effective.

Physiology of Laughter

Humor is cognitive and intellectual. Mirth is the emotional response to humor. Laughing, giggling, chortling, guffawing, tittering, smiling are what we call the behavioral responses to humor (Robinson, 1991). They produce changes in our physiology. Dr. William Fry's research states that "mirth and its mirthful behavior has impact on most of the major physiological systems of the body" (Fry, 1986, p.84). One actually feels better after one laughs or after one cries because of changes in body and brain chemistry. We operated from the basic assumption that those who abuse drugs came to us with neurophysiological deficits, primarily in the areas of dopamine, serotonin, and norepinephrine. We believed that most substance abusers suffered from dysphoric moods. And we believed that catharsis (laughter, tears, anger) could potentially serve as a mechanism for rebalancing brain neurochemistry. We covered the following effects with our clients to substantiate our objective to develop their humor skills.

- Reduction of tension occurs through laughter.
- Laughter offers an aerobic experience, which is sometimes called "internal jogging."
- Both blood pressure and heart rate can decrease after laughter to below the pre-laughter baseline (Fry & Savin, 1982).
- There is greater coordination between the right and left hemispheres following a laughter experience producing a more holistic consciousness (Svebak, 1982) .
- Humor and laughter both significantly increase levels of salivary immune globulin A, a vital immune system protein which is the body's first line of defense against respiratory disease as identified in the early research of McClelland (as cited in Long, 1987, and Dillon & Minchoff, (1985-1986).
- Adrenalin gets excreted when people laugh which increases memory, alertness, creativity and learning (Fry, 1986; Goldstein, 1987).
- Laughter stimulates the circulatory system including the heart muscle (Fry, 1986).
- Laughter increases production of catecholamines which stimulates the production of endorphins in the brain

190

- Laughter increases oxygen consumption (Svebak, 1975, 1977).
- We believe that neuro-transmitters are excreted, like dopamine, norepinephrine and serotonin as well as opiates and enkephalins which help people feel better just about being alive (Fry, 1986).
- Laughter enables the brain to rebalance itself chemically after deficits caused by substance abuse, withdrawal and excessive seriousness.
- Often with laughter came tears in our cathartic therapy group. The two eruptions of spontaneous emotions are closely connected. So we also covered the physiological benefits of tears.
- Emotional tears carry the same toxins as cells under stress and we decrease some of the stress hormones by crying (William Frey, II, University of Minnesota, 1985).

Perspective

Humor shifts our perspective so that we can take our work in life seriously or our recovery seriously, while we take ourselves lightly. People who take themselves very very seriously often wind up seriously ill. They sometimes end up seriously relapsed. Relapse is an important issue for people recovering from the disease of alcoholism and drug addiction.

Taking one's recovery in life seriously while taking oneself seriously is a deadly combination. So a major skill for our clients to learn was how to take your recovery in life seriously while you take yourself lightly. Another thing we know about humor is that it is about having a skill set (Metcalf, 1992). Humor is cognitive and intellectual. It is not something you are born with or born without. It is something you develop over a period of time. So humor is about having a skill set that you can turn to when your life feels like it is going to fall apart from chaos, change and crisis.

Humor changes the look of circumstances before the circumstances get any better. Humor is used to shift perspective. We relied on Annette Goodheart, PhD's model in this regard (Goodheart, unpublished work). She suggests that emotion or feeling combined with catharsis enables us to rethink our situation which in turn produces more sensible action (emotion/feeling + catharsis > rethink> sensible action). The neuro-chemical balancing that accompanies catharsis is part of what enables .the reframing. Humor can free us from our need to be overly serious, perfectionistic or controlling. Metcalf (1992) characterizes this as learning to access joy to cope with adversity. The tension release that accompanies laughter often has a cognitive component where the burdens being carried do not feel as heavy. Troubles do not seem as intimidating. People feel better able to flow with turn of events once they adopt a humorous perspective.

It is common for people with an addictive disease to face obstacles regarding laughing. Many associate it with being laughed at viciously. We never-ever used humor in the group to laugh at a patient or to make fun of his or her symptoms. Laughing *with* someone rarely does harm, but laughing *at* someone can cause great pain and suffering. Besides preventing further injury, we worked to heal some old wounds. About 85% of the women we have seen in inpatient treatment have suffered early sexual abuse as children. Often times that sexual abuse was perpetrated with a sadistic parent who used humor in a way that was very damaging, frightening, and overwhelming. Humor is often confused with aggression, teasing or tickling, as well. Women in particular have found it helpful to do a Humor Inventory (HI) of past experiences (Metcalf, 1992). Metcalf's work with taking humor inventories inspired our process.

Most of us grow up with strict rules about not being silly and absurd. You've heard most of the following: "Grow up; get serious; wipe that stupid smile off your face; act your age." Those reoccur in adulthood: "You can't be working; you're having too much fun; what's all this laughing about?" Those are things that get internalized into what has been termed "terminal seriousness" or "terminal professionalism" (Metcalf, 1992, p. 147). It is not necessary to look for deeply buried memories. The idea is to get a clear picture of each person's humor history so that they can make as many conscious choices about their "Humor Perspective" as possible. Often patients can answer the inventory questions within ten minutes and come up with information that was an eye-opener for them.

Humor Support Group

Each group would begin with a brief overview of the nature of catharsis and healing, shame and addiction, as well as shame and recovery (Bradshaw, 1988). We reviewed how shame takes up a lot of energy and it keeps us from being in the moment. We emphasized the need to take risks in recovery, in relationships, and in living our dreams. We also included spirituality as a component of the cathartic or humor experience. Humor enables our spirits to stay fluid and not be easily broken. We routinely formed dyads to share what some of their early experiences had been with humor. Participants inevitably uncovered a piece of their history that they had forgotten. Frequently those experiences were painful. Either the client was being harmful or someone else was laughing at them, using sarcasm, hostile humor or a prank that was hurtful. The fact that patients did their own uncovering gave them a sense of efficacy as well as material to work in our group or other settings. We used a variety of exercises which invited projective responses and revealed a client's concerns and feelings in the moment. Bernie Siegel's "art therapy" exercises with oncology patients was a fertile source for much of this (Siegel, 1989). We also used Siegel's exercise where patients describe their favorite

192

animal, color, and body of water, and explain why they chose those answers. Then they are asked to describe how it would be for them to enter a room where everything is white. We used this exercise to help patients interpret how they were feeling in the areas of self, support, sexuality, creativity, and spirituality (Siegel, 1989).

It has been my experience that newly sober alcoholics and addicts have so much pain and so much shame that they can barely stay in their skin. The first three months, even the first year, is full of memories of their own behavior and painful recollections of past traumas. They have to face their whole life ahead of them, to make amends and to start over again. The whole process is overwhelming. Many people relapse and do not come back. They need to be equipped for "flood control" when the deluge of feelings overtakes them. Humor is one piece of the pie that might keep them hanging on in the darkness, when there really seems to be no light. We talked for several sessions on a number of different subjects using Bernie Siegel recommendations of "seven things to do if you have pain" (Siegel, 1989) and Annette Goodheart's "incorrect myths about laughter and tears" (Goodheart, unpublished works). We talked at length about the emerging field of mind-body medicine and the power of our outlook on our own healing. The projective responses also provided hours of discussion as material that surfaced met people's needs to make sense of their own inner turmoil. One of the most helpful intervention tools for addicts is to show them ways to be "connected." Humor is about feeling connected and feeling fluid. All this flowed nicely as we taught people to reach out to others to get some stability without rigidity in their lives.

We taught people how to be silly like they had not been in a long time. The idea books and props for this aspect of the work were extensive at the time, and the volume continues to multiply. We would get colored chalk and draw on the sidewalk. We skipped around the entire hospital, in and around different wings and units and then played hopscotch. I think both male and female patients loved this exercise more than any others because it was so child-like, joyous and free. At the same time we also wore little comic headbands with bouncing antennas I call "beeboppers." Having experiential props and outdoor exercises in the cathartic therapy groups seemed to be well received by most everyone. Also, in these groups, we listened to music, danced sometimes, drew pictures, journal-ized, sometimes only focused on our breath in silent meditation, participated in native American "healing circles." Sometimes we told stories. Sometimes we held "listening circles." Sometimes we just wept. We provided a safe place where people could explore all the concepts mentioned here: having fun, being silly, feeling unconnected, exploring grief, exploring internal workings through projective tests, learning new skills for coping in times of chaos, change, and crisis. We hung out together. We practiced a humor skill technique I call "Hangin' Baby." We practiced being a human being with other beings. Our clients were given the opportunity to allow some old shame to surface as it naturally

193

does in early recovery, and not drink or use drugs over it, but to be present with it, talk about it, laugh and cry about it.

Conclusion

This group took place over a three-year period. I wish that, when we had started this group, we had planned for a research component. Patients rated this as the "most favorite group" on program evaluations. Variations in individual responses appeared to be related to the amount of risk taking each was willing to attempt either verbally, physically or experientially in the group. In the last year of the group, the focus of the group changed as we spent more time teaching patients how to just "be." We explored how to be present, to witness their own experience and those of their peers. We called this "Being Mindful." Being still long enough to listen to their own inner voice is even more crucial for the recovering person given their disease. However, I think it is critical for all human beings to be aware of their thoughts and feelings, regardless of how turbulent and contradictory they are.

I wish all patients in every health care setting could have the option of attending a group or class or experience like this one. Through the exploration of humor, they could learn information about themselves that would be helpful to them in their daily lives, to cope with life on life's terms. With a small amount of information, we can make a big difference healing ourselves with humor. It has long been my desire that every person who comes to us in the health care setting be in true partnership with us, that we use the opportunity of their entering the health care system as a vehicle for learning and transformation. In the case of recovering individuals who are in such a physical, mental and spiritual crisis, allowing them the experience of exploring their own soul through a humor and healing program, or cathartic therapy group can be transformative. We can develop "care partnerships" where each benefits from the healing experience.

Since humor is really about having a flexible spirit, and being able to flow like water, it is a perfect adjunct to traditional treatment modalities and interventions used in treating the addicted individual. "Humor interventions" fit nicely into the third step of Alcoholics Anonymous (1976) which concerns itself with the concept of "surrender" and letting go.

Bibliography

Alcoholics Anonymous, 3rd edition. (1976). New York: World Services.

Bradshaw, J. (1988). *Bradshaw on healing the shame that binds you*. Deerfield Beach, FL: Health Communications.

Dillon, J., & Minchoff, B. (1985-86). Positive emotional states and enhancement of the

194

immune system. *International Journal of Psychiatry in Medicine,* 15(1), 13-18.

Freud, S. (1905/1961). Jokes and their relation to the unconscious. In J. Strachey (Trans. and Ed.), *The complete psychological works of Sigmund Freud, vol. VIII.* London: Hogarth Press.

Frey, W. H., II. (1985). *Crying: The mystery of tears.* Minneapolis: Winston Press.

Fry, W. F., Jr. (1986). Humor, physiology and the aging process. In L. Nahemow, K.A. McCluskey-Fawcett, & P. E. McGhee (Eds.), *Humor and aging* (pp.81-89). Orlando, FL: Academic Press.

Fry, W. F., Jr., & Savin, M. (1982). Mirthful laughter and blood pressure. Paper presented at the Third International Conference on Humor, Washington, DC.

Gallant, D. (1987). *Alcoholism: A Guide to Diagnosis, intervention, and treatment.* New York: Norton.

Goldstein, J. H. (1987). Therapeutic effects of laughter. In W. F. Fry, Jr., & W. A. Salameh (Eds.), *Handbook of humor and psychotherapy: Advances in the clinical use of humor* (pp. 1-19). Sarasota, FL: Professional Resource Exchange.

Goodheart, A. (1988). Laughter and humor. Paper presented at the Laughter Therapy Training Institute, Santa Barbara, CA.

Long, P. (1987). Laugh and be well? *Psychology Today,* 21,10, 28-29.

Metcalf, C. (1992). *Lighten up.* Reading, MA: Addison-Wesley.

Robinson, V. M. (1991). *Humor and the health professions,* 2nd edition. Thorofare, NJ: Slack.

Siegel, B. (1989). *Peace, love & healing.* New York: Harper & Row.

Svebak, S. (1975). Respiratory patterns as predictors of laughter. *Psychophysiology,* 12, 62-65.

Svebak, S. (1977). Some characteristics of resting respiration as predictors of laughter: In A. J. Chapman & H. C. Foot (Eds.), *It's a funny thing, humour* (pp.101-1-4). Oxford: Pergamon.

Svebak, S. (1982). The effect of mirthfulness upon amount of discordant right-left occipital EEG alpha. *Motivation and Emotion,* 6, 133-143.

CHAPTER XVI

SURVIVOR HUMOR AND DISASTER NURSING

by Sandra E. Ritz, RN, MSN, MPH

Nurses and disasters — the combination does not sound like much fun, nor does it sound very funny. Yet, there is humor going on amid the disaster rubble. Question: What's the new area code for Los Angeles? Answer: 911 (overheard in L.A. two days after January 1994 earthquake). Nurses are involved as disaster workers and often as survivors as well. Any of us can suddenly and without warning be called to action in a disaster. Depending on where you live, you will face some sort of natural disaster, like a hurricane (now playing: Gone with the Wind); flood (the new zip code for Des Moines, Iowa: 50H2O); tornado; volcano; earthquake; etc. (What are the four seasons in L.A.? Earthquake, fire, flood, and mudslides). Or it could be a man-made disaster, like a war: "Good evening, all three of you out there who still have batteries"-Sarajevo radio broadcast by former Yugoslavia comedy troupe ("Sarajevo's 'Hit Parade,'" 1993); or a riot (pick from zillions of Rodney King or LAPD jokes); multiple deaths (Jeffrey Dahmer jokes, WACO jokes, etc.); radiation accident (pick any joke about glowing in the dark); airplane crash; multiple vehicle accident; technological accident; epidemic, etc.

As a nurse, you feel compelled to help in a disaster; in fact, you may be stuck at your place of work. You are torn between your allegiance to helping people in need and wanting to locate your family and make sure they are safe. You work long hours in sometimes horrendous conditions. "Toto, I don't think we're in Kansas anymore." (comment made when first going outside after Hurricane Iniki in Kauai). You experience sensory overload; noise is always a problem; oppressive heat and offensive odors often occur with lack of safe water and electricity.

"I smell so bad that my Sure deodorant is undecided", (Des Moines Register, "I'm a Floody Mess" contest to try to keep the city's spirits up after the water system failed during the 1993 floods (Buxman, K., personal communication, July 19, 1993).

Crowded conditions make solitude a distant memory. Flexibility and creativity are essential skills, as the conditions change constantly. Supplies are frequently inadequate, safety is a constant concern and the demands are physically exhausting. "Whenever you feel a tremor in California, you should do two things; get under a doorway, and make sure the doorway is in Cleveland" (comic Argus Hamilton, as cited in Farhi, 1994, p. A-14) You deal with people experiencing high emotions, multiple injuries, and tremendous losses. You may be experiencing the same and have to keep working.

197

At Henry Mayo Newhall Memorial Hospital during the 1994 Los Angeles earthquake, the doctor could not get in, so a nurse who had never delivered a baby before delivered Bob and Laura Mugno's first baby by flashlight. They nicknamed the 7 pound, 8 ounce baby "Rocky" ("New baby gets," 1994, p. A-10).

The use of humor as a coping strategy in a disaster can help relieve tension, manage stress, and reframe your perspective.

It's not all tragedy. You have to like the way the earthquake has brought this city together. I was driving down Sunset Boulevard and I noticed a white man, a black man and a Hispanic man all looting together (Jay Leno, as cited in Farhi, 1994, p.A-14).

I refer to gallows, black, and/or sick humor used in the context of a disaster and/or major crises as "survivor humor." This is the humor generated by survivors and workers that "laughs with" the survivors. It is a type of humor that helps one cope and also gives one hope. It is not ethnic humor that "laughs at" the survivors and/or puts them down. Instead, it enhances the feeling that "we're all in this together." I also try to avoid the term victim as much as possible, as I find it negative. Instead, I support the optimistic term of survivor. Survivor humor may help you find the absurdity in the adversity so that you will not lose hope in what feels like a hopeless situation — especially when you may have already lost everything else. "I doubled my real-estate portfolios. I now have a north house and a south house," said U.S. attorney Nora M. Manella after her L.A. townhouse was split in two by the January 1994 earthquake (Staff, Newsweek, 1994, p. 15).

Survivor Humor

The secret source of humor itself is not joy but sorrow. There is no humor in heaven.
Mark Twain

In Laughter in Hell: The Use of Humor During the Holocaust, Lipman (1991) acknowledged that "nothing about the Holocaust was funny," but referred to humor as the "currency of hope." He explained that during the Holocaust, humor was ". . . both a psychological weapon and a defense mechanism. It was a social bond among trusted friends. It was a diversion, a shield, a morale booster, an equalizer, a drop of truth in a world founded in lies. In short, a cryptic redefining of the victims' world" (pp. 8, 10).

Victor Frankl (1959) was a psychiatrist and survivor of Auschwitz who observed that humor was an essential factor in the prognosis for survival. The capacity to laugh at oneself and one's predicament provided detachment from the horror, yet paradoxically forced one to recognize it and be able to maintain a sense of purpose.

While we were waiting for the shower, our nakedness was brought home to us; we really had nothing now except our bare bodies — even minus hair; all we possessed, literally, was our naked existence . . . Thus the illusions some of us still held were destroyed one by one, and then, quite unexpectedly, most of us were overcome by a grim sense of humor. We knew that we had nothing to lose except our so ridiculously naked lives. When the showers started to run, we all tried very hard to make fun, both about ourselves and about each other. After all, real water did flow from the sprays! (Frankl, 1959, pp. 22, 24).

Freud (1960) saw humor as cathartic, a tension-lessening element of life; laughter as the mind's way of dealing with incongruous. He saw repressed feelings as the unconscious source of anxiety and tension, and that humor provided a momentary liberation. Freud identified "Galgenhumor," or gallows humors, as the crudest case of humor with the example of "a rogue on his way to an execution on a Monday remarking, 'Well, this week's beginning nicely' and asking for a scarf for his bare throat so as not to catch cold" (Freud, 1960, p. 229). Humorous pleasure from this Galgenhumor resulted from an economy of feeling: Pity is inhibited because the criminal makes nothing of the situation and humor is touched by the rogue's indifference. This gallows humor is grim humor, sometimes called "bravado in the face of death" (Ziv, 1984).

Obrdlik (1942) provided the first sociological study of humor in his report on gallows humor in Nazi-occupied Czechoslovakia. Gallows humor was seen as a type of humor that arises in connection with a precarious or dangerous situation and is an index of strength or morale on the part of oppressed peoples. Rather than just an expression of cynicism as demonstrated by Freud, Obrdlik viewed gallows humor from the innocent victims of oppression as an expression of hope and wishful thinking. Gallows humor functioned to ridicule with irony, invectives, and sarcasm as a means to bolster the morale and resistance of the victims and undermine the morale and influence of the oppressors. Obrdlik also noted that the oppressors' reaction to gallows humor is a reliable index of their strength: If ignored, they are strong; if the oppressors react with anger, reprisals and punishment, they are not sure of themselves.

One Nazi sees another walking out of the rabbi's home. "Why were you in a Jew's home?" he asks.

"I'm having the rabbi teach me Yiddish," the first Nazi answers. "That way I can listen when they are talking and discover their devious plans."

"That's really clever of you."

"Yes," boasts the linguist, pointing to his head. "That's using my tochis."

("Tochis" is Yiddish for buttocks.) (Lipman, 1991, p. 180).

Gallows humor uses irony to acknowledge dehumanizing, life-threatening circum-

199

stances and seeks to transform them into something human, delightful, and worthy (Koller, 1988). This gallows humor is used by survivors to build morale and confront the oppressor that seeks to subdue the human spirit. Koller (1988) notes that, "Even on the gallows, a prisoner can confront executioners with gallantry, poise, disdain, and high courage. His or her bearing, manner, grace, and self-respect transcends the taking of his or her life" (p. 10).

"I forgot to duck" and "I hope my surgeon is a Republican" (Ronald Reagan after an attempted assassination).

Survivor humor is an active defense mechanism that helps to cope with threats and fears instead of surrendering to them. It emphasizes the absurd that makes us laugh so that we will not cry. It is an attempt to shock ourselves out of the horror and anxiety. Laughing and even sometimes obscene comments serve the survivor's needs to cover his embarrassment and humiliation, although outsiders may not find it funny at all. It provides a sense of mastery over that which is out of one's control. For example, survivor T-Shirts, many with humorous pictures, are printed up and worn by many survivors in an affected community.

After the Santa Barbara, California fires, survivors from a neighborhood where all of their homes (except for the brick fireplaces) were reduced to ashes made up and wore T-shirts that read "My chimney is bigger than your chimney!" (D. Myers, personal communication, January 24, 1994).

To share a laugh together is a major social bond, and to move past our troubles, we resort to humor (Koller, 1988). The use of humor as a coping mechanism in disasters can provide some form of tension release and allow a re-interpretation (or reframing) of a situation or event (Moran, 1990). Not just used to help people cope, survivor humor also helps people maintain hope.

Coping humor is a valid and essential use of humor . . . [Humor] is a generator of energy, allowing one to "hang in there." By itself it cannot sustain the human spirit. If our humor is limited to laughing at the hopeless, in time it will become sarcastic, cynical and destructive. (Eberhart, 1986, cited in Fry, 1987, p. 61)

Lipman (1991) views humor as a form of spiritual resistance among the oppressed. He noted that during the Holocaust, "religion and humor served a like — though not identical—purpose: the former oriented one's thoughts to a better existence in the next world, the latter pointed to emotional salvation in this one . . . Both gave succor and provided an intellectual respite beyond the immediate physical surroundings" (pp. 11-12).

Hand-painted signs go up throughout a community immediately after a disaster, most with positive and encouraging messages. Some are spiritual, as in Kauai after

Hurricane Iniki: "Mahalo (Thank you in Hawaiian) God and everyone!" Some border on pornographic, such as "Iniki, one hell of a blow job!" On a home reduced to ruins after the Oakland Firestorm, a sign said "Fire Sale." Signs during the Midwest floods of 1993 included "Corn sold by the gallon"; "No fishing" in parking lots; and "Welcome to Missouri, now the 'Row-me state.'"

On a community level, humor can serve to redirect focus so that the hardships of disaster can be turned into causes of involvement (Laube, 1985). Also, just as a family caught in a private disaster may need humor for individual respite care, the promotion of positive humor may be indicated in a large-scale disaster for "community respite" (Ritz, 1993). Radio stations are often the sole means of communication for a community immediately following a large-scale natural disaster. Along with the provision of essential information for disaster relief, there can also be survivor humor on the airwaves for some collective comic relief. "At Ichitachi Quickie Mart, we haven't raised our prices since the hurricane — our prices were always this high!" (comedy skit on KONG radio, Kauai, soon after Hurricane Iniki (Cataluna, 1992). Survivor humor on the radio can provide collective acknowledgement of the frustrations and release from the tensions in an affected community. For example, language and cultural differences between survivors and relief workers can be stressful following a disaster. A respected celebrity and/or leader in the community who is able to express the humor in the situation can be an inspiration for optimism, patience, and hope.

> "Hi, I'm Cheryl from Cold-Hand Insurance Company. I'm here to look at your home. Are you Mrs. Kam-a-ka?"
> "No, that's Mrs. Kamaka . . .never mind girl, you call me auntie. . ."
> "Tell me, was there any damage done to your davenport, your living area, your veranda, your portecochere or your daybed?"
> "No, but I had damage on top my sofa, inside da parlor, da lanai, da garage, and on top of my pune'e." (Pune'e is Hawaiian for couch or single bed.) (comedy skit on KONG radio, Kauai, soon after Hurricane Iniki, Cataluna, 1992)

Dundes (1987) considers jokes a standard folklore genre. He believes that no piece of folklore continues to be transmitted unless it means something, and that where there is anxiety, there will be jokes to express that anxiety. His research on sick humor cycles and stereotypes revealed that people joke about only what is most serious and that one person's tragedy may become a point of projection or catharsis for the fears and anxieties of others. So, people joke about what they are most anxious about and sick humor will reflect the fears of a people at a given time. With television and newspaper coverage of all major disasters, virtually everyone becomes an unwilling witness (Emmons, 1986). The joking is a defense mechanism to cope with disaster and to distance oneself from the tragedy.

Nilsen (1993) believes that the most common type of gallows humor is the "disaster joke." These jokes, such as those about the Challenger explosion, appear immediately following a major disaster and spread quickly across the country. Few of these jokes are actually new. Instead they are recycled jokes with altered names and places that indicate that the jokes may not be about the actual events at all. "The hostility of the joke, or of the teller, is not directed toward the victims and topical references but rather to some psychically significant theme underlying the jokes. . . death, deformation, disease, and illness" (Smyth, 1986, p. 252).

Humor can moderate the relationship between stressful events and psychological distress (Martin & Lefcourt, 1983; Nezu, Nezu, & Blissett, 1988). Humor and laughter have been referred as the "antidote to adversity", as they play an important role in the maintenance of both psychological and physiological health in the face of stress (Lefcourt & Martin, 1986). A humorous perspective can enhance flexibility and creativity while learning to adapt to enforced changes. The spontaneous joking, silly quips, and sometimes cynical one-liners made by disaster survivors and relief workers are a method of coping with the overwhelming stress, as well as maintaining hope in the affected community. By taking a nonserious approach to very serious matters, the disaster survivor can neutralize the horror of the trauma and even make it possible to rise above it (Ziv, 1984). The bitter reality of the disaster cannot be altered; however, what can be altered is one's attitude toward it. This survivor humor provides a sense of mastery over death and any other subject that arouses fear.

Disasters

Disasters strike without discrimination, often without warning, and cause extensive destruction, death, injury, deprivation, and devastation. A disaster is a situation in which available resources are overwhelmed and can no longer cope. Rapid mobilization of resources from outside the affected community are required. In fact, disasters now are not classified according to the number of casualties, but by the level of resources needed to meet demands adequately (Burkle & Kinney, 1993).

A major disaster occurs in the world every 8 1/2 days, with most of these occurring in third-world countries and of moderate size with 100 to 200 casualties (Burkle & Kinney 1993). However, the death rates and economic losses in United States disasters have recently climbed sharply due to the high costs associated with technologically based societies and rapid increase in population density into hazardous areas (Waters, Selander, & Stuart, 1992).

Disaster Survivor Stress

The mental health needs in major disasters in the United States were recognized as a significant area of concern for the first time with the passage of the The Disaster Relief Act of 1974 (Public Law 93-288). This act mandated that the National Institute of Mental Health (NIMH) provide mental health crisis counseling services and training as part of the disaster relief effort. The training includes basic principles of crisis intervention and supportive treatment and includes outreach procedures and "curbstone therapy" (Farberow & Frederick, 1978).

The great majority of post-disaster problems are essentially problems of living and readjustment (Farberow & Frederick, 1978). Contrary to the stereotypical Hollywood disaster movie, people do not disintegrate in response to disaster. Survivors are normal people who are under temporary emotional stress. Their observed responses to disaster stress are "normal reactions to an extraordinary and abnormal situation, and are expected under the circumstances" (Myers, 1992, p. 3). Grief reactions are also a normal part of recovery from disaster (Zunin & Zunin, 1991, cited in Myers, 1992).

204

Factors viewed as essential in a survivor's recovery and that will lead to the reestablishment of equilibrium include: (a) the relief from stress; (b) the ability to talk about the experience; and (c) the passage of time (Hartsough & Myers, 1985). The aim for human service workers in a disaster is to help the survivor resume his or her own independent functioning by supporting usual coping mechanisms and available personal resources (Farberow & Frederick, 1978). Interestingly, humor is not identified as a "usual coping mechanism" or an "available personal resource." Mental health services provided for support through the stresses of long-term recovery emphasize the individual's adaptation to changed conditions. Additionally, the anticipation of a favorable recovery is crucial for all individuals, as without it, community and individual demoralization and decline are likely to occur.

In contrast to the treatment of the individual post-disaster, the social problem model approach to disaster phenomena does not assume that disasters are necessarily bad in their consequences. Golec (1980, cited in Quarentelli, 1985, p. 201) observed that the very term "victim" connotes an adverse consequence. Quarentelli (1985) notes that some "have in fact argued for positive consequences of disasters" and that it is the "second disaster" that arrives by way of the post-impact relief efforts that may contribute substantially to the negative consequences for victims (p. 196). In this view, disaster response organization inefficiency, disparity in allocation of resources, and efforts to obtain services create the increase in disaster survivor stress. The implication is that individual survivors may not manifest stress if the community response is organized to meet their needs.

Disaster Worker Stress

There has been increased concern for the welfare of disaster and emergency workers, as no one who sees a disaster is untouched by it — including the workers (Myers, 1992). Exposure to traumatic stimuli and the demands of disaster work may cause workers to show signs of emotional and psychological strain. In a study of the psychological impact of disaster on rescue personnel who treated victims of an apartment building explosion, 80% had at least one symptom of posttraumatic stress disorder (PTSD), with the most frequently reported symptom being intrusive thoughts about the disaster (Durham, McCammon, & Allison, 1985). "I suffer from "PISS": Post Iniki Stress Syndrome" (T-Shirt worn by nurse working in Hurricane Iniki disaster relief on Kauai).

One way of addressing this disaster worker stress is Critical Incident Stress Debriefing (CISD). A critical incident stress is any situation faced by emergency personnel that causes them to experience unusually strong emotional reactions having the potential to interfere with their ability to function at the scene or later (Mitchell, 1983). The debriefing process helps those involved with a critical incident by mitigating or lessening the impact of the event (Rubin, 1990). In recent years, increased concern over the well-being of emergency workers has been demonstrated at the organizational level by the implementation of formal CISD programs to prevent the development of longer-term stress reactions (Moran, 1990). CISD is a method of post-disaster stress management for disaster workers. A growing awareness of worker stress has led to the recent development and implementation of stress management programs for Federal Emergency Management Association (FEMA) workers at ongoing disasters, such as the 1993 Midwest Floods (Myers & Zunin, 1993, August) and the 1993 Florida Winter Storms (Myers & Zunin, 1993, March).

Training programs and simulation exercises are being developed for primary prevention to keep disaster workers from experiencing some of the stress in the first place, or that might enhance efforts at dealing with the situations that confront them (Lystad, 1985). Recommendations have been made that pre-disaster stress management courses, which could include a variety of stress reduction techniques, be provided for emergency workers. However, the use of humor for stress reduction is not addressed. Also, there are no humor guidelines provided to disaster workers except for a rare one-sentence reference in a few of the federal and state disaster training booklets, i.e., "laughter is the best medicine" or to "avoid grim humor."

Although there are studies that investigate emergency worker stress, research specific to disaster nursing is minimal to date. The results of a preliminary study have suggested that nurses are required to make difficult choices during national emergencies and may be at risk for experiencing psychological distress following a disaster (Waters et al., 1992). Nurses are often required to remain at patients' bedsides prior to, during, and after a disaster. This often separates nurses from their own families at a vulnerable time, creating a role conflict and contributing to their stress. During the disaster, they must cope with their concern for their own survival, that of the patients under their care, as well as that of their family, co-workers, and friends.

ODE TO BURNOUT:

YES, I'M FINE.
I'M REALLY FINE.
SO MUCH TO DO,
SO LITTLE TIME.

I AM, I'M FINE.
REALLY JUST FINE.
SO MANY TO HELP,
SO LITTLE TIME.

TRUST ME, I'M FINE.
IT'S NOT A JOKE.
I'M REALLY JUST FINE.
BUT DO YOU SMELL SMOKE?

Among nurses who served in Vietnam, life and death decisions based on inadequate information, hospital bombings, fatigue, severe trauma in patients, and lack of emotional support produced increased rates of PTSD (Sandecki, 1987, and Shovar, 1987, cited in Waters, et al., 1992). Major stressors for nurses working during Hurricane Celia in Corpus Christi in 1970 included excessive physical demands, concerns for safety, inadequate supplies, and concerns for their family's safety (Laube, 1973). Home care nurses who were both disaster victims and caregivers for other victims following Hurricane Hugo experienced grief, anger, and frustration about their losses, as well as conflict between their family and work-related responsibilities (Chubon, 1992).

Reports in the nursing literature reveal some of the intense stress nurses have faced in recent disasters. During Hurricane Andrew, nurses in the impact zone pulled patients from room to room throughout the storm to avoid exploding windows and ceilings that buckled while water poured through the roof ("Hurricane Andrew Puts...," 1992). When a back-up generator at Deering Hospital failed, "nurses manually bagged five respirator

207

patients for 12 hours" (p. 98). At Homestead Hospital, while gales of up to 160 mph broke windows, and power and water were lost, the staff managed to deliver seven babies by flashlight. Hurricane Andrew closed four hospitals and nine nursing homes and left 250,000 people homeless, including many nurses. Three weeks later, the island of Kauai was devastated by Hurricane Iniki. Public health nurses searched neighborhoods in Kauai and Florida for those in need of care, and staffed clinics 15 to 18 hours a day ("In Hurricanes' Wake. . .," 1992). Nurses who were members of the Disaster Medical Assistance Teams reported that the key lessons learned included "the need to be flexible [as] change is the most common occurrence in a disaster," and the need to be adequately prepared and be completely self-sufficient (Gaffney, Schodorf, & Jones, 1992, p.79). Nurses provided the lifeline to many of the 1993 Midwest flood's victims ("In the Midwest's. . .," 1993). This was a "slow-motion disaster," and nurses who had been victims themselves provided "curbside mental health" to help ease the psychological trauma to flood victims who were very emotional and fatigued. Some other examples of nurse-survivors coping with disasters include the violent 1991 Kansas tornadoes (Prilliman, Solis, Swartz, & Conley, 1993), a volcano eruption (Sloan, 1990), and the 1994 Los Angeles earthquake ("New Baby Gets. . .," 1994).

Humor as a Form of Nursing

Researchers across many disciplines refer to humor as a coping strategy (Bellert, 1989; Freud, 1960; Fry, 1987; Haig, 1986) and a defense mechanism (Grotjahn, 1957; Robinson, 1991). Robinson (1991) refers to the use of gallows humor by both patients and health professionals as "medical humor." In a study of the social functions of humor among the staff of a mental hospital, Coser (1960) found that the use of humor highlights or creates group consensus and at the same time permits all to withdraw together briefly from the seriousness of the concerns that face the group. Kuhlman (1988) found that gallows humor used on a maximum security forensic unit provided a way for staff to better interact with aggressive patients, was a bolster for staff solidarity, and functioned as a coping mechanism and as a way of "being sane in an insane place" (p. 1085). Warner (1991) found that student nurses in a psychiatric hospital used humor as a coping response to regulate stressful emotions and/or alter a stressful person-environment relationship. Humor is recommended as a coping strategy for nurses combating job-related stress in the CCU (Lieber, 1986) and for oncology nurses Simon (1989).

Field research by nurses involved in disaster relief following Hurricane Hugo revealed that humor was the second most frequently observed coping strategy among the survivors (Weinrich, Hardin, & Johnson, 1990); the most common one was talking about their experiences. Retelling the events repeatedly helps the survivor to gain mastery over

208

them. Home care nurses who were both disaster survivors and caregivers after Hurricane Hugo routinely provided continuing support to one another (Chubon, 1992). In a study of 79 rescue and hospital personnel involved in an apartment building explosion, 42% reported the use of humor as a coping behavior (Durham, et al., 1985). Of those that used humor, 79% found that humor as a coping behavior was helpful. Molitor (1993) reported that "Laughter is free and can be heard often" among Hurricane Andrew nurse-survivors (p. 41a). A Disaster Medical Assistance Team going to St. Croix after Hurricane Hugo that was faced with logistical and transportation problems "found considerable humor in the question of what the military proposed to do with us" (Lewis-Rakestraw, 1991, p. 162). American military nurses who lived and worked through the months of combat and horrendous conditions of Bataan in World War II "used humor and a sense of normalcy to maintain their mental balance" (Norman & Elfried, 1993, p. 123).

To cope with the stress under conditions of disaster and refugee care, Burkle (1983) recommended that health care professionals:

> . . . develop the ability to use what we know are the three most adaptive defense mechanisms: (1) Suppression; the ability to let things "bounce off your chest." Avoid repression or the immediate internalization of surrounding emotional and physical threats to your ego. (2) Acceptance; things will happen over which we have absolutely no control nor can we possibly change. Don't ruminate about what "could have been." (3) Develop a sense of humor, not so much the ability to find humor in adversity, but rather the ability to laugh at oneself and one's own vulnerability (p. 803).

Martin and Lefcourt (1983) found that having the ability to notice potentially humorous situations was not sufficient to reduce stress. It was active humor, the ability to produce humor and not just react or appreciate it, that was found to be positively related to performance under stress (Bizi, Keinan, & Beit-Hallahmi, 1988). Rosenberg (1991) also found that the ability to produce humor that is spontaneous and situationally relevant is critical in stress reduction (p. 201). Medical research suggests the physiological changes that occur with laughter may be effective in reversing the classical stress hormone response. So, not only an effective psychological release from stress, but humor may also help maintain good health during the prolonged stress of a disaster. For example, 10 minutes of solid belly laughs cause the blood's sedimentation rate (a sign of inflammation) to decrease (Cousins 1979, 1989). Mirthful laughter initially causes a slight increase and then subsequent longer lowering effect on blood pressure (Fry & Savin, 1988). Fry likens laughter to physical exercise, as 20 seconds of laughter can double the heart rate for 3 to 5 minutes, the equivalent of 3 minutes of strenuous rowing (Cousins, 1989). Berk, et al. (1989) found changes in neuroendocrine and stress hormones during mirthful laughter. Martin and Dobbin (1988) utilized measurements of IgA in saliva to demonstrate evidence of a stress-moderating effect of humor. Lefcourt, Davidson-Katz, and Kueneman (1990) demonstrated that humor has an enhancing effect on immune system functioning, supporting the findings of Dillon, Minchoff, and Baker (1985-86) who showed that positive emotional states enhance the immune system. Cogan, Cogan, Waltz, and McCue (1987) demonstrated that laughter and relaxation can increase the discomfort threshold, the ability to withstand pain. Dillon and Totten (1989) presented research findings that positive psychological factors, including humor, influenced the immunocompetence and health of breast-feeding mothers and infants.

Nurses involved in a disaster can use survivor humor as a healthy coping strategy to relieve tension, manage stress, reframe perspective, and maintain hope. Because a disaster overwhelms normal resources, there are outside resources that quickly arrive to help the affected community. Nurses must work together and cooperate with strangers under horrendous conditions. The social benefits of humor come into play when dealing with the influx of disaster relief workers, as people who can laugh with each other can work together. Humor can relieve the tension in a group working together, enhance communication, and encourage the flexibility, adaptability, and creativity required in a disaster setting.

Beyond using humor for themselves and with their coworkers, nurses can also use humor as a therapeutic intervention with disaster survivors. There are four identified emotional phases that survivors experience following a disaster: heroic, honeymoon, disillusionment, and reconstruction (Farberow & Frederick, 1978). Preliminary field investigations suggest that these phases may be used as a guideline for humor assessment of the disaster survivor. For example, survival is the basic concern in the heroic phase, so humor is spontaneously produced by the survivor to relieve tension and overcome fear.

Most of the disaster survivors' humor reported by the media occurs during the second or "honeymoon" phase. It can last from 1 week to 3 to 6 months post-disaster and is a state of recovery optimism (Farberow & Frederick, 1978). The third, or "disillusionment" phase can last from 2 months to 1 to 2 years. This is a time of anger, resentment, and disappointment. In contrast to the honeymoon phase where humor is prevalent, in this third phase the survivor is quite bitter and could easily misinterpret and take offense at attempts at humor. The survivor in this phase often feels oppressed by the many agencies and organizations that have invaded the community. A sense of powerlessness can be expressed through gallows humor that uses satire, ridicule, and irony aimed at disaster workers and others perceived to be in power. The fourth, or "reconstruction" phase involves rebuilding, recovery and acceptance. Humor returns slowly, aided by community activities, rituals such as anniversary celebrations, and social support.

Awareness of these phases in the survivor can assist the nurse who chooses to use humor as a coping strategy when working in a disaster. If nurses working on disaster relief are also disaster survivors, this awareness can be applied to them as well. They can identify if they and the disaster survivor-clients may be out of "sync" with their phases and preferred types of humor. There are so many frustrations for survivors after a disaster, and some of the relief efforts can feel demeaning. Awareness of the need for survivor humor in oneself and in the survivors, and sensitivity to appropriate timing and use, are essential for disaster nurses who choose to use survivor humor in a therapeutic and positive manner. Those who appropriately and actively produce survivor humor will be better able to cope with the severe stress, as well as maintain and generate hope.

Bibliography

Bellert, J. L. (1989). Humor: A therapeutic approach in oncology nursing. *Cancer Nursing*, 12(2), 65-70.

Berk, L. S., Tan, S. A., Fry, W. F., Napier, B. J., Lee, J. W., Hubbard, R. W., Lewis, J. E., & Eby, W. C. (1989). Neuroendocrine and stress hormone changes during mirthful laughter. *The American Journal of the American Sciences*, 298(6), 390-396.

Bizi, S., Keinan, G., & Beit-Hallahmi, B. (1988). Humor and coping with stress: A test under real-life conditions. *Personality and Individual Differences,* 9(6), 951-956.

Burkle, F. M., Jr. (1983, October). Coping with stress under conditions of disaster refugee care. *Military Medicine,* 148, 800-803.

Burkle, F. M., Jr., & Kinney, M. L. (1993). The personalized disaster plan narrative: An effective teaching tool for hospitals. *Journal of Emergency Nursing,* 19(3), 254-257.

Cataluna, L. (Speaker). (1992). *Hurricane Iniki comic relief* [Cassette Recording]. Kapaa, HI: Small Cat Productions.

Chubon, S. J. (1992). Home care during the aftermath of Hurricane Hugo. *Public Health Nursing,* 9(2), 97-102.

Cogan, R., Cogan, D., Waltz, W., & McCue, M. (1987). Effects of laughter and relaxation on discomfort thresholds. *Journal of Behavioral Medicine,* 10(2), 139-144.

Coser, R. L. (1960). Laughter among colleagues: A study of the social functions of humor among the staff of a mental hospital. *Psychiatry,* 23, 81-95.

Cousins, N. (1979). *Anatomy of an illness.* New York: Norton.

Cousins, N. (1989). *Head first: The biology of hope.* New York: Dutton.

Dillon, K. M., Minchoff, B., & Baker, K. H. (1985). Positive emotional states and enhancement of the immune system. *International Journal of Psychiatry in Medicine,* 15(1), 13-18.

Dillon, K. M., & Totten, M. C. (1989). Psychological factors, immunocompetence, and health of breast-feeding mothers and their infants. *Journal of Genetic Psychology,* 150(2), 155-162.

Dundes, A. (1987). *Cracking jokes: Studies of sick humor cycles and stereotypes.* Berkeley, CA: Ten Speed Press.

Durham, T. W., McCammon, S. L., & Allison, E. J., Jr. (1985). The psychological impact of disaster on rescue personnel. *Annals of Emergency Medicine,* 14, 664-668.

Emmons, S. (1986, May 30). Sick jokes: Coping with horror. *Los Angeles Times,* pp. 26, 30.

Farberow, N. L., & Frederick, C. J. (1978). Training manual for human service workers in major disasters. Washington, DC: National Institute of Mental Health, DHHS Publication No. (ADM), 90-538.

Farhi, P. (1994, January 21). Quakes: Laughing at despair. *Honolulu Advertiser,* p. A-14.

Frankl, V. (1959). *Man's search for meaning: An introduction to logotherapy.* New York: Pocket.

Freud, S. (1960). *Jokes and their relation to the unconscious.* (J. Strachey, Trans. and Ed.). London: Norton. (Original work published 1905).

Fry, W. F. (1987). Humor and paradox. *American Behavioral Scientist*, 30(1), 42-71.

Fry, W. F., & Savin, W. M. (1988). Mirthful laughter and blood pressure. Humor 1(1), 49-62.

Gaffney, J., Schodorf, L., & Jones, G. (1992). DMATs respond to Andrew and Iniki. *Journal of Emergency Medical Services*, 17(11), 76-79.

Grotjahn, M. (1957). *Beyond laughter.* New York: McGraw-Hill.

Haig, R. A. (1988). *The anatomy of humor.* Springfield, IL: Thomas.

Hartsough, D. M., & Myers, D. G. (1985). *Disaster work and mental health: Prevention and control of stress among workers.* Washington, DC: National Institute of Mental Health, Center for Mental Health Studies of Emergencies, DHHS Publication No. (ADM), 87-1422.

Hurricane Andrew puts Florida's hospitals to the test and leaves hundreds of nurses homeless. (1992). *American Journal of Nursing,* 92(10), 96, 98, 100-102.

In hurricanes' wake, Florida's and Hawaii's stressed survivors turn to public health nurses for healing. (1992). *American Journal of Nursing*, 92(11), 92-93.

In the Midwest's still unfolding tragedy, nurses are the lifeline to many of the flood's victims (1993). *American Journal of Nursing,* 93(9), 73, 81.

Koller, M. R. (1988). *Humor and society: Explorations in the sociology of humor.* Houston, TX: Cap and Gown Press.

Kuhlman, T. L. (1988). Gallows humor for a scaffold setting: Managing aggressive patients on a maximum-security forensic unit. *Hospital and Community Psychiatry,* 39(10), 1085-1090.

Laube, J. (1973). Psychological reactions of nurses in disaster. *Nursing Research,* 22(4), 343-347.

Laube, J. (1985). Emotional consequences of disasters. In J. Laube & S. A. Murphy (Eds.), *Perspectives on disaster recovery* (pp. 150-178). Norwalk, CT: Appleton-Century-Crofts.

Lefcourt, H. M., Davidson-Katz, K., & Kueneman, K. (1990). Humor and immune-system functioning. *Humor,* 3(3), 305-321.

Lefcourt, H. M., & Martin, R. A. (1986). *Humor and life stress, Antidote to adversity.* New York: Springer.

Leiber, D. B. (1986). Laughter and humor in critical care. *Dimensions of Critical Care Nursing,* 5(3), 162-170.

Lewis-Rakestraw, L. (1991). Response of the New Mexico disaster medical assistance team in St. Croix after Hurricane Hugo. *Journal of Emergency Nursing,* 17(3), 162-164.

Lipman, S. (1991). Laughter in hell: The use of humor during the holocaust. Northvale, NJ: Jason Aronson.

214

Lystad, M. (1985). *Innovations in mental health services to disaster victims.* Washington, DC: National Institute of Mental Health, Center for Mental Health Studies of Emergencies, DHHS Publication No. (ADM), 90-1390.

Martin, R. A., & Dobbin, J. P. (1988). Sense of humor, hassles, and immunoglobulin A: Evidence for a stress-moderating effect of humor. *International Journal of Psychiatry in Medicine,* 18(2), 93-105.

Martin, R. A., & Lefcourt, H. M. (1983). Sense of humor as a moderator of the relation between stressors and moods. *Journal of Personality and Social Psychology,* 45(6), 1313-1324.

Mitchell, J. T. (1983). When disaster strikes . . . the critical incident stress debriefing process. *Journal of Emergency Medical Services,* 8, 30-36.

Molitor, L. (1993). Coping, caring, and heroism in the wake of Hurricane Andrew. *Journal of Emergency Nursing,* 19(3), 37A-42A.

Moran, C. (1990). Does the use of humor as a coping strategy affect stresses associated with emergency work? *International Journal of Mass Emergencies and Disasters,* 8(3), 361-377.

Myers, D. (1992). Key concepts of disaster mental health. Technical assistance to disaster crisis counseling planners and administrators. Washington, DC: National Institute of Mental Health Contract #91MF23504101D.

Myers, D., & Zunin, L. M. (1993, March 28-April 14). Stress management program, after-action report; 1993 Florida Winter Storms, Disaster Field Office; Tampa, FL. FEMA-982-DR-FL.

Myers, D., & Zunin, L. M. (1993, August 6-September 18). Stress management program, after-action report; 1993 Midwest Floods, Federal Emergency Management Agency, Central Processing Unit; Kansas City, Missouri. FEMA-995-DR-MO, FEMA 996-DR-IA; FEMA 998-DR-NE; FEMA 1000-DR-KS.

New baby gets a rocky start in this world. (1994, January 21). *Honolulu Star-Bulletin,* p. A-10.

Nezu, A. M., Nezu, C. M., & Blissett, S. E. (1988). Sense of humor as a moderator of the relation between stressful events and psychological distress: A prospective analysis. *Journal of Personality and Social Psychology,* 54(3), 520-525.

Nilsen, D. (1993). *Humor scholarship: A research bibliography.* Westport, CT: Greenwood Press.

Norman, E., & Elfried, S. (1993). The Angels of Bataan. *Image: Journal of Nursing Scholarship,* 25(2), 121-126.

Obrdlik, A.J. (1942). Gallows humor: A sociological phenomenon. *American Journal*

Prilliman, K., Solis, G., Swartz, M., & Conley, K. (1993). Disaster response: A review

215

of the April 26, 1991, Kansas tornado. *Journal of Emergency Nursing*, 19 (3), 209-211.

Quarentelli, E. L. (1985). An assessment of conflicting views on mental health: The consequences of traumatic events. In C. R. Figley (Ed.), *Trauma and its wake: The study and treatment of post-traumatic stress disorder* (pp. 173-215). New York: Brunner/Mazel.

Ritz, S. (1993). Disaster relief. *Laugh it up*, 7(4),1-2.

Robinson, V. M. (1991). *Humor and the health professions*, 2nd edition. Thorofare, NJ: Slack.

Rosenberg, L. (1991). A qualitative investigation of the use of humor by emergency personnel as a strategy for coping with stress. *Journal of Emergency Nursing*, 17(4), 197-203.

Rubin, J. G. (1990). Critical incident stress debriefing: Helping the helpers. *Journal of Emergency Nursing*, 16(4), 255-258.

Sarajevo's "hit parade" humor helps war-weary citizens cope. (1992, July 6). *Honolulu Star-Bulletin*, p. D-5.

Simon, J. M. (1989). Humor techniques for oncology nurses. *Oncology Nursing Forum*, 16(5), 667-670.

Sloan, K. A. (1990). Volcano! Disaster management. *Journal of Emergency Nursing*, 16(4), 263-268.

Smyth, W. (1986). Challenger jokes and the humor of disaster. *Western Folklore*, 45, 243-60.

Staff. (1994, January 31). Perspectives. *Newsweek*, p. 15.

Warner, S. L. (1991). Humor: A coping response for student nurses. *Archives of Psychiatric Nursing*, 5(1), 10-16.

Waters, K. A., Selander, J., & Stuart, G. W. (1992). Psychological adaptation of nurses post-disaster. *Issues in Mental Health Nursing*, 13, 177-190.

Weinrich, S., Hardin, S. B., & Johnson, M. (1990). Nurses respond to Hurricane Hugo victims' disaster stress. *Archives of Psychiatric Nursing*, 4(3), 195-205.

Ziv, A. (1984). *Personality and sense of humor*. New York: Springer.

CHAPTER XVII

HUMOR'S ROLE IN TERMINAL ILLNESS

by Kaye Ann Herth, PhD, RN, FAAN

One inch of joy surmounts of grief a span, Because to laugh is proper to the man.
Rabelais, 1952, p. 5.
Humor, like hope, allows one to acknowledge and endure what is otherwise unendurable.
Sheehy, 1981, p. 387.

The health-care literature contains little reference to the role or impact of humor on the terminally ill or on those providing care to the terminally ill. Nurses have recognized the great need and are in the forefront in exploring this critical area. This chapter provides an overview of the work in this area completed by nurses and identifies implications for practice and areas needing further investigation.

The subject of death and dying connotes for most an attitude of seriousness, not one that allows for or invites lightheartedness. Few studies exist that explore the role of humor during terminal illness despite humor becoming more widely accepted for its positive physiological, sociological, and psychological effects in a variety of other clinical settings and populations. Nursing is at the forefront of applying humor in clinical practice arena. The therapeutic role of humor on client populations within the critical care setting (Leiber, 1986), the oncology setting (Bellert, 1989; Erdman, 1991), the rehabilitation setting (Schmitt, 1990), and the mental health setting (Davidhizar & Bowen, 1992; Pasquali, 1990; Raber, 1987) are reported within the nursing and health care literature. Humor as it relates to specific age groups, children (Smith, 1986) and older adults (Herth, 1993a,b; Hulse, 1994; Maliniski, 1991; Simon, 1988; Sullivan & Deanne, 1988; Tennant, 1990) is also being studied by nurse researchers. McCloskey and Bulechek (1992) include humor and humor-promoting activities in the first nursing intervention classification system developed.

Interest in the possible therapeutic role of humor in the terminally ill population is relatively recent, and may be in partial response to the current hospice movement in this country. The hospice model, different from the traditional medical model, emphasizes providing holistic care to dying individuals and their family members/significant others, and in helping the terminally ill to live as fully as possible until death (Dobratz, 1990). A review of recent hospice and palliative care journals and regional and national hospice

217

conferences indicates a growing interest in the potential therapeutic role of humor in the case of dying individuals, their family, and their health care providers.

Barriers

Barriers continue to exist in the exploration of and therapeutic use of humor during a terminal illness. Death in the American culture is viewed by many individuals with fear and anxiety. There is a cultural and religious expectation that the dying be treated with dignity and respect, and that a muted display of positive emotions be maintained. This overall attitude of solemnity dampens any possibility for lightheartedness. Comedians have tried to lighten our death anxiety by poking fun at death, but many people feel that laughing about anything dealing with dying or death is definitely beyond the bounds of what is acceptable. This is not the case in many other cultures where death is accepted as the natural course of events and where humor is not only allowed but encouraged (Klein, 1986).

Cultural expectations are often compounded by the tremendous physical, emotional, and social pain and loss that the dying individuals and their loved ones face daily (Killeen, 1991). The unrelenting physical deterioration and the loss of bodily functioning affects all those involved including family, significant others, and the health care providers. The seriousness of this situation and the possibility of being perceived as lacking sensitivity to the pain involved is seen by those caring for and about the terminally ill person as a barrier to the inclusion of humor. This basic concern is further compounded by the lack of research on the effects of humor and the application of humor to practice with the seriously ill or terminally ill population. A study of nurses' attitudes toward humor (Simon, 1989) found that, while humor was strongly valued by individual nurses in their personal lives, there was hesitancy and uncertainty on its appropriate application in professionals dealing with clients facing the serious stresses of acute and terminal illness.

Anecdotal accounts exist describing the helpfulness of humor during the terminal phase of an illness, but research studies are almost nonexistent. Inferences are often made as to the physiological, psychological, and sociological role of humor in the terminally ill population based on humor's role in healthy and chronically ill populations. Health care providers, families, and the terminally ill individuals themselves are becoming more interested and vocal about the potential role of humor during this very stressful time in their lives.

Perceptions of Health Care Providers

The perceptions of health care providers, based on clinical experiences in working with the terminally ill, provide the first step towards identifying the therapeutic role of humor in terminally ill individuals and their family members. It is important to note that the descriptions provided by health care professionals do not always correspond to the terminally ill persons' views or their family's views. Several hospice nurses/health care providers have identified physiological, psychological, and interactive benefits of humor to their terminally ill clientele, families, and coworkers based on direct observations gathered through years of working with terminally ill individuals. Graham and Cates (1989), both nurses with extensive experience in the hospice field, suggest that humor provides treatment of the whole person, encourages the expression of a range of emotions, facilitates coping with the pain and loss, and provides a positive means of framing life even when life is limited. Killeen (1991), a social worker within a hospice home care setting, proposes that humor adds to the terminally ill individuals' inventory of positive coping skills, enables the recognition and acknowledgment of the person rather than the sick role, allows for greater closeness, and can enable the terminally ill individual to have internal control when the external situation seems out of control. Barnum (1990), a nurse and editor of the journal Nursing and Health Care, believes that humor provides a momentary escape into a place of freedom and power. This escape may be especially important to the terminally ill individual or family members who are experiencing intense pain and multiple losses. Moody (1978) and Samra (1985) contend that humor makes us better by enabling us to stand aside from things and get a different perspective.

Klein (1986), a noted lecturer and author on humor, suggests that humor facilitates the release of tension and thus can be a very effective way of coping with failing body functions and confused emotions. The major focus of Klein's work is on the therapeutic role of humor with the family members and professional caregivers. Based on interviews of family members caring for their dying loved ones, Klein identified that humor serves as a positive means to transcend a stressful situation. As one family caregiver expressed to Klein, "Humor has a force of its own; like prayer, it transforms you" (Klein, 1986, p. 44). Klein suggests that, for the professional caregiver who encounters numerous deaths, humor can be a socially acceptable way of releasing frustration and helplessness (p. 44). Victor Frankel (1963), a noted psychiatrist and survivor of the Nazi Germany concentration camps, described inventing one humorous story a day in his struggle to stay alive and cope with the appalling conditions in the concentration camp. In his book Man's Search for Meaning, Frankel described humor as ". . . affording an ability to rise above any situation, even if only for a few seconds" (Frankel, 1963, p. 68).

Perceptions of the Terminally Ill

The question remains whether the terminally ill perceive humor as an appropriate and effective strategy in light of the magnitude of the emotional physical pain and loss. Schmitt (1990) asked that same question of individuals undergoing serious changes in bodily function and image in a rehabilitation setting. Schmitt interviewed patients in a rehabilitation hospital regarding their perception of laughter and its effect on their mood, their opinion of nurses who laugh with patients, and the appropriateness of laughter in this setting. Results from 35 surveys indicated that the patients welcomed laughter and perceived nurses who laughed with their patients to be therapeutic. However, these individuals were not terminally ill.

A review of the literature found only one research study that directly examined humor from the perspective of the terminally ill individual and that particular study was conducted by the author (Herth, 1990). The study involved interviewing 14 terminally ill adults (prognosis 6 months or less to live) from two hospice home care programs regarding their perceptions of and experiences with humor. The purpose was to clarify the concept of humor and its contributions during terminal illness from the perspective of those who are terminally ill. Data were collected through the use of an audiotaped semistructured interview conducted in the terminally ill participants' homes. The participants were found to be eager and open in their discussion of humor. Many expressed that the opportunity to share their feelings about something positive made them feel like "a real person again." Most verbalized that humor enabled them to see things more positively and to put a new light on their situation. More than half also expressed that humor allowed them to ask questions that they might otherwise not ask and to hear instructions they might otherwise be too anxious to hear. Several verbalized that the constant seriousness present in their environment made them feel isolated and as if they were "already dead." The data obtained from the recorded interviews were content analyzed using the data reduction method. Themes that occurred repeatedly were clustered into categories that best represented the participants description of the therapeutic benefits of humor in their lives. The categories were identified as connect-edness, perspective, hope, joy, and relaxation. Based on these categorizations, humor was viewed as forming a bridge that facilitated transition through difficult times. The majority of participants expressed that humor helped them to maintain a sense of belonging, to experience a feeling of relaxation, to empower their hope and joy, and to alter their perceptions in overwhelming situations. Based on the participants' responses, humor was conceptualized as having both an attitude and an action component that elicited for these participants a feeling of warmth inside, a sense of lightheartedness and delight, and at times hearty laughter (Herth, 1990). Over and over again, the participants expressed that humor enabled them to feel "alive" and thus for them was a life-enhancer and life-enricher even though their time was very limited.

220

Perceptions of Family Members

Terminal illness places heavy demands on the family unit, the individual family members, and their interrelationships. The stress of a dying family member is usually unmatched to any other stress previously experienced and affects all aspects of family dynamics. There is much written in the literature on the burden placed on the family caregiver, but little on how family caregivers find the courage and strength to continue on. The question remains whether humor has any role in so grave a situation from the standpoint of those family members giving care to their dying loved one. A review of the literature found no studies that directly examined the role of humor in the family caregiver, although several studies indirectly identified the important role of humor (Herth, 1993a,b; Miller, 1991). In studies of hope in caregivers, humor was identified by the family caregivers as a hope enhancing strategy both for themselves and for their dying loved ones (Herth, 1993a,b; Miller, 1991). Humor was described as enabling the family caregiver to relabel the stress and gain perspective, as distracting the individual from painful feelings and allowing for a temporary escape from the burdens thereby making reality more tolerable, and as enabling hope and thus allowing the dying individual and family to focus on quality of life, the achievements in life, and the legacy of the dying individual.

Implications for Practice

Throughout the research literature, the adaptive, coping, and communicative functions of humor are identified and the need to incorporate humor into the caregivers' clinical practice is stressed. Jourard (1970), a noted psychologist, suggests that caregivers have the power to be either "dispiriting" to those in their care, or "inspiriting" to those in their care. Dispiriting is defined by Jourard as "accelerating the ill individuals' rate of dying"; inspiriting as an "invitation to continue living" (p. 269). Jourard suggests that health care professionals can intervene by using techniques designed to inspirit. The question, however, remains: How does the clinician use humor therapeutically to inspirit those individuals experiencing the terminal phase of an illness?

(Assessment Guidelines.) Humor may be one tool that health care professionals, particularly nurses, can use to inspirit the terminally ill individual. Using humor as a therapeutic tool must begin with doing an assessment of individual/family, their environment and their situation. This assessment has been identified as involving five key areas: values/beliefs, intent (appropriateness), timing, receptiveness, and respon-siveness (Astedt-Kurki & Liukkonen, 1994; Herth, 1990; Hunt, 1993; Killeen, 1991 Leiber, 1986; Robertson, 1991; Simon, 1989; Sullivan & Deane, 1988).

221

Assessment always begins with a careful examination of health care providers' values and beliefs as they relate to the specific therapeutic intervention/tool the providers plan to use with their clients. It is important that the values and beliefs of health care professionals be congruent with the methodology/tool they are using. Health care providers considering the therapeutic use of humor in their practice need to carefully examine their own views and values regarding humor before attempting to incorporate it into their practice. The caregiver must place a high positive regard on humor's potential usefulness in order to most effectively use it (Robinson, 1991). The intent of using humor must be clearly delineated. Pasquali (1990) identifies three key questions that test the intent of the humor in a particular situation: Does the humor take into account the level of and effect on anxiety? Does it have as its goal clarification rather than masking of feelings? Is the humor oriented to laughing with rather than at a person? (p. 32). These questions, if answered in the affirmative, suggest that the use of humor is appropriate in particular situations.

Timing has also been identified as a key to the effective use of humor (Herth, 1990; Leiber, 1986; Samra, 1985; Simon, 1989). A study completed by the author of this chapter (Herth, 1990) found responsiveness to humor to be unique to each individual and, with only two exceptions, there were no specific right or wrong times for implementation. The exceptions noted were that humor should not be interjected when serious dialogue is initiated or when an acute crisis is present. These findings were substantiated in findings with other clinical populations (Erdman, 1991; Leiber, 1986; McGhee & Goldstein, 1983; Simon, 1988, 1989). It is important to also note that humor is not an appropriate intervention with family members at the time of death, although later at the funeral it may be very appropriate to share some of the humorous and joyous incidents in that individual's life.

I remember attending the funeral of a 68-year-old gentleman I had cared for through the home hospice program for about 4 months. This particular gentlemen had a great sense of humor and had always been the "life of a party." Prior to entering the sanctuary of the church, the family, close friends, and myself were secluded in a room just off to the side. The silence in the room was deafening. The minister asked if anyone wanted to ask or say anything before we went into the church. Remembering his joy for living, I asked if anyone could think of specific times they had spent with him that brought a sense of delight and joy to the heart that we could share before entering the sanctuary. One of the family members shared a really humorous, joyous time they had together, and immediately other members shared similar experiences. The family and friends soon recognized that this gentlemen would want his funeral to be a celebration of his life and his joy for living. There was a marked change in the atmosphere after that sharing. Several weeks later, several family members and friends told me how much it had meant to share the joyous moments at the funeral, and how important this was to them as they were working through the grieving process.

Closely aligned to timing is receptiveness and responsiveness. People's capacity to engage in humorous exchange is a valuable indicator of their emotional state. Those who are in severe pain or extremely depressed are not receptive or responsive to humor, nor is it appropriate to interject humor in those situations. Killeen (1991) stresses the importance of assessing the meaning of humor in the person's life prior to illness as that may influence the receptiveness of the individual to any humorous intervention. The author (Herth, 1984) developed a formal assessment questionnaire entitled, "Funny Bone History" (FBH). This tool was designed to assess individuals' past and present history of humor use and to identify what makes them laugh. Knowing what makes people laugh is believed to be an important clue based on the fact that there are many types of humor and a variety of responses to humor. The "Funny Bone History" asks what kinds of things make the subjects laugh and then asks them to think specifically how they could put more humor or lightheartedness into their life (see Table 1).

Table 1.
Funny Bone History

What was the last time you had a good laugh?
What kinds of things make you laugh?
How often do you laugh?
How do you feel when you laugh?
What role did humor play in your family while growing up?
Imagine yourself as a comedian. Which one would you choose to be and why?
When was the last time you played?
What could you do today that would make you laugh?
If you put more play and laughter in your life, how would you feel?
Do you find humor a source of relaxation?
Each time you laugh in the next week, write down what made you laugh.
                                        Kaye Herth (1984)

The FBH questionnaire is designed to be incorporated into the traditional health history or taken separately if appropriate. The tool was used by the author in a clinic

223

setting with individuals across the health spectrum, ranging from those individuals in fairly good health to those in the terminal stage of an illness. The FBH is presently being used in a variety of health care settings (pain clinics, oncology outpatient clinics, AIDS support groups, etc.) throughout the United States. Bellert (1989) also developed a formal assessment tool to examine patient's attitudes and practices regarding humor. Although not specifically designed for the terminally ill, her tool could be used by that population. Specific areas assessed on this survey include a history of whether individuals laugh a lot or a little, an assessment as to whether the amount of laughter in their life has changed since illness, and specifics as to how humor may have helped them cope with a painful situation in the past. The survey concludes with asking if they would like to add more humor into their life and in what one area would they like to add humor and why. Both of these tools have a definite role in assessing humor appreciation and use in terminally ill individuals. The use of a formal tool, however, may not always be possible or appropriate. Killeen (1991) suggests that, for those situations where a formal tool may not be appropriate, it may be just as effective to use a more informal style of listening for references to humor and then following up when individuals describe how they have coped in the past and what situations made them laugh.

Any attempts to initiate humor must consider personality, culture, background, and levels of stress, depression, and pain. The terminally ill participants in the study conducted by the author (Herth, 1990) suggested that humorous overtures should begin very slowly with lighthearted actions such as a warm smile, a wink, or a playful comment. This approach enables the existing level of receptivity to humor to be validated. The participants also stressed that the sharing of humor needs to occur within a caring framework and one that is built on a comfortable level of trust. The "core conditions" of caring were described as warmth, authenticity, and empathy. As one young dying mother told me, "Caring helps me to make real connections, those connections made at the heart that allow me to both laugh and cry depending on my need at the time."

Openness to fun on the clinicians' part can provide the opportunity for the seriously ill individual to open up to humor. Once people sense that humor is acceptable, they will often feel free to bring forward their own humor style. Humorous and playful interactions can occur throughout the care-giving process. It is important to note that these humorous interventions should be intermittent and interspersed with the full range of human emotions in order to make difficult situations manageable. Continuous humor is no more appropriate than continuous sadness. The clinicians' use of humor and an eye for the incongruous or unexpected provides a model of such intervention for the family, according to Graham and Cates (1989). This use of self, often referred to as modeling, may give permission to the family to interact playfully, both with the ill individual and with each other in the individual's presence. Graham and Cates caution, however, that

224

the humor of the terminally ill and their family must be accepted in a nonjudgmental manner and that demeaning or offensive humor should not be tolerated. Sumners (1990) aptly described positive humor as ". . . . a form of intellectual play characterized by spontaneous or supportive behaviors that connote kindness and geniality, and carries a message of affection, caring, and humaneness" (p. 198). I recall a young man who was in the last stages of liver cancer. When I visited him, the jaundice was so intense that his entire body looked like egg-yolk yellow. He reported that the hoped-for treatment was not possible, that his ex-wife was already closing in for part of his estate, that his lawyer had said, "Don't worry, you're basically bankrupt," and that the pain was becoming intolerable. For some reason, my spontaneous response was, "Other than that, how's your week been?" I was immediately concerned that I had been inappropriate. However, the young man was laughing so hard I could hardly understand him as he said, "Thank goodness, someone still thinks I am alive! I am so tired of everyone treating everything so seriously."

Intervention Strategies. Although humor most often occurs spontaneously, in some instances it may be consciously planned. Several authors (Ackerman, Henry, Graham, & Coffey, 1993; Erdman, 1991; Herth, 1984; Hunt, 1993; Killeen, 1991; Robinson, 1991; Simon, 1988, 1989) have suggested specific strategies and ways to create a humorous environment and thereby integrate humor into practice. Specific items include sharing cartoons, jokes, humorous anecdotes, bumper stickers, tapes and books with a humorous theme, recommending the viewing of comedy movies and recording video-tapes of funny television shows or family antics, making available or having within sight "objects" that bring forth a smile, and encouraging the playing of games that bring out laughter. One young man I remember became a champion at nerf basketball from his bed during the final weeks of his life. He loved to watch family members and nurses try to shoot the ball from a reclining position and would laugh heartily. Other items include inviting the terminally ill individuals and/or their family to identify and engage in those things they could do in 5 or 10 minutes that would bring them joy, and to keep a joy journal. The joy journal is a written record of those specific things that brought a smile that day. Another useful activity involves developing a "joy jar" in which cartoons, silly pictures, comic characters, and those sayings that make the individual smile/laugh are placed and kept; these can then be pulled out when a smile or laugh is needed. Killeen (1991) describes her use of "bubble therapy" and "the magic wand" to encourage the playful spirit of the terminally ill person to emerge. Simon (1989), based on her work with oncology patients, suggests the use of imagery. In imagery, the individual is encouraged to visualize people wearing "silly" faces or clothes, anything that brings a smile. The author has found the use of milestoning — using familiar items, music or photos, any sensory stimulus that encourages individuals to talk about the pleasant times

225

and memories they have had in life. Milestoning might involve asking people to describe what happened at the first Birthday Party which they can remember, or their funniest date, or what pranks they played on classmates or at their best friend's wedding. This can be an effective way to generate lightheartedness. Another idea that the author has found useful and which has been utilized by a number of health care professionals is encouraging the seriously ill to develop a "joy bag" ("Laughter Kit" or "First Aid Kit"). The individuals are encouraged to put anything into a bag they have chosen that lifts their spirit and brings them joy or laughter: a music box, a favorite book, tape recordings, photos, or special mementos. The items in the bag represent support, joy, and renewal. I have found that two other items also elicit lightheartedness in the terminally ill: singing telegrams performed by friends and neighbors, and developing a picture collage that represents the most fun times in the individual's life or consists of a collection of silly pictures that makes the individual chuckle.

Evaluation Guidelines. Evaluation as to the appropriateness and effectiveness of the humor on the individual's and/or family's quality of life is essential to assess. Several authors have suggested guidelines. However, the number one rule of thumb, is that, if you are using humor and it doesn't connect you with the person or enable the person to experience some joy, then don't use it.

Staff Support. All authors cautioned that the effective use of humor is a skill that must be valued and nurtured in oneself in order to use it effectively with self and others (Cohen, 1990; Metcalf, 1987; Woodhouse, 1993). Killeen (1991) and Metcalf (1987) suggest that humor must be nurtured and supported in the staff who are repeatedly exposed to suffering, grief, and loss as they work with dying individuals and their family members. This is particularly necessary in view of the need to constructively deal with the stress and maintain a balanced perspective of life. Metcalf's definition of humor as ". . . a developed, nurtured perspective; a perspective that allows you to take yourself lightly, while taking your work or your problem seriously" (p. 20) is essential to understanding the importance of humor to the health care provider. Resources for staff include the provision of both informal and formal supports throughout the day. These supports may be something as simple as colleagues sharing levity together to planned activities such as humor boards, theme days, dress-up days, button days, sticker days, and funny glasses day. The use of a humor consultant can be a helpful strategy to reinforce the positive aspects of humor for the care providers. I have found that keeping a feather close at hand either at my desk or on a mirror will remind me to keep things light.

Limitations in Using Humorous Approaches

It is important to note that not all humor is beneficial; in fact, under certain circumstances, humor can be detrimental to the terminally ill, their family members, or the health care providers. It is crucial to differentiate between therapeutic and destructive humor. Destructive humor includes that which mocks, "puts down," or excludes individuals or interferes with sharing and communicating. Humor that is empathic, genuine, and respectful and occurs in a caring environment is usually therapeutic. The noted nurse expert on humor, Vera M. Robinson (1991), cautions the health care professional to remember that humor is one of many tools and is not to be used at the exclusion of other tools.

Future Direction

The study of humor's role during terminal illness is only in its infancy; and there is little available empirical data at this point in time. It also remains uncertain how much humor research can be extrapolated from research done in other disciplines using healthy subjects to the care of the terminally ill. The therapeutic use of humor with the terminally ill, families, and their care providers poses many questions worthy of further investigation. The nature of humor in the care of the dying, whether in the hospice, home, or hospital setting, needs to be defined and further developed. There is a need for more definitive and rigorous investigation as to the use of humor by those of various ethnic backgrounds, culture, and age groups during terminal illness. Reliable and valid methods and tools for studying humor must be developed and tested if we are to validate humor's contribution during the final stage of illness.

Nursing is at the forefront in the investigation of humor in the terminally ill population. Further research is needed to explore the impact and influence of humor on the terminally ill and their family members'/significant others' perceived quality of life. The reported physiological and psychosocial effects of laughter identified in other clinical populations warrant future study in the terminally ill population and their family/ caregivers. Humorous interventions need to be studied for effectiveness among and between terminally ill individuals. The possible benefit of one humorous intervention over another (humorous films or movies vs. reading or listening to jokes, cartoons, or funny stories) needs to explored. Research questions such as "What makes the humor successful?" or "What factors destroy humor or cause the attempt to fail?" invite investigation.

Finally, humor as a therapeutic approach among hospice nurses and other nurses caring for dying individuals needs to be examined. Does humorous communication among hospice nursing staff members help to prevent burnout and improve staff morale? Do specific planned humorous activities increase the nursing staff's ability to use humor therapeutically with their clients? These are difficult questions to answer, yet they are vital to the quality of care provided to terminally ill individuals and their families. Only by conducting further research specific to the terminally ill population will the therapeutic value of humor to hospice nurses, terminally ill individuals, and their families be determined and the quality of life in those whose time is limited be improved.

Although this chapter contains little hard quantitative scientific evidence, it does include the broad fund of qualitative data gained from the many individuals who have shared their experiences with humor during the terminal stage of their illness or that of their loved ones during those final days/months with myself and other nurse authors. This chapter is offered with the hope that it will encourage those caring for and about the terminally ill to explore the potential therapeutic value of humor. Frankel (1963) said, "Everything can be taken from a man but one thing, the last of the human freedoms — to choose one's attitude in any given situation, even if only for a few seconds" (p.69).

Bibliography

Ackerman, M., Henry, M., Graham, K., & Coffey, N. (1993). *Nursing Forum*, 28(4), 9-17.

Astedt-Kurki, P., & Liukkonen, A. (1994). Humor in nursing care. *Journal of Advanced Nursing,* 20, 183-188.

Barnum, B. (1990, February). Losses and laughter. *Nursing and Health Care*, 13(1), 59.

Bellert, K. (1989). Humor: A therapeutic approach in oncology nursing. *Cancer Nursing*, 12(2), 65-70.

Cohen, M. (1990). Caring for ourselves can be funny business. *Holistic Nursing Practice*, 4(4), 1-11.

Davidhizar, R., & Bowen, M. (1992). The dynamics of laughter. *Archives of Psychiatric Nursing,* 7(2), 132-137.

Dobratz, M. (1990). Hospice nursing: Present perspectives and future directives. *Cancer Nursing,* 13(2), 116-122.

Dugan, D. (1989). Laughter and tears: Best medicine for stress. *Nursing Forum,* 24(1), 18-26.

Erdman, L. (1991). Laughter therapy for patients with cancer. *Oncology Nursing Forum*, 18(8), 1359-1363.

Frankel, V. (1963). *Man's search for meaning.* New York: Pocket Books.

Groves, D. (1991). A merry heart doeth good like a medicine. *Holistic Nursing Practice*, 5(4), 49-56.

Graham, L., & Cates, J. (1989, January/February). Responding to the needs of the terminally ill through laughter and play. *American Journal of Hospice Care*, 6(1), 29-30.

Herth, K. (1984). Laughter: A nursing Rx. *American Journal of Nursing*, 84(8), 991-992.

Herth, K. (1990). Contributions of humor as perceived by the terminally ill. *American Journal of Hospice Care*, 7(1), 36-40.

Herth, K. (1993a). Humor and the older adult. *Applied Nursing Research*, 6(4), 146-153.

Herth, K. (1993b) Hope in the family caregiver of terminally ill people. *Journal of Advanced Nursing*, 18, 538-548.

Hulse, J. (1994). Humor: A nursing intervention for the elderly. *Geriatric Nursing*, 13(2), 88-90.

Hunt, A. (1993). Humor as a nursing intervention. *Cancer Nursing*, 16(1), 34-39. Jourard, S. (1970). Living and dying. *American Journal of Nursing*, 70, 269-275.

Killeen, M. (1991, May/June). Clinical clowning: Humor in hospice care. *American Journal of Hospice and Palliative Care*, 83), 23-27.

Klein, A. (1986). Humor and death: You've got to be kidding. *American Journal of Hospice Care*, 3(4), 42-45.

Leiber, D. (1986). Laughter and humor in critical care. *Dimensions of Critical Care Nursing*, 5(3), 162-170.

Maliniski, V. (1991). The experience of laughing at oneself in older couples. *Nursing Science Quarterly*, 4(2), 69-75.

McCloskey, V., & Bulechek, G. (1992). *Nursing interventions classifications*. St. Louis: Mosby.

Metcalf, C. (1987). Humor, life, and death. *Oncology Nursing Forum*, 14(4), 19-21.

McGhee, P., & Goldstein, J. (1983). *Handbook of humor research: Applied Research*, vol. II. New York: Springer.

Miller, J. (1989) Hope inspiring strategies of the critically ill. *Applied Nursing Research*, 2(1), 23-29.

Miller, J. (1991). Developing and maintaining hope in families of the critically ill. *ACCN: Clinical Issues*, 2(2), 307-315.

Mindess, H. (1971). *Laughter and liberation*. Los Angeles, CA: Nash Publishing.

Moody, R. (1978). *Laugh after laugh: The healing power of humor*. Jacksonville, FL: Headwaters Press.

Pasquali, D. (1990). Learning to laugh: Humor as therapy. *Journal of Psychosocial*

Nursing, 28(3), 31-35.

Rabelais, F. (1952). Gargantua and Pantagruel. Chicago: *Encyclopedia Britannica.*

Raber, W. (1987). The caring role of the nurse in the application of humor therapy to the patient experiencing helplessness. *Clinical Gerontologist, 7*(1), 3-11.

Robinson, V. (1986). Humor is a serious business. *Dimensions of Critical Care Nursing, 5*(3), 132-133.

Robinson, V. (1991). *Humor and the health professions.* Thorofare, NJ: Slack.

Samra, C. (1985, Fall). A time to laugh. *Journal of Christian Nursing,* 15-19.

Schmitt, N. (1990). Patients' perception of laughter in a rehabilitation hospital. *Rehabilitation Nursing,* 15(3), 143-146.

Sheehy, G. (1981). *Pathfinders.* New York: Bantam.

Simon, J. (1988). Humor and the older adult: Implications for nursing. *Journal of Advanced Nursing,* 13, 441-446.

Simon, J. (1989). Humor techniques for oncology nurses. *Oncology Nursing Forum,* 16(5), 667-670.

Smith, D. (1986). Using humor to help children with pain. *Children's Health Care,* 14(3), 187-188.

Sullivan, J., & Deane, D. (1988). Humor and health. *Journal of Gerontological Nursing,* 14(1), 20-24.

Sumners, A. (1990). Professional nurses' attitudes toward humor. *Journal of Advanced Nursing, 15(2), 196-200.*

Tennant, K. (1990). Laugh it off: The effect of humor on the well-being of the older adult. *Journal of Gerontological Nursing,* 16(12), 11-17.

Tesler, M., Wegner, C., Savedra, M., Gibbons, P., & Ward, A. (1981). Coping strategies of children in pain. *Issues in Comprehensive Pediatric Nursing,* 5(3), 351-359.

Woodhouse, D. (1993). The aspect of humor in dealing with stress. *Nursing Administration Quarterly,* 18(1), 80-89.

CHAPTER XVIII

HUMOR IN PERIOPERATIVE NURSING
by Kathleen B. Gaberson, RN, PhD
and
Janice M. Parfitt, RN, MSN

Many nurses are familiar with humor used in operating room settings. In the high-pressure environment of the operating room, humor is frequently used to relieve stress and anxiety among members of the surgical team. Since many of the jokes cracked around the OR bed are of the "black" or "gallows" variety of humor, it is particularly important to avoid giving the impression that surgical staff are making light of what the patient views as a serious, life-or-death situation. With the increasing number of procedures being performed under local or intravenous/conscious sedation, this type of joking in the OR must be minimized to avoid upsetting patients.

Patients who overhear a surgeon or nurse joking during a surgical procedure might question that person's professionalism. However, as Goffman (1961) suggested, the ability to joke during a complicated performance may be an indication of the professional's role distance. That is, the extent to which professionals are able to distance themselves from role behavior is a measure of the comfort they feel in the role. If this concept is valid, the scrub nurse who engages in social conversation or joking while preparing suture and passing instruments is demonstrating comfort in the role and is able to distance the self from the behavior required of a scrub nurse.

In spite of the pervasive use of humor by perioperative nurses to cope with their own stress, there is little evidence in the literature that humor is used as a nursing intervention with patients before, during, or after surgery. Two studies have been reported (Gaberson, 1991; Parfitt, 1990) that tested the effects of humorous interventions on recall of preoperative teaching and on preoperative anxiety. These studies will be discussed in the next section of this chapter.

Humorous Preoperative Teaching

A common teaching strategy for providing preoperative instruction is the use of printed teaching materials, although the effectiveness of these materials has not been adequately researched. One way of altering printed teaching materials is to add humor, but before this strategy can be recommended, the effect of humor on recall of information

231

must be determined. Parfitt (1990) reported results of a study in which cartoons were used to test the effect of humor on the recall of preoperative instruction about postoperative exercise routines. An experimental two-group pretest-posttest research design was used to determine if the use of a humorous preoperative teaching technique affected the recall of instructions about postoperative exercise routines.

Instrument. Recall of information about postoperative exercise routines was measured by a researcher-developed instrument called the Postoperative Exercise Routine-Knowledge Test (PER-KT). The test consisted of nine true or false statements that measured knowledge about three postoperative exercise routines: coughing and deep breathing, turning, and ambulating. A panel of perioperative nurse experts established the content validity of this tool. Alternate forms of the PER-KT were used for the pretest and posttest.

Sample. The convenience sample was comprised of 24 subjects whose surgeons had given permission for their patients to be asked to participate in this research study. The subjects were scheduled for general surgery procedures and admitted to one 320-bed community hospital at least the day before their surgeries. They were adults, ages 21 to 76 years, who could read, write, and speak English. The first 18 subjects were randomly assigned to either the control or treatment group. The last 6 subjects were assigned to the treatment group to ensure equal group size.

Methods. Control group subjects read a preoperative instruction booklet with information about the three postoperative exercise routines. Treatment group subjects read the same preoperative instructions illustrated with three cartoons, one for each exercise routine. A professional graphic artist was employed to develop the cartoons. The researcher provided the artist with ideas and guidelines to create the cartoons. They were to be patient-related, use very few words, and be overtly funny. In a pilot test of these materials, six patients' reactions to the cartoons confirmed their construct validity. The pretest, treatment, and posttest phases of the study took place in the subjects' hospital rooms. The researcher performed all preoperative teaching on an individual basis. The researcher briefly explained the purpose of the study, and subjects signed a consent to participate. All subjects were pretested with the PER-KT. Each subject was then given the appropriate teaching booklet to read. Immediately after reading the booklets, all subjects were posttested with the alternate form of the PER-KT. Subjects were unaware that there were actually two methods of instruction until after the data were collected.

Results. Participant characteristics revealed that the control and treatment groups were equivalent on age and type of surgery. Although the control group had more women, and men predominated in the treatment group, this difference was not \ believed to be important. Mean scores for the PER-KT pretest and posttest were calculated for the control group and treatment group, and gain score means for each group were determined.

232

The results of a t-test on the mean gain scores revealed that the treatment group gained more knowledge than the control group, but the difference was not statistically significant ($t = -1.02$, $df = 22$, $p > 0.05$). However, the test score data analysis revealed some interesting results. The control group mean score was higher than that of the treatment group on the pretest, but the treatment group posttest mean score was higher than that of the control group. Subjects in both groups answered more than half of the test items correctly on the posttest, and all subjects' posttest scores were higher than their pretest scores.

Discussion. These results indicated that subjects who used the humorous teaching booklet were able to recall more information about the postoperative exercise routines than subjects who were not exposed to the cartoons. However, because the findings were not significant, it could not be said that humor helped subjects to recall information more easily. Alternative explanations for these findings may exist. Because the differences between group mean scores were small, a larger sample may be necessary in order to detect these differences. Future research studies should include a larger number of subjects. Another consideration is that the PER-KT may not have been sensitive enough to measure real differences in knowledge of postoperative exercise routines. The validity of this instrument might be improved by increasing its difficulty, and adding items may increase reliability.

There were several limitations to this research study. Two variables that were impossible to control were the length of preoperative stay and the subjects' exposure to other sources of preoperative teaching. Because this was intended to be an initial study, only the recall of written information was examined; no attempt was made to test subjects' abilities to perform the exercise routines. These factors should be considered in the design of future studies.

The use of humor as an adjunct to preoperative teaching needs further research, but the results of this study do not suggest that humorous teaching strategies should be avoided.

The Effect of Humor on Preoperative Anxiety

Preoperative anxiety is a problem for most surgical patients. Excessive anxiety is thought to interfere with learning (Rothrock, 1989), affect the need for preanesthetic medication and anesthesia (Totas, 1978), and increase distress related to postoperative pain (Acute Pain Management Guideline Panel, 1992). A nursing intervention that reduces preoperative anxiety may reduce the incidence of complications and shorten hospital stays, thereby reducing the cost of surgical patient care. Few nursing research studies have investigated the effectiveness of nursing interventions to reduce preoperative

233

anxiety. Studies investigating the effects of tranquil music on preoperative and postoperative anxiety (Kaempf & Amodei, 1989; Moss, 1987; Steelman, 1990) demonstrated some reduction in anxiety, although the results cannot be generalized.

Humor has been studied as a means of managing stress and relieving anxiety (Dixon, 1980; Safranek & Schill, 1982), but before Gaberson's 1991 pilot study, no nursing research to study the effect of humorous distraction on preoperative anxiety had been reported. Gaberson tested the following hypothesis: Among preoperative patients who listen to a humorous audiotape, patients who listen to tranquil music, and patients who wait without auditory distraction for 20 minutes, there will be significant differences in self-reported levels of preoperative anxiety (in descending order: no intervention, music, humor). This investigation was a pilot study designed to test the research procedures and to determine the feasibility of conducting a larger test of the same hypothesis. The sample size was intentionally small and the setting was limited to one hospital.

Sample. The sample consisted of preoperative patients who were awaiting same-day surgery. Fifteen male and female subjects who met the inclusion criteria were recruited in the Same-Day Surgery waiting room. Eligible research subjects were patients aged 21 years or older who were admitted for same-day, elective surgical procedures. The patients' surgeons gave their consent for their participation and the patients gave their written informed consent to join the study. Permission to conduct the pilot study was also obtained from the hospital Research and Human Subjects Committee and from the Duquesne University Institutional Review Board. Potential subjects were excluded from the study if they did not speak, understand, and read English, if they had a hearing loss which prevented them from using a cassette player with earphones, or if they had taken any medication with an anti-anxiety effect within 24 hours prior to admission. Patients having diagnostic surgery were also excluded from the study, because they were expected to have higher state anxiety levels as compared to the general population of surgical patients (Scott, 1983).

Instrument. The dependent variable, preoperative anxiety, was measured with a Visual Analog Scale (VAS), a 10-cm horizontal line with the left end of the line labeled "no sensation" and the right end labeled "as much as could possibly be." This instrument was reported by Vogelsang (1988) to be a valid and reliable self-report measure of preoperative anxiety. Subjects were instructed to mark the line at the point which represented their current level of apprehension, tension, nervousness, or worry in anticipation of surgery. The score was the distance in cm from the left end of the line to the subject's mark.

Methods. This study used an experimental, three group post-test research design. Subjects who met inclusion criteria were randomly assigned to one of two treatment groups or the control group; each group contained 5 subjects. Group 1 was the control group, Group 2 received the musical intervention, and Group 3 received the humorous intervention. The dependent variable of this study was preoperative anxiety. The independent variable was a 20-minute wait in the Same-Day Surgery waiting room, during which time subjects in the two treatment groups listened to audiotapes on a cassette tape player and the control group subjects received no additional intervention.

The musical and humorous audiotapes were selected in the following manner. The musical selection, "Omni Suite" by Steven Bergman, was used because it met the standards of tranquil music as defined by Bonny and McCarron (1984). The humorous audiotape was selected from a variety of comedy tapes that were evaluated by 17 individuals who were similar to the subjects who would later participate in the pilot study. Each evaluator listened to two tapes and rated them on a 5-point "funniness" scale (Wilson, Rust, & Kasriel, 1977). The tape receiving the highest rating was a combination of Bill Cosby comedy routines from two albums, "Revenge" and "Wonderfullness." This tape was used as the humorous distraction.

Data collection days were scheduled in cooperation with the Same-Day Surgery unit director and were varied within the week to control for a possible "day" effect. On data collection days, the Same-Day Surgery schedule was checked for patients whose surgeons had consented, and these patients' medical records were read for evidence that they met inclusion criteria for the study. Patients who met inclusion criteria were given a brief oral explanation of the study and asked to participate. Those who agreed signed the consent form. Subjects were randomly assigned to one of the three groups. Each subject in a treatment group was given an audiocassette tape player and a headset, and asked to listen to a humorous tape or a tranquil music tape for 20 minutes. Earpieces of the headsets were cleaned with alcohol wipes between uses. Subjects in the control group received no additional intervention during the 20-minute waiting period. During the intervention period, necessary demographic data were obtained from subjects' medical records (age, gender, type of surgery). Following the intervention (waiting or listening to a tape), the subject was given oral instructions for completing the Visual Analog Scale, and was asked to mark the scale as previously described. If a subject was called into the Same Day Surgery unit before data collection was complete, that subject was dropped from the sample. After data collection, all treatment group subjects were asked whether they had ever heard the tapes before; all subjects reported that the music and humor tapes were new to them.

Results. The ages of subjects ranged from 23 to 76 years. The nine female and six male subjects were scheduled for a variety of general, orthopedic, ophthalmic, and vascular surgical procedures. The mean anxiety scores in all groups were fairly low, but the humor group reported the lowest level of anxiety (mean = 1.40) and the control group reported the highest level (mean = 2.76), as predicted by the research hypothesis.

235

However, a one-way analysis of variance revealed that this difference was not statistically significant ($F = 1.48$, $p = .267$). Therefore, the research hypothesis was not supported. However, a moderate effect size (.496) suggests that the lack of significance was due to the small sample size.

Discussion. In this sample, the use of humorous distraction was at least as effective as tranquil music in reducing preoperative anxiety. Subjects who experienced no intervention during their wait before surgery reported the highest levels of preoperative anxiety. However, because of the lack of significance, further research is needed to test the effect of humorous distraction on preoperative anxiety before findings can be generalized beyond this sample. Consistent with Steelman's (1990) findings, the self-reported anxiety levels of all subjects in this study were lower than might be expected from a review of the literature. As Steelman suggested, this finding might be related to the use of a self-report measure. Subjects may have been using denial as a coping mechanism, although observation of subjects during this pilot study revealed no behavioral signs of excessive anxiety. Since the purpose of the pilot study was to test research procedures and the sample size was limited, statistically significant results were not anticipated. The research procedures were found to be valid, and a larger multisite study of the effect of humorous distraction on preoperative anxiety was recommended.

Since a nursing intervention which reduces preoperative anxiety has the potential to reduce the incidence of perioperative complications and shorten hospital stays for surgical patients, further nursing research should be done to study the effects of humorous distraction on preoperative anxiety.

Conclusion

These two studies reported findings that suggest that humor can be used as a nursing intervention in perioperative settings, although the research results cannot be widely generalized. In an effort to build a stronger research base, the following questions may be used to guide future studies of the value of humor as a perioperative nursing intervention:
1. What types of humor are most effective in preoperative teaching and in reducing preoperative anxiety?
2. What is the most appropriate time to use humor as a preoperative teaching strategy? As a means of reducing preoperative anxiety?
3. Do the reactions of perioperative patients to humorous nursing interventions depend on the gender of the patient?
4. Are there differences in perioperative patients' reactions to humorous nursing interventions related to the age of the patient?

5. Is the use of humor as a preoperative nursing intervention more effective with individuals or groups of patients?
6. When using humor to reduce preoperative anxiety, does the effect vary if patients are permitted to select a humorous distraction according to their own preferences?
7. Does humor have an effect on postoperative outcomes?
8. Do patients perform their postoperative exercise routines better if a humorous teaching strategy was used?
9. Do patients report less postoperative anxiety and pain if humorous distraction is used?

Bibliography

Acute Pain Management Guideline Panel (1992). Acute pain management: Operative or medical procedures and trauma (AHCPR Pub. No. 92-0032). Rockville, MD: Agency for Health Care Policy and Research, Public Health Service, U.S. Depart ment of Health and Human Services.

Bonny, H. L., & McCarron, N. (1984). Music as an adjunct to anesthesia in operative procedures. *Journal of the American Association of Nurse Anesthetists*, 52, 55-57.

Dixon, N. F. (1980). Humor: A cognitive alternative to stress? In I. G. Sarson & C. D. Spielberger (Eds.), *Stress and anxiety,* vol. 7 (pp 281-289). Washington, DC: Hemisphere.

Gaberson, K. B. (1991). The effect of humorous distraction on preoperative anxiety: A pilot study. *AORN Journal,* 54, 1258-1264.

Goffman, E. (1961). *Encounters: Two studies in the sociology of interaction.* Indianapolis: Bobbs-Merrill.

Kaempf, G., & Amodei, M. E. (1989). The effect of music on anxiety: A research study. *AORN Journal*, 50, 112-118.

Moss, V. A. (1987). The effect of music on anxiety in the surgical patient. *Perioperative Nursing Quarterly*, 3, 9-16.

Parfitt, J. M. (1990). Humorous preoperative teaching: Effect on recall of postoperative exercise routines. *AORN Journal*, 52, 114-120.

Rothrock, J. C. (1989). Perioperative nursing research, Part I: Preoperative psychoeducational interventions. *AORN Journal*, 49, 597-619.

Safranek, R., & Schill, T. (1982). Coping with stress: Does humor help? *Psychological Reports,* 51, 222.

Scott, D. (1983). Anxiety, critical thinking, and information processing during and after breast biopsy. *Nursing Research,* 32, 24-28.

Steelman, V. (1990). Intraoperative music therapy: Effects on anxiety, blood pressure.

AORN Journal, 52, 1026-1034.

Totas, M. L. (1978). The emotional stress of the preoperative patient. *Journal of the American Association of Nurse Anesthetists*, 46(2), 27-30.

Vogelsang, J. (1988). The Visual Analog Scale: An accurate and sensitive method for self-reporting preoperative anxiety. *Journal of PostAnesthesia Nursing*, 3, 235-239.

Wilson, G. D., Rust, J., & Kasreil, J. (1977). Genetic and family origins of humor preferences: A twin study. *Psychological Reports*, 41, 659-660.

CHAPTER XIX

CHILDREN AND HUMOR

by Janet Hardy Boettcher, RN, C, PhD, FAAN

There is general agreement in the literature that humor provides some relief from the everyday stress and strain of life for both adults and children. Humor is expressed in the form of laughter and smiling for people of all ages. Humor seems to be one of the few biologic phenomena that is distinctively human (Robinson, 1977). As far back as Biblical days, Proverbs 17:22 admonishes us that "A cheerful heart is good medicine, but a crushed spirit dries up the bones." Humor is good for the spirit, for children as well as adults; humor is a positive attribute, promoting flexible thinking, good feelings, reducing tension and anxiety, fostering good communication, and even improving the ability to learn and understand (Fern, 1991).

Humor also seems to contribute to health and an overall sense of well-being. Laughter provides excellent exercise for the muscles in the face, arms, legs, chest ,and stomach-besides reducing stress. Some believe that laughter actually releases pain-reducing chemicals that relieve minor aches and pains (Harrison, 1988). Fry (1981) has studied humor's physiologic effects extensively and reports that laughter improves health status and helps fight disease by improving circulation, strengthening muscle tone, reducing tension, stress, depression, and reducing violent behaviors. Cousins (1979) has written about how humor has helped to prolong his life, even with a diagnosed terminal illness, as well as to reduce the pain during his illness.

How humor is perceived and expressed by children is an important consideration in stressful times. Humor is definitely a positive function for children. Not only does it lessen anxiety and relieve tension, but it facilitates communication, promotes positive self-esteem and good feelings, encourages flexible thinking, and possibly even enhances learning and understanding (Fern, 1991).

Only through understanding the child's perspective of everyday life, as well as in times of hospitalization and illness, can we maximize the therapeutic value of humor. This chapter will include a review of some of the concerns adults have regarding humor in children, in addition to selected aspects of play in the ill and hospitalized child. It is difficult to dissect humor in the life of the child. In the case of children, the perspectives of the adults caring for them and providing their health care have much influence over their use of humor. There are some important differences between the situations of

239

children and adults; such as: (a) children usually do not seek the health care, an adult brings them to it sometimes under great protest; (b) children have developmentally varying cognitive and language skills that may interfere severely with their ability to verbalize or explain their anxieties or concerns; (c) the adults have greater control over the environment of the child; and (d) children are accustomed to playing and generally do so with little encouragement (Ventis & Ventis, 1989).

Every situation in life, even death, is subject to humor (Robinson, 1977). Humor tends to be spontaneous, making it difficult to document and study. Put too much inspection on the situation, and the humor disappears. Try to observe it, and it goes away. Humor draws on cognitive differences and past experiences. Individual differences in appreciation and comprehension are observed (Shaeffer & Hopkins, 1988).

Rather like observing the wind, a universal definition of humor has remained elusive. It seems best to identify humor by what can be observed. Laughter has often been used as an indicator that humor has occurred. Most of the humor within a health care setting is usually situational rather than formal. Jokes, witticisms, and pleasantries are all part of the picture (Emerson, 1963). Humor is a powerful human attribute that can be used to bond people together or can be used as a weapon that tears cruelly at the human spirit. How to cultivate a sense of humor is probably one of the key components to improving health for both the children and the adults in their world.

Humor is a form of intellectual play that seems to be founded on incongruence. Predictability, therefore, becomes part of what constitutes humor. Humor often results when our prediction is contradicted by some incongruence in the facts (Shaefer & Hopkins, 1988). A playful context or mindset is also important for an incongruence to be humorous (McGhee, 1979). Thus, creativity is also related to having a "sense of humor." Studies measuring creativity or divergent thinking have been positively linked with humor comprehension. In a study of 51 school-aged children, metaphor comprehension was a strong predictor of humor comprehension for the 13-year-olds, while divergent thinking was the strongest predictor for the 7-year-olds (McGhee & Panoutsopoulou, 1988). The study results indicated that cognitive skills were most important in determining whether one "gets the joke," but other factors yet to be determined relate to the "funniness" of the joke.

Sarcasm and ridicule are forms of hostile humor and have little place in the adult world and none in the child's world. Sarcasm can be unmerciful. The etymology of the word is revealing: Sarkasmos, fr. sarkazein, "to tear flesh" — razor-like words cutting deep into the psyche. Children know when they feel it, and it is not funny to the victim (Bryant & Zillmann, 1989). Likewise, ridicule has been shown to be a personally costly and morally questionable corrective form of humor that is effective with school aged children, but not pre-schoolers.

240

Theoretical Considerations

A theoretical understanding of humor for all age groups has also been perplexing. Humor and laughter may be viewed as representing a "broad-spectrum" coping strategy that is helpful in coping effectively with the stresses and strains of life. If viewed as an appraisal-focused coping strategy, a humorous view to a stressful situation may enable the child to view the situation from another perspective and see it as less threatening and thus less stressful (Dixon, 1980). Some theorists, taking a cognitive approach to humor, consider the very essence of humor is the perception of incongruity in two disparate trains of thought that are brought together in a novel and surprising manner (Koestler, 1964; Suls, 1983). In order to "get the joke," the child makes a rapid shift that changes the significance of the original view. O'Connell (1976) points out that a person with a good sense of humor notices the ludicrous parts of life's situations and is better able to cope effectively with those situations which may or may not be malleable. People with a good sense of humor are capable of seeing more than one view of things, and thus are not locked into their perception of a situation (Martin, 1988).

Dixon (1980) views humor and laughter as an "emotion-focused" coping strategy that has a cathartic effect to release pent-up emotions. Humor can be maladaptive as a means of defending against reality through repression or denial. However, humor that recognizes reality but refuses to succumb to it can buffer the feelings of anger, depression and fear. This liberating view of humor was purported by Freud (1928) who saw jokes and wit as a way of expressing repressed aggressive and sexual impulses and yet found humor generally positive and life-affirming. Freud (1928) stated that, by means of humor, "one refuses to undergo suffering, asseverates the invincibility of one's ego against the real world, and victoriously upholds the pleasure principle, yet all without quitting the ground of mental sanity" (p. 217). Freud viewed this healthy form of humor as a function of the superego reassuring the anxious ego and asserting in the face of hardship. The Freudian view suggests that children who develop a healthy sense of humor are those whose parents provide a model of positive acceptance and security rather than a harsh and overly demanding set of prescriptions.

Chapman (1983) has viewed humor as a problem-focused coping strategy. Humor often diffuses problems and conflicts. It is important to remember that humor can be a two-edged sword, and children must be taught to distinguish between healthy, appropriate, and derisive humor. McGhee (1979) has observed that humor development in children parallels Piaget's postulated stages of cognitive development in children. From this theoretical perspective, children must develop particular cognitive abilities in order to comprehend various forms of humor. Loeb and Wood (1986) have devised a developmental model of humor that parallels Erikson's well known eight stages of

241

psychosocial development, suggesting that humor is one method that children use to deal with conflicts arising from developmental crises of trust versus mistrust, autonomy versus shame and doubt, etc. Levine (1977) has expanded on the mastery component of humor and related it to internal locus of control issues indicating that those children who have a sense of mastery in their lives display more mirth and humor than children who have less control. Brown, Wheeler and Cash (1980) take a social-learning approach to understanding humor. This focuses on the effects of the environment on the individuals humorous behavior. Children who have positive role models of humor and who are reinforced for their attempts at humor are more likely to acquire a strong sense of humor characterized by laughter and joking.

Developmental Aspects of Humor

Because humor is cognitively related, it definitely develops in stages and is related directly to the mental age of the individual. In adults, all stages are visible, but it is generally age-related in children (McGhee, 1979; McGhee & Lloyd, 1981). McGhee (1979) has proposed four developmental stages of humor.

Stage 1: Infants and young toddlers experience laughter but that may be more of a release of tension than actual humor; it is difficult to know in the preliterate child. Usually during the second year of life, we find children capable of performing incongruous acts and experiencing humor. Slapstick humor and crazy antics represent the earliest stages of humor observed in children.

Stage 2: Older toddlers and young preschoolers who have become verbal enter a new stage of humor. It may be similar to and may overlap, but the characteristic difference is that a verbal statement can create the incongruity that the child finds so funny. Verbal gaming enters the picture as nonsensical names or rhyming can be added to the incongruity to make the humor. "Off the wall" verbal creations, such as those made so famous in the Dr. Seuss books, use fantasy figures and absurd antics are examples of this verbal dimension. Children enjoy catching on to the repetitious pattern that often emerges in these verbal renditions. Stages 1 and 2 are very important beginning backgrounds for future humor development. Even in very young children with poor language control, evidence of humor and language is evident as soon as children develop the ability to use symbols. Nilsen (1983) reports an example of this use of symbols in a 2-year-old playfully picking up a spoon, holding it to his ear and pretending to be talking on the telephone or with equal glee pointing to the cat and saying "doggie, doggie" and laughing. The humor is obviously focusing on the mismatching. The mismatching stimulates curiosity and "puzzlement" which is enjoyable because it is acknowledgement that the distortion exists in a playful or pretend manner.

242

Stage 3: Around pre-school age, 3 years, the child's thinking is advanced to the stage where the child can sense humor in conceptual incongruity. Very young children may miss the background material necessary to develop the humor.

Stage 4: There may be more than one meaning, and things certainly may not be what they seem. The child has developed sufficient cognitive ability to "play mental gymnastics, reversing observed actions or understanding multiple word meanings" (Shaefer & Hopkins, 1988, p. 91). The acquisition of concrete operational thinking as well as acquisition of formal operation in the Piagetian sense, contributes to the comprehension of humor. Jokes specifically related to Piagetian conservation and class inclusion were funnier to children who had mastered these concepts (McGhee & Panoutsopoulou, 1988).

Humor and play are closely bound together for children. A review of activities that are developmentally appropriate is helpful to consider when thinking about promoting humor in children's lives. Table 1 shows a good review of play materials and social play activities for infants as described by Geismar-Ryan (1986, p. 26).

Table 1

Review of play materials and activities

Age	Type of Humor	Examples of Children's Books
Infant/Toddler	Sensory Stimulation Direct physical participation	The secret birthday message (Carle, 1972) Zoo City (Lewis,1976)
Early/Childhood/ Preschool	Clowning, slapstick, nonsense, expressions, chants	Henry and the red strips (Christlow, 1982) "Who," said Sue, "Said who" (Rashin, 1973)
Early Childhood	Add:insults, practical jokes jokes, hostile humor	The quicksand Book (de Paola, 1977) April Fools (Krahn, 1974) I'll fix aAnthony (Viorst, 1969)
Middle Childhood	Add: riddles, word play conventional jokes	Socko! Every riddle your feet will ever need (Manes, 1982); Dr. Gloom's monster jokes and puzzles (Whitney, 1981); The illustrated treasury of humor for children (Hendra,1980)

Table 2 provides an excellent summary of selected play activities for children of varying ages from toddler through school-age as reported by Vessey and Mahon (1990, p. 330).

Table 2:

Play materials and social activity.

Toy Situation	Infant Social Activity	Games To Play
Absence of play materials	Distant Social Signals vocalizing, smiling, gesturing, visually regarding	Name games, singing, fingerplays, pat-a-cake, peek-a-boo
	Physical contact, touching	Body part games
Fine motor play materials cubes and containers, shape sorters, popbeads	Direct involvement in peer play: taking, showing, exchanging, side-by-side play, duplicating action	Filling and dumping, building, in and out games, "trade" games
Social/language play: phones, books, hats, dolls	Direct involvement in peer play: offering, accepting, exchanging, duplicating action	Phone play, "reading", dress-up, doll play
Gross motor play materials: large balls, rocking boat, climbing steps, tunnels	Direct involvement in peer ball rolling, chasing, leading, following	Roll and chase, follow the leader, peek-a-boo, row-row-row your boat

For it to be humorous, children must feel a sense of detachment. If the identification is too close or if they are left out, humor will not be present, instead it can be painful (McGhee & Lloyd, 1981). In many stories it is more enjoyable for children if the "small one" in the story is also the "smart" one. Children often enjoy feeling superior to their "younger selves" (represented by the story character) and are relieved to know that they have grown (Alberghene, 1989). There are also differences between boys' and girls' responses as they age beyond infancy and young preschoolers (Honig, 1988). Boys tend to be most comfortable when they can "produce" the humor and girls when they can "respond" (McGhee & Lloyd, 1981). By age 6, boys show more silly rhyming, including naughty words as well as playful, untrue, and exaggerated statements. Boys make more behavioral humor such as clowning and throwing themselves on the floor. Boys laugh and girls smile. Boys appreciate hostile and bathroom humor more than girls, and then by adolescence replace that with sexual jokes (Honig, 1988). Children as young as 7 seem to regard joke telling as a male activity.

The ability to grasp metaphor is important in humor comprehension. Very young children can discern metaphor, and the ability is related to information processing skills and knowledge. Since metaphor understanding involves moving knowledge from one conceptual domain to another, the child's ability to do the required cognitive functions is important. Some children as young as 4 years of age have shown the ability to understand metaphors when allowed to enact them with toys. Knowledge of the linguistic form, knowledge of the concepts and concreteness, are involved with metaphor comprehension (Williams, 1989). As expected, young children can understand metaphors based on physical or perceptual similarities easier than abstractions.

As children age, their humor tends to quickly involve the complex issues that relate to adults with the familiar themes of sex, aggression and feelings of superiority or embarrassment (Nilsen, 1983). Children worldwide use such jokes, rhymes, and wisecracks that may be shocking to adults and are used to explore such taboo subjects as sexual variation, body functions, and the sex act. For young children, toileting is an area of concern. Young school-aged children, for example, love rhymes such as this one:

I see England, I see France. I see Betsy's underpants.

They aren't green, they aren't blue.

They're just filled with number two. (Nilsen, 1983).

Another example: "The King of France, wet his pants. Right in the middle of his wedding dance." And continuing on to make it a jump rope rhyme, "How many puddles did he make? One, two, three, etc." (Nilsen, 1983). A remaking of a nursery rhyme done as a joke by 12-year-olds goes like this:

Jack and Jill went up the hill

To fetch a pail of water.

Jill forgot to take her pill

And now she's got a daughter. (Nilsen, 1983).

Teachers and others in authority are often the subjects of school-aged and teenaged language humor. One parody often heard is one that goes like this:

Row, row, row your boat

Gently down the stream

Throw your teacher overboard

And you will hear her scream.

Often teachers are given names such as "Electrodehead" or "B-Flathead". Some children referred to a strict math teacher as "Busty" Barton. "Are you going out with 'Busty' tonight?" and laughing madly (Nilsen, 1983). Or this rhyme, "God made the bees, the bees made the honey; we do the work, the teacher gets the money." These are all ways to poke fun at the authority figures, vent some hostility and the laughter relieves some tension. Then life goes on with the adults in charge and the children subservient to the adults. These jokes seem to negate the influence of the authority figures, but in actuality they are open acknowledgements of the power of adults over children.

Language jokes that children use on their peers often influence and shape their own social structure and pecking order. They are ways to bond, to determine who's "in" and who's "out" and for reprimanding transgressions. Some frequently heard examples are:

Liar, liar, pants on fire, hanging from a telephone wire.

Tattle tale, tattle tale, hanging by a bull's tale.

Cry baby, cry baby, stick your finger in your eye, tell your mother it wasn't I.

And for newcomers, they may hear: "Two's company, three's a crowd, four on the sidewalk is not allowed." Newcomers with different names may be subjected to name distortions, such as a boy named "Marty Miller" was called "Farty Killer" incorporating the body functions along with the distortion itself (Nilsen, 1983). Some of these newcomer, outsider jokes are in effect exaggerations that are part of folklore and stereotypes. Children with disabilities may be the target of such jokes. Adults should not always ignore the messages they hear in this type of humor. Education and explanation may be needed to help children understand that what they really doing to another in the name of fun may not be much fun for the other person. Because it is not abnormal does not necessarily mean it is acceptable on a continuing basis and in all situations.

Humorous books for children are available for all age groups and can be an important part of the daily life of the child, sick or well. Table 3 adapted from Tamashir (1979) and presented in an article about children's literature by Jalongo (1985, p. 112) provides an excellent summary of appropriate humorous children's literature.

Table 3:

Selected activities for children of varying ages

Toddlers

Washable crayons

"Sand" play substituting oatmeal or rice

"Painting" using large brush and pail (water optional)

Pegboard and hammer

Inflatable bopper clowns

Toddler picture books such as:

Hill, E. (1986). *Spot goes to the hospital*. New York, NY: Putnam.

Freeman, D. (1968) *Corduroy*. New York, NY: Penguin.

Preschoolers

Plain rag dolls that each child "personalizes" with magic markers

Dress up play using discarded or toy medical equipment, uniforms, and scrub clothes

Finger painting with pudding

Crayons and paper

Books such as:

Sendak, R.(1963) *Where the wild things are*. New York: Harper & Row

Kent, J. (1975) *There is no such thing as a dragon*. New York: Western

Mayer, R.(1987) *There's and alligator under my bed*. New York: Dial

School-aged children

Puppets

Doll hospital with miniature equipment and figurines

Drawing supplies, Etch-a-Sketch

Blank books for writing or drawing stories

Blank audiotapes for telling stories

Interactive videogames

Nerf basketball

Books such as:

Anderson, H.C. (1985) *The ugly duckling*. New York: Green Willow Books

Williams, R. (1985) *Velveteen rabbit*. New York: Knopff

Mayer, M. (1968) *There's a nightmare in my closet*. New York: Dial

Irony, satire, understatement, exaggeration-all forms of distortion humor that adults usually understand readily contain mixed messages and much ambiguity making them more difficult for young children to comprehend. The novelty may be interesting, but there is much danger of being misunderstood and the child receiving misinformation (Bryant & Zillman, 1988). Teachers from elementary through college report using humor advantageously with their students, with funny stories being the most frequently cited form. Beyond the elementary level, these jokes included hostile and sexual humor (Bryant & Zillmann, 1985). Children are used to humor being used in all realms of their lives, and it is clearly the responsibility of the adults to make it appropriate for their age level.

Humor and Clinical Pediatrics

Hospitalized children often do not have control over what happens to their bodies and can feel powerless, even betrayed and definitely vulnerable. Music, laughter, play, storytelling-all of these are combined with humor and can do much to lift children's spirits and promote healing (Grimm & Pefley, 1990). Humor and play for children are inextricably linked together.

D'Antonio (1989) compares hospitalization for a child as "similar to the effect of visiting a newly-discovered planet to the adult" (p. 157). Nothing is really the expected or the same as at home. Even though treatments may be lifesaving, they can be dehumanizing to the child. Feelings of lack of control and depersonalization are common. Children fear pain and may incorporate parts of the treatment paraphernalia (i.e., the intravenous tubing or the cast as a part of themselves) and cry or respond negatively whenever these are approached, even though they cause no pain. Hospitalized children have been shown to be in fear of drugs, safety, and loss of home (Astin, 1977). Children are unsure of how to interact with nurses and other health care providers. Hospitalized children are afraid of abandonment, death, losses of body parts, intrusions of body space, injury, mutilation, and hostile new environments. These fears are not necessarily based on the reality of their condition. Abused children have special problems because of suspiciousness about any physical contact (Malone, 1966). In addition, children experiencing restricted physical activities due to treatments or disease may also experience increased tension due to inability to participate in rough and tumble play as is appropriate to their age, and may need some alternative outlet for this lack of gross motor activity (Pellegrini & Perlmutter, 1988).

Children in the hospital can benefit from the use of fantasy and humor to assist them in reducing the tensions brought about by the fears associated with the hospitalization. The humor can be a way to help them resolve the conflicts. The use of a professional

248

clown has been demonstrated to benefit the physical condition of the child (Long, 1987). A clown has social license to poke fun at the frightening physicians, nurses, treatments, and events that are threatening the child. A clown can do and say things that are acceptable because we all know that clowns are intended to make us laugh.

In making developmental considerations regarding humor for hospitalized children, the chronological age and thinking age of the child must both be considered for maximum effectiveness. For example, it is not uncommon for the preschool aged child to view the treatment of another child as something that is done to all children and thus fear for their own situation. There is a lack of differentiation between concept and perceptual content from preoperational thinking; fears of taking "all my blood" or "Are you going to do that to me?" or "I've got little worms in my head like apples" (Pidgeon, 1977). These all stem from not really understanding what is wrong with them that is requiring treatment. Attributing cause to things that happened by coincidence at the time of the illness is also common, for example, a newly diagnosed diabetic 10 year old attributed her illness to her grandfather's death. The adolescent may exhaust all possibilities in arriving at the solution to the cause of illness. D'Antonio (1989) cited one 16-year-old as stating that she could pass the test to become a doctor because "I've been examined so much that I know every part of me."

One hospital nursing staff developed a tape and book series "In The Hospital" (available from Moose School Records, tel. 213-455-2318) that covers a variety of issues including: (a) separation from parents, family, school and friends; (b) humor, friendship, and misunderstanding the cause of illness; (c) facing the reality of physical problems and being different; (d) self-esteem needs; (e) powerlessness; (f) loss of privacy and embarrassment; (g) using imagery to facilitate the healing process; (h) fears about the hospital; (i) loss and disappointment; (j) motivation; and (k) exploring inner resources and developing hope (Grimm & Pefley, 1990). Some of the titles of the programs included "Let's Face It!" (which promotes sensitivity to others and self-esteem), "Samit and the Dragon" (which uses imagery to promote the healing process), "Needle-ee, Noodle-ee" (helps children with hospital fears and fantasies), and "Take A Step" (which seeks to provide empowerment to the children through motivation).

Humor and Play Therapy in Hospital Settings

Play has been characterized as the work of the child. Therefore, the well-known increased fears and stressors associated with hospitalization mean that the absence of play is as serious emotionally as not eating or drinking is physically (Bolig, 1984; Piaget, 1947). How the child talks about play, type of play, content of play, what toys are used, the activity level, the affect or mood, as well as repetition, are all meaningful for the adult

249

to observe to get an understanding of what pressures the child is under and which type of role-playing can serve to help cope with the hospitalization and illness.

Children's play is thought to be a reflection of the individual's efforts toward mastery of developmental and situational hurdles (Oremland, 1988). The traumas associated with hospitalization certainly fall within this realm. It is helpful to review several examples of games that are enjoyed by children all over the world to get an example of their meaning. "Peek-a-boo" is a game in which very young children express delight as they and then reappear. Adults usually initiate this game, but it is often the children who make the reunion after the separation. They gain control as they repeatedly overcome the anxieties of the separation. The game "This Little Piggy" is fun for the young child who has just realized the differences in body parts. The adult singles out fingers or toes and the game climaxes with reintegration of all the digits back into the complete body (Oremland, 1973). Preschoolers often build blocks for the thrill of knocking them down, the thrill coming from the power of making the crash occur. These are fun not only because of the positive adult interaction, but also because the child is demonstrating power and mastery through symbolic play activities. Humor and playfulness are an integral part of these physically-oriented activities for the young child.

It has been suggested that young children do not "tell" what they think or feel or believe, and that children's play constitutes a language which is similar to adults' grammar and vocabulary (Fraiberg, 1959; Woltman, 1960). Play is a way to reconstruct, reenact, and understand. Directions as to how to incorporate play into the care of infants and toddlers has been stressed as important for hospitalized young children who may be deprived of normal playful periods and interactions with their parents due to therapy and lack of availability (Goldberger, 1988). Some of the restrictions common to health care areas are: (a) enforced passivity; (b) medical equipment incorporated into body image; and (c) intrusive treatments such as surgery. Medical play may be initiated by the adult, but is sustained by the child. Medical play is enjoyed by the child, often accompanied by laughter and subsequent relaxation. Humor is incorporated even though intense emotions and aggression are represented (McCue, 1988). Types of medical play activities can be divided into four categories for older children: (a) role rehearsal/role reversal, (b) medical fantasy play, (c) indirect medical play, and (d) medically related art. Models or actual hospital equipment may be used to support these activities.

Some instruments have been developed to attempt to measure play more effectively. The Children's Playfulness Scale is one of those tools (Barnett, 1991). The scale is a measurement of play as viewed as an internal personality construct. Many have observed that the child can be viewed as a projective system whose play is an expression of the individual child's personality and cognitive style (Barnett, 1991). This tool focuses on the identification of the underlying components of the playfulness construct (physical spontaneity, social spontaneity, cognitive spontaneity, manifest joy and sense of humor) as opposed to specific behaviors. Another tool that may be useful is the Rubin Play Observation Scale (Rubin, 1977, 1982a, 1982b). The Rubin tool focuses on the play behaviors themselves and is presented in a developmental and social context (see Chapter XX for an extensive listing of tools).

Humor is often a closely interwoven part of the play that helps to make it enjoyable. The play and the humor both provide benefits to the child by helping the child reveal fears in a socially acceptable non-threatening way. For example, an 8-year-old immobilized boy who had been hit by a car was asked by his nurse, "You ran in front of a car, huh?" and the child replied, "No, it ran in front of me" (Edison, 1976). Children who have had surgery may refer to their "zipper up the front". One child transplant patient referred to himself as being just like a used car, "I've got used parts" (Neff, 1973). To best utilize humor with children, it is important to be sensitive to their own life experiences and developmental ages, and take the initial clues from them.

The line between laughter and tears is often close and is often related to intensity. Tickling can be funny in one instance and even incorporated into the physical assessment. Yet if tickling is prolonged or introduced at the wrong time, it can cause tears rather than laughter. The role of the adult can be either that of the sensitive straight man or the humorist. The role always should involve the adult being emotionally available, sensitive, understanding, and accepting so that it is safe for the child to express feelings.

Giving cues that humor is acceptable even in nonhumorous situations enhances security in children and lets them know that the adults are indeed human and can see them as human beings also. Humorous communications by the adult such as verbal play on words, jokes, witticisms, cartoons, clowning, and practical jokes can be evaluated for effectiveness by the reactions of amusement such as giggles, smiles, chuckles, and laughter. Cues often help the child to understand that humor and/or play is on the way. "Let's play doctor and nurse," "Let me tell you a story about. . .," or "You know, sometimes funny things happen . . . ." These are all examples of cues to set the stage. For humor to occur, there must be that important matching of the message and the recipient (D'Antonio, 1984).

It is also helpful to incorporate the concepts related to play and humor in the actual design and decor of the pediatric unit. Much has been written about colors and design, but for the child's area it is also important to consider all elements of the room-floors, walls, ceilings, horizontal and vertical supports, objects, forms, and architectural details-as interactive surfaces that can be explored with eyes, hands, toys, etc. Stop thinking in terms of function alone, and start thinking also in terms of the activities of interest to children to promote their ability to enjoy the area as much as possible (Olds, 1988).

There are no rules saying that this "new planet" they must experience must be dull, boring, and frightening. Aesthetically rich environments dedicated to the child's point of view can promote positive, healing interactions. Unlike adults who seem to focus on goals and purposes, children seem to be especially sensitive to all of the qualitative aspects of their world and delight in the colors, light, sound, touch, texture, movement, form, and rhythm in the environment and people around them. Environments especially designed to promote mind-body healing through play and humor for child health care areas are available from Anita Olds & Associates, Environmental Facilities for Children, 10 Saville Street, Cambridge, MA 02138.

Humor in the Life of the Terminally Ill Child

Death is hidden from children in our modern society, making it unfamiliar to them. However, children are still concerned about death, especially those with a terminal diagnosis. Although our society tries to view death as something for the old, children experience many conditions that often lead to death — leukemia, cancer, cystic fibrosis, and muscular dystrophy being some of the most frequent causes (Ainsa, 1981). Age-appropriate play therapy can be useful in providing insight into the child's feelings, perceptions, and needs for understanding. Not only must children cope with the life-threatening illness, but they must also deal with separation from family, friends, school, as well as intrusive procedures and side effects from treatments and medication that are often more painful and disturbing than the illness itself (Gibbons & Boren, 1985).

Playing through anxiety is helpful for pre-school and school-aged children (Rucker, Thompson, & Dickerson, 1978). Art, music, storytelling, writing, talking into a tape recorder — all can be enjoyable for the child by reducing the levels of anxiety and promoting peaceful transition to death (Kubler-Ross, 1975). If the problem is faced, growth is possible. The child's mood needs are what should guide the activities in the last days. Although the adults may be sad, the young child is capable of enjoying humorous events until the very last moment.

One pediatric oncology hospital unit developed an ongoing storytelling group for children aged 5-10 years (Krietemeyer & Heinery, 1992). Some of the tactics used were: (a) storymaking: a story is written specifically for a child to address their individual needs; (b) mutual storytelling: listening to the child's story, analyzing the themes, then retelling a healthier version with alternatives and solutions to the dilemmas indicated by the child; and (c) fantasy play: stress reduction by reading visual fantasies from the book Put Your Mother on the Ceiling: Children's Imagination Games (DeMille, 1985). Trained therapists also used free fantasy and the creation of mental images through hypnotherapy (Krietemeyer & Heinery, 1992). An example of a group story was "The Wolf Who Killed Children on Chemotherapy." The children used felt figures and worked

252

together to develop the story and the plot. As the story progressed, one brave man went after the wolf with a gun, but the wolf got away and was still roaming about.

Even children in restricted isolation rooms who have received bone marrow transplants for cancer therapy can find anxiety reduction and increased ability to cope with their situation through the use of humor and creative imagination that is encouraged by their caregivers (Gottlieb & Portnoy, 1988). One example that illustrates using imaginary escape from a confining situation is 4-year-old Annie, who dealt with isolation in part by focusing on a plain white hospital sheet that was allowed to be a part of her fantasy life. When the blanket was on the floor it was a beach blanket; when it was on her bed draped over the headboard, it was a tent in the woods (Gottlieb & Portnoy, 1988). Some terminally ill children play out roles that they may not get to actually experience; for instance, Gottlieb & Portnoy (1988) reported that one 10-year-old child with leukemia took on the persona of a teenager, playing loud rock and roll music, dressing in sunglasses and typical teen clothes.

Summary

For children and the adults responsible for their care at home and in the clinical setting, it is important to recognize, stimulate, and reinforce a healthy display of humor as a part of the child's daily life. Children have cognitive, physical, social, and psychological changes related to their developmental age and this relates directly to their ability to comprehend and enjoy humor. Humor is inextricably linked with children's play and is as important to the child as breathing is to the physical survival.

Language, verbal skills, art, fantasy — all relate to humor expression in children and can be beneficial to the child struggling with the usual feelings associated with growing up in our fast paced culture. It can also be helpful to the child experiencing the additional stressors associated with illness, hospitalization, medical treatments, and terminal illness.

Humor is a normal part of our lives as human beings and is an important part of the life of the child. Parents and health care providers will do well to take humor and play very seriously in caring for their young charges in all situations, but especially in assisting children in coping with the intrusions and limitations imposed by illness and modern medicine. Humor can be an important part of the healing process.

Bibliography

Alberghene, J. (1989). Humor in children's literature. *Journal of Children in Contemporary Society*, 20, 1-2, 223-245.

Ainsa, T. (1981, summer). Teaching the terminally ill child. *Education*, 101, 4, 397-401.

Astin, E. (1977). Self-reported fears of hospitalized and non-hospitalized children aged ten to twelve. *Maternal-Child Nursing Journal*, 6,17-24.

Barnett, L. (1991). The playful child: Measurement of a disposition to play. *Play & Culture*, 4, 51-74.

Bolig, E. (1984). Play in hospital settings. In T. Yawkey & A. Pellegrini (Eds.), *Child's Play: Developmental and Applied* (pp. 323-343). Hillsdale, NJ: Erlbaum.

Brown, G., Wheeler, K., & Cash, M. (1980). The effects of a laughing versus a nonlaughing model on humor responses in preschool children. *Journal of Experimental Child Psychology*, 29, 334-339.

Bryant, J., & Zillmann, D. (1989). Using humor to promote learning in the classroom. *Journal of Children in Contemporary Society*, 20,1-2, 49-77.

Carle, E. (1972). The secret birthday message. New York: Crowell.
Chapman, A. (1983). Humor and laughter in social interaction and some implications for humor research. In P. McGhee & J. Goldstein (Eds.), *Handbook of humor research*, vol. 1 (pp. 135-157). New York: Springer.

Christelow, E. (1982). *Henry and the red stripes*. New York: Clarion.

Cousins, N. (1979) *Anatomy of an illness*. New York: Bantam.

D'Antonio, I. (1984). Therapeutic use of play in hospitals. *Nursing Clinics of North America*, 19, 2, 359.

D'Antonio, I. (1989). The use of humor with children in hospital settings. *Journal of Children in Contemporary Society*. 20,1-2, 157-169.

de Paola, T. (1977). *The quicksand book*. New York: Holiday.

Dixon, N. (1980). Humor: A cognitive alternative to stress. In I. Sarason & C. Spielberger (Eds.), *Stress and Anxiety, vol. 7* (pp. 281-289). Washington, DC: Hemisphere.

Ebmeier, J. (1982). Manifestations of guilt in an immobilized child. *Maternal-Child Nursing Journal*, 4, 109-115.

Edison, C. (1976). Reintegration of ego functioning during recovery from a cerebral insult. *Maternal-Child Nursing Journal*, 7,87-98.

Emerson, J. (1963). Social functions of humor in a hospital setting. PhD Dissertation. Berkeley, CA: University of California.

Fern, T. (1991, September). Identifying the gifted child humorist. *Roeper Review*, 14(1), 30-34.

Fraiberg, S. (1959). *The magic years*. New York: Scribner.

Freud, S. (1928). Humour. Reprinted in J. Strachey (Trans. and Ed.), *Collected Papers of Sigmund Freud*, vol. 5. New York: Basic Books, 1959.

254

Freud, S. (1960). *Jokes and their relation to the unconscious.* (J. Strachey, Trans. and Ed.) New York: Norton (Original work published 1905).

Fry, W. (1981). Doctor proves that laughter helps the health. *San Antonio Star*, p. 22.

Geismar-Ryan, L. (1986). Infant social activity: The discovery of peer play. *Childhood Education,* 63(1), 24-29.

Gibbons, M., & Boren, H. (1985). Stress reduction: A spectrum of strategies in pediatric oncology nursing. *Nursing Clinics of North America,* 20(1), 83-103.

Goldberger, J. (1988). Issue-specific play with infants and toddlers in hospitals: Rationale and intervention. *Children's Health Care,* 16(3), 134-141.

Goodman, J. (1983). How to get more smileage out of your life: Making sense of humor, then serving it. In P. E. McGhee & J. H Goldstein (Eds.), *Handbook of humor research,* vol. II (pp. 1-21). New York: Springer.

Gottleib, S., & Portnoy, S. The role of play in a pediatric bone marrow transplantation unit. *Children's Health Care,* 16(3), 177-181.

Grimm, D., & Pefley, P. (1990, July-August). Opening doors for the child "inside." *Pediatric Nursing,* 16(4), 368-369.

Harrison, D. (1988). *My ducks are really swans: Learning from the ups and downs of life.* Nashville, TN: Broadman.

Hendra, J. (1980). *The illustrated treasury of humor.* New York: Grosset & Dunlap.

Jalongo, M. (1985). Children's literature: There's some sense to its humor. *Childhood Education,* 62(2), 109-114.

Koestler, A. (1964). *The act of creation.* London: Hutchinson.

Krahn, F. (1974). *April fools.* New York: Dutton.

Krietemeyer, B., & Heinery, S. (1992). Storytelling as a therapeutic technique in a group of school-aged oncology patients. *Children's Health Care,* 21(1),14-20.

Kubler-Ross, E. (1975). *Death:The final stage of growth.* Englewood Cliffs, NJ: Prentice-Hall.

Levine, J. (1977). Humour as a form of therapy: Introduction to symposium. In A. Chapman & C. Foot (Eds.), *It's a funny thing, humour* (pp. 127-137). Oxford: Pergamon Press.

Lewis, S. (1976). *Zoo city.* New York: Greenwillow.

Loeb, M., & Wood, V. (1986). Epilogue: A nascent idea for an Eriksonian model of humor. In L. Nahemow, K. McCluskey-Fawcett, & P. McGhee (Eds.), *Humor and aging* (pp. 279-284). Orlando, FL: Academic Press.

Long, P. (1987). Laugh and be well. *Psychology Today,* 21,10, 28-29.

Manes, S. (1982). *Socko! Every riddle your feet will ever need to know.* Rutherford, NJ: Coward.

Martin, R. Humor and the mastery of living: Using humor to cope with the daily stresses of growing up. *Journal of Children in Contemporary Society*, 1(2), 135-154.

McCue, K. (1988). Medical play: An expanded perspective. *Children's Health Care*, 16(3), 157-161.

McGhee, P. (1979). *Humor: Its origin and development*. New York: Free Press.

McGhee, P., & Chapman, A. (Eds.) (1980). Children's humour. New York: Wiley.

McGhee, P., & Lloyd, S. (1981). A developmental test of the disposition theory of humor. *Child Development*, 52, 925-931.

McGhee, P., & Panotsopoulou, T. (1990). The role of cognitive factors in children's metaphor and humor comprehension. *Humor*, 3(4), 379-402.

Neff, J. (1973). Psychological adaptation to renal transplant. *Maternal-Child Nursing Journal*, 2, 111-119.

Nilsen, A. (1983). Children's multiple uses of oral language play. *Language Arts*, 60(2), 194-201.

O'Connell, W. (1976). Freudian humour: The eupsychia of everyday Life. In A. Chapman & H. Foot (Eds.), *Humour and laughter: Theory, research, and applications*. Oxford: Pergamon Press.

Olds, A. (1988). Designing for play: Beautiful spaces are playful places. *Children's Health Care*, 18, 3, 218-222.

Oremland, E. (1973). The jinx game. *Psychoanalytic Study of the Child*, 16(3), 419-431.

Oremland, E. (1988). Mastering developmental and critical experiences through play and other expressive behaviors in childhood. *Children's Health Care*, 16(3),150-156.

Pellegrini, A., & Perlmutter, J. (1988). The diagnostic and therapeutic roles of children's rough-and-tumble play. *Children's Health Care*, 16(3), 162-168.

Piaget, J. (1947). *The psychology of intelligence*. London: Routledge & Kegan.

Pidgeon, V. (1977). Characteristics of children's thinking and implications for health teaching. *Maternal-Child Nursing Journal*, 6, 1-8.

Raskin, E. (1973). *Who said Sue, said whoo?* New York: Atheneum.

Robinson, V. M. (1991). *Humor and the health professions*, 2nd edition. Thorofare, NJ: Slack.

Rubin, K. (1977). Play behaviors of young children. *Young Children*, 3, 16-24.

Rubin, K. (1982a). Nonsocial play in preschoolers: Necessarily evil? *Child Development*, 53, 651-657.

Rubin, K. (1982b). Social and social-cognitive developmental characteristics of young isolate, normal, and sociable children. In K. Rubin & H. Ross (Eds.), *Peer Relationships and Social Skills in Childhood* (pp. 211-219). New York: Springer.

Rucker, M., Thompson, L., & Dickerson, B. (1978, May). Puppet life and death education. *The Clearing House,* 51(9), 458.

Shaeffer, M., & Hopkins, D. (1988, Winter). Miss Nelson, knock-knocks, and nonsense: Connecting through humor. *Childhood Education,* 65,(2), 88-93.

Suls, J. (1983). Cognitive processes in humor appreciation. In P. McGhee & J. Goldstein (Eds.), *Handbook of humor research,* vol. 1 (pp. 39-57). New York: Springer.

Tamashiro, R. (1979). Children's humor: A developmental view. *Elementary School Journal,* 80, 68-75.

Ventis, W., & Ventis, D. (1989). Guidelines for using humor in therapy with children and young adolescents. *Journal of Children in Contemporary Society,* 20(1-2), 179-197.

Vessey, J., & Mahon, M. (1990). Therapeutic play and the hospitalized child. *Journal of Pediatric Nursing,* 5(5), 328-333.

Viorst, J. (1969). *I'll fix Anthony..* New York: Harper.

Whitney, S. (1981). *Dr. Gloom's monster jokes and puzzles.* San Diego: Harcourt Brace Jovanovich.

Williams, P. (1989). Going west to get east: Using metaphors as instructional tools. *Humor and Children's Development,* 20(1-2), 79-98.

Wolfenstein, M. (1954). *Children's humor: A psychological analysis.* Glencoe, IL: Free Press.

Woltman, A. (1960). Spontaneous puppetry by children as a projective method. In A. Robin & M. Haworth (Eds.), *Projective techniques with children* (pp. 305-312). New York: Grune & Stratton.

CHAPTER XX

WORKING TOOLS

by Kathleen S. Cannella, RN, CS, MN, MS, PhD

Planning humor interventions and facilitating humorous interactions may be supported by using one or more tools or instruments designed to assess humor. These tools may be categorized as descriptive or quantitative.

Humor, an elusive concept, has been very difficult to measure. In large part this has been related to the difficulties involved in defining humor. This is evidenced by the number of instruments developed for the study of humor. These instruments measure various aspects of humor in different populations, usually through a self-report, paper and pencil format. The majority of these instruments claim to measure sense of humor, defining it in terms of humor appreciation.

Focus of Tools

Humor Appreciation. Sense of humor has been defined and investigated most frequently in terms of appreciation of particular forms of humorous stimuli, such as jokes and cartoons, in particular content categories. Generally the content of humor comprising these instruments can be categorized as one or more of the following types: neutral, salient, taboo, nonsensical, hostile, sexual, and incongruity-resolution. Consistent preferences for certain content or themes have been thought to reflect certain underlying personality characteristics.

According to Ruch and colleagues (1988a, 1988b, 1990), the stimulus or demand should also be appraised in terms of its aversiveness, defined as negative reactions to humor such as indignation, embarrassment, and boredom. Humor appreciation was viewed as the combined effect of both funniness and aversiveness. No other instrument was found to include a similar component in its measurement of humor appreciation.

Usually subjects are asked to complete 5 to 7 point Likert-type scales, rating the funniness or amount of amusement perceived in response to a series of verbal jokes or cartoons. One of these instruments also includes an external behavior rating of children's spontaneous facial mirth in response to a series of cartoons as well as a rating of their understanding of the point of each cartoon. Another requires children to complete drawings by selecting one of two drawings which yield nonsensical or hostile humor

259

from the completed drawing.

Humor Comprehension. Humor comprehension refers to the ability to perceive and understand the humorous meaning(s) of stimuli. Cognitive abilities influence the ability to comprehend stimuli in a humorous fashion. As their cognitive abilities increase, children enjoy increasingly complex humor stimuli.

Humor as a Response. Other instruments have focused on humor as a response. Many of these instruments have focused on behaviors such as laughing and smiling, measured through self-report or behavioral ratings in general or in response to particular stimuli. Martin and Lefcourt (1984) purposefully used a behavioral definition of humor in the development of the Situational Humor Response Questionnaire to avoid the debates over the processes and theoretical approaches involved in humor, and thus increase its applicability.

Humor Creation/Production. Humor creation/production is the ability to actively create/produce/use humor, as opposed to simply enjoy or appreciate it. Some scholars have differentiated between the ability to create humor and the ability to reproduce humor, regardless of environmental input. Humor creation is the active creation of humorous stimuli/responses, whereas humor reproduction is the use of previously learned humorous messages, such as particular jokes.

Other Aspects of Humor. Other measurement tools have focused on the evaluation of humorous messages, attitude towards humor, humor as a coping strategy, and therapeutic level of humor used. Relatively few tools have focused on these aspects. While many tools have been designed to measure one aspect of humor, others focus on two or more aspects of sense of humor.

Use of These Tools

The paper and pencil tools are relatively easy to administer and could be given to individuals or groups. The other tools are more cumbersome to administer and require one-on-one, rather than group, administration. While this is often feasible in clinical situations, it may be problematic in conducting research with large groups of subjects.

These tools are in various stages of development and use. While some are in the initial stages of development and/or have only been used by their author(s), others have been widely disseminated and used over a long period of time. In particular, three instruments, the Sense of Humor Questionnaire (Svebak, 1974), the Coping Humor Scale (Martin & Lefcourt, 1983), and the Situational Humor Response Questionnaire (Martin & Lefcourt, 1984), have been frequently used in studies focusing on the relation of humor to one or more aspects of physical and/or mental health and well-being. Lefcourt and Martin (1986) suggested that these scales seemed to measure somewhat different aspects of sense of humor, and that, as such, they could be used together as a battery of tools to provide a more complete assessment of sense of humor.

In contrast, Thorson and Powell (1991) assert that sense of humor is a multidimensional construct that has not been measured well, even with the set of instruments recommended by Lefcourt and Martin (1986). Thorson and Powell noted that the "use of any or a combination of all of the three scales examined in the present study would not seem to give an accurate picture of humor in the broadest sense (p. 701). They developed a multidimensional sense of humor scale to overcome the problems they identified with other measures.

Beyond the brief overview of tools to assess humor presented above, the purpose of this chapter is to acquaint readers with the number and variety of humor assessment tools that have been used in clinical and/or research situations, and to facilitate readers' use of one or more of these tools. While the search and retrieval of humor assessment tools for this chapter was not exhaustive, a large number of humor assessment tools were reviewed. Selected characteristics of these tools are presented in the following tables. While these tools represent the majority of those that have undergone revision and further testing; a selection of those in the early stages of development are also described.

Bibliography

Ackermann, M. H., Henry, M. B., Graham, K. M., & Coffee, N. (1994). Humor son, humor too: A model to incorporate humor into the health care setting (revised). *Nursing Forum*, 29(2), 15-21.

Anderson, C. A., & Arnoult, L. H. (1989). An examination of perceived control, humor, irrational beliefs, and positive stress as moderators of the relation between negative stress and health. *Basic and Applied Social Psychology*, 10(2), 101-107.

Bellert, J. L. (1989). Humor: A therapeutic approach in oncology nursing. *Cancer Nursing*, 12(2), 65-70.

Bizi, S., Keinan, G., & Beit-Hallahmi, B. (1988). Humor and coping with stress: A test under real-life conditions. *Personality and Individual Differences*, 9, 951-956.

Brodzinsky, D. M., & Rubien, J. (1976). Humor production as a function of sex of subject, creativity, and cartoon content. *Journal of Consulting and Clinical Psychology*, 44, 597-600.

Campinha-Bacote, J. (1989). How's your laugh life? Cited in J. Campinha-Bacote (1995). Ho-ho-listics-The role of culture and humor. In K. Buxman & A. LeMoine (Eds.), *Nursing perspectives on humor* (pp. 177-182). New York: Power Publications.

Cannella, K. S., Opitz, M, & Missroon, S. (1993, February). The effectiveness of humor as a teaching strategy in initial research courses. Paper presented at the Southern Nursing Research Society, Birmingham, AL.

Crawford, M., & Gressley, D. (1991). Creation, caring, and context: Women's and men's account of humor preferences and practices. *Psychology of Women Quarterly*, 15, 217-231.

Cohen, M. (1990). Caring for ourselves can be funny business. *Holistic Nursing Practice*, 4(4), 1-11.

Deaner, S. L., & McConatha, J. T. (1993). The relation of humor to depression and personality. *Psychological Reports*,2, 755-763.

Deckers, L, & Ruch, W. (1992). The Situational Humour Response Questionnaire SHRQ as a test of "sense of humour": A validity study in the field of humour appreciation. *Personality and Individual Differences*, 13, 1149-1152.

Derks, P., Staley, R. E., & Haselton, M. G. (1994). "Sense" of humor: Perception or intelligence? Paper presented at the Symposium on "Approaches to the Sense of Humor: Concepts and measurement, 1994 International Society for Humor Studies Conference, Ithaca, New York.

Dillon, K. M., Minchoff, B., & Baker, K. H. (1985). Positive emotional states and enhancement of the immune system. *International Journal of Psychiatry in Medicine*, 15, 13-17.

Erdman, L. (1991). Laughter therapy for patients with cancer. *Oncology Nursing Forum*, 18, 1359-1363.

Feingold, A. (1982). Measuring humor: A pilot study. *Perceptual and Motor Skills*, 54, 986.

Feingold, A. (1983). Measuring humor ability: Revision and construct validation of the Humor Perceptiveness Test. *Perceptual and Motor Skills*, 56, 159-166.

Felker, D. L., & Hunter, D. M. (1970). Sex and age differences in response to cartoons depicting subjects of different ages and sex. *Journal of Psychology*, 76, 19-21.

Gavanski, I. (1986). Differential sensitivity of humor ratings and mirth responses to cognitive and affective components of the humor response. *Journal of Personality and Social Psychology*, 51(1), 209-214.

Groch, A. S. (1974). Generality of response to humor and wit in cartoons, jokes, stories and photographs. *Psychological Reports*, 35, 835-838.

Hampes, W. P. (1992). Relation between intimacy and humor. *Psychological Reports*, 71, 127-130.

Henkin, B., & Fish, J. M. (1986). Gender and personality differences in the appreciation of cartoon humor. *Journal of Psychology*, 120(2), 157-175.

Herth, K. A. (1984). Laughter: A nursing rx. *American Journal of Nursing*, 84, 991-1992.

Herth, K. A. (1993). Humor and the older adult. *Applied Nursing Research*, 6, 146-153.

Herth, K. A. (1995). Humor's role in terminal illness. In K. Buxman & A. LeMoine (Eds.), *Nursing perspectives on humor* (p. 217-30). New York: Power Publications

Khoury, R. M. (1977). Sex and intelligence differences in humor appreciation: A re-examination. *Social Behavior and Personality*, 5, 377-382.

King, P. J., & King, J. E. (1973). A children's humor test. *Psychological Reports*, 33, 632.

Kirkland, J. (1974). Warm-up and fatigue effects in jokes rated by concrete and abstract persons. *Social Behavior and Personality*, 2(2), 161-165.

Kohler, G. (1994). Factorial and correlational study of current sense of humor scales. Paper presented at the Symposium on Approaches to the Sense of Humor: Concepts and measurement, 1994 International Society for Humor Studies Conference, Ithaca, New York.

Kuhlman, T. L. (1985). A study of salience and motivational theories of humor. *Journal of Personality and Social Psychology*, 49(1), 281-286.

Labott, S. M., Ahleman, S., Wolever, M. E., & Martin, R. B. (1990). The physiological and psychological effects of the expression and inhibition of emotion. *Behavioral Medicine*, 16, 182-189.

Labott, S. M., & Martin, R. B. (1987). The stress-moderating effects of weeping and humor. *Journal of Human Stress*, 13, 159-164.

Labott, S. M., & Martin, R. B. (1990). Emotional coping, age, and physical disorder. *Behavioral Medicine*, 16, 53-61.

Labott, S. M., Martin, R. B., & Eason, P. S. (1989, April). Emotional expression and physical symptomatology. Presented at the Eastern Psychological Association, Boston, MA.

Lefcourt, H. M., Davidson-Katz, K., & Kueneman, K. (1990). Humor and immune system functioning. *Humor: International Journal of Humor Research*, 3(3), 305-321.

Lefcourt, H. M., & Martin, R. A. (1986). *Humor and life stress: Antidote to adversity.* New York: Springer.

Martin, R. A., & Dobbin, J. P. (1988). Sense of humor, hassles, and immunoglobulin A: Evidence for a stress-moderating effect of humor. *International Journal of Psychiatry in Medicine*, 18(2), 93-105.

Martin, R. A., & Lefcourt, H. M. (1983). Sense of humor as a moderator of the relation between stressors and moods. *Journal of Personality and Social Psychology*, 45, 1313-1324.

Martin, R. A., & Lefcourt, H. M. (1984). Situational humor response questionnaire: Quantitative measure of sense of humor. *Journal of Personality and Social*

Psychology, 47, 145-155.

Mindess, H., Miller, C., Turek, J., Bender, A., & Corbin, S. (1985). *The Antioch humor test: Making sense of humor.* New York: Avon.

McGhee, P. E. (1976). Children's appreciation of humor: A test of the cognitive congruency principle. *Child Development, 47*, 420-426.

Nezu, A. M., Nezu, C. M., & Blissett, S. E. (1988). Sense of humor as a moderator of the relation between stressful events and psychological distress: A prospective analysis. *Journal of Personality and Social Psychology, 54*, 520-525.

O'Connell, W. E. (1960). The adaptive functions of wit and humor. *Journal of Abnormal and Social Psychology, 61*, 263-270.

O'Connell, W. E. (1962). An item analysis of the wit and humor appreciation test. *Journal of Social Psychology, 56*, 271-276.

O'Connell, W. E. (1964a). Resignation, humor, and wit. *Psychoanalytic Review, 51*, 49-56.

O'Connell, W. E. (1964b). Multidimensional investigation of Freudian humor. *Psychiatric Quarterly, 38*, 1-12.

O'Connell, W. E. (1969). Creativity in humor. *Journal of Social Psychology, 78*, 237-241.

O'Connell, W. E. (1976). Freudian humour: The eupsychia of everyday life. In A. J. Chapman, and H. C. Foot (Eds.), *Humour and laughter: Theory, research and applications* (pp. 313-329). New York: Wiley.

Opitz, M. P. (1988). Humor in Teaching Research. Cited in K. S. Cannella, M., Opitz, & S. Missroon (1993, February). The effectiveness of humor as a teaching strategy in initial research courses. Paper presented at the Southern Nursing Research Society, Birmingham, AL.

O'Quin, K. (1994). Sociability and social skill related to the sense of humor: A multitrait, multimeasure approach. Paper presented at the Symposium on "Approaches to the Sense of Humor: Concepts and measurement, 1994 International Society for Humor Studies Conference, Ithaca, New York.

O'Quin, K. (1991). Is the sense of humor multidimensional? Paper presented at the 1991 International Society for Humor Studies Conference, Ontario, Canada.

Overholser, J. (1992). Sense of humor when coping with life stress. *Personality and Individual Differences, 13*, 799-804.

Pasquali, E. A. (1995). Humor for mentally ill patients. In K. Buxman & A. LeMoine (Eds.), *Nursing perspectives on humor* (pp.161-176). New York: Power Publications.

Paulson, T. L. (1989). *Making humor work: Take your job seriously and yourself lightly.* Menlo Park, CA: Crisp Publications.

Porterfield, A. L. (1987). Does sense of humor moderate the impact of life stress on psychological and physical well-being? *Journal of Research in Personality*, 21, 306-317.

Powell, L. Items for evaluating humor. *Psychological Reports*, 58, 323-326.

Prerost, F. J., & Brewer, R. E. (1977). Humor content preferences and the relief of experimentally arouse aggression. *Journal of Social Psychology*, 103, 225-231.

Rim, Y. (1988). Sense of humour and coping styles. *Personality and Individual Differences*, 9, 559-564.

Robinson, V. M. (1977). *Humor and the health professions:*Thorofare, NJ: Slack.

Ruch, W. (1983). Humor-test 3 W-D (Form A, B, and K). Unpublished manuscript, University of Dusseldorf, Department of Psychology, Dusseldorf, FRG.

Ruch, W. (1988). Sensation seeking and the enjoyment of structure and content of humour: Stability of findings across four samples. *Personality and Individual Differences*, 9, 861-871.

Ruch, W. (1993). Temperament, Eysenck's PEN system, and humor-related traits. Unpublished manuscript.

Ruch, W., & Hehl, F.J. (1988). Attitudes to sex, sexual behaviour and enjoyment of humour. *Personality and Individual Differences*, 9, 983-994.

Ruch, W., McGhee, P. E., & Hehl, F.J. (1990). Age differences in the enjoyment of incongruity-resolution and nonsense humor during adulthood. *Personality and Aging*, 5, 348-355.

Ruxton, J. P., & Hester, M. P. (1987). Humor: Assessment and interventions. *Clinical Gerontologist*, 7(1), 13-21.

Safranek, R., & Schill, T. (1982). Coping with stress: Does humor help? *Psychological Reports*, 51, 222.

Salameh, W.A. (1983). Humor in psychotherapy: Past outlooks, present status, and future frontiers. In P. E. McGhee & J. H. Goldstein (Eds.), *Handbook of humor research*, Volume I: Basic issues (pp. 61-88). New York: Springer.

Sumners, A.D. (1990). Professional nurses' attitudes toward humor. *Journal of Advanced Nursing*, 15, 196-200.

Sumners, A. D. (1988). Humor: Coping in recovery from addiction. *Issues in Mental Health Nursing*, 9, 169-179.

Svebak, S. (1974a). A theory of sense of humor. *Scandinavian Journal of Psychology*, 15, 99-107.

Svebak, S. (1974b). Three attitude dimensions of sense of humor as predictors of laughter. *Scandinavian Journal of Psychology*, 15, 185-190.

Svebak, S. (1974c). Revised questionnaire on the sense of humor. *Scandinavian Journal of Psychology*, 15, 328-331.

Svebak, S. (1975). Styles in humour and social self—images. *Scandinavian Journal of Psychology*, 16, 79-84.

Svebak, S. (1993). Sense of Humor Scale—Revised. Cited in G. Kohler (1994). Factorial and correlational study of current sense of humor scales. Paper presented at the Symposium on Approaches to the Sense of Humor: Concepts and measurement, 1994 International Society for Humor Studies Conference, Ithaca, New York.

Thorson, J. A., & Powell, F. C. (1991). Measurement of sense of humor. *Psychological Reports*, 69, 691-702.

Thorson, J. A., & Powell, F. C. (1993a). Development and validation of a multidimensional sense of humor scale. *Journal of Clinical Psychology*, 49, 13-23.

Thorson, J. A., & Powell, F. C. (1993b). Sense of humor and dimensions of personality. *Journal of Clinical Psychology*, 49, 799-809.

Thorson, J. A., & Powell, F. C. (1994). Psychometric properties of the Multidimensional Sense of Humor Scale. Paper presented at the Symposium on Approaches to the Sense of Humor: Concepts and measurement, 1994 International Society for Humor Studies Conference, Ithaca, New York.

Trice, A. D., & Price-Greathouse, J. (1986). Joking under the drill: A validity study of the CHS. *Journal of Social Behavior and Personality*, 1, 265-266.

Yovetich, N. A., Dale, J. A., & Hudak, M. A. (1990). Benefits of humor in reduction of threat-induced anxiety. *Psychological Reports*, 66, 51-58.

Zigler, E., Levine, J., & Gould, L. (1966a). Cognitive process in the development of children's appreciation of humor. *Child Development*, 37, 507-518.

Zigler, E., Levine, J., & Gould, L. (1966b). The humor response of normal, institutionalized retarded, and noninstitutionalized retarded children. *American Journal of Mental Deficiency*, 71, 472-480.

Zigler, E., Levine, J., & Gould, L. (1967). Cognitive challenge as a factor in children's humor appreciation. *Journal of Personality and Social Psychology*, 6, 332-336.

Ziv, A. (1979a). Sociometry of humor: Objectifying the subjective. *Perceptual and Motor Skills*, 38, 431-432.

Ziv, A. (1979b). L'Humour en Äducation: Approche psychologique. Paris: Editions Sociales Franiaises. Cited in A. Ziv (1984) *Personality and sense of humor*. New York: Springer.

Ziv, A. (1983). The influence of humorous atmosphere on divergent thinking. *Contemporary Educational Psychology*, 8, 68-75.

Ziv, A. (1989). Using humor to develop creative thinking. In P. E. McGhee (Guest Ed.), Humor in children's development: A guide to practical applications. *Journal of Children's Development*, 20(1/2), 99-116.

Contributing Authors and Editors

Aust, Carolyn H., RN, MS
Chapter XII: Humor in the Aging Society
622 Glacier Dr, Grand Junction, CO 81503; tel. 303-242-8766
Carolyn Aust is the Director of Gerontological Services at St. Mary's Hospital and Medical Center. She is also Chairman and Charter Board Member of an adult day care center. Carolyn is a member of Sigma Theta Tau and was named Nurse of the Year in 1992 by the Colorado Nurses Association. She was recently appointed Delegate to the White House Conference on Aging for May 1995.

Boettcher, Janet Hardy, RN, C, PhD, FAAN
Chapter XIX: Children and Humor
100 Vista Ridge, Radford, VA 24141; tel. 703-731-3376
Janet Boettcher received her BSN degree in 1967 from the University of Virginia, Charlottesville; her MS degree in parent-child nursing from Medical College of Virginia, Richmond; and her PhD in nursing from the University of Texas, Austin. She is currently chair and associate professor of the School of Nursing, Radford University, Radford, VA. Her research interests include reducing infant mortality and rural health care. She has been married to Rev. Kenneth Boettcher since 1967.

Buxman, Karyn, RN, MS,
Editor; Introduction: How the Book Came to Be
Founder, HUMORx, P.O. Box 1273, Hannibal, MO 63401-1273; tel. 800-8HUMORX (800-848-6679); email 74762.2032@compuserve.com
Karyn Buxman is a leading international expert in therapeutic humor. She has over 18 years of first-hand experience in humor and nursing. Now, as a full-time speaker and humorist, Karyn has found a way to share her passion and mission in life with folks of all ages (even the humor-impaired). She is a contributing editor and vice-president of Journal of Nursing Jocularity as well as editor for Therapeutic Humor, the newsletter for the American Association of Therapeutic Humor. Other organizations include the International Society of Humor Studies, Sigma Theta Tau, American Nurses Association, and National Speakers Association. Karyn has been published in a variety of publications, including Nursing91, American Journal of Nursing, and Journal of Psychosocial Nursing. She has also produced numerous audio- and videotapes, including Health Care FUN-damentals, Wit Happens, and Humor: The Good, The Bad, & The Ugly. She is currently looking for ways to use humor to achieve her ultimate life goals: world peace and thin thighs.

Campinha-Bacote, Josepha, PhD, RN, CS, CTN
Chapter XIV: Ho-Ho-Listics — The Role of Culture and Humor
921 Oregon Trail, Wyoming, OH 45215; tel. 513-761-0074
Josie Campinha-Bacote is the President and Founder of Transcultural C.A.R.E. Associates, a private consultation service which focuses on clinical, administrative, research, and educational issues in transcultural health care and mental health. She is certified by the American Nurses Association as a Clinical Nurse Specialist in psychiatric and mental health nursing, and by the Transcultural Nurses Society as a Certified Specialist in Transcultural Nursing. She has been the recipient of several national and international honors, including the Distinguished Lecturer Award from Sigma Theta Tau, and the Ethnic/Racial Minority Fellowship Award from the National Institute of Mental Health.

Cannella, Kathleen S., RN, CS, MN, MS, PhD
Chapter V: Humor — An Educational Strategy, and Chapter XX: Working Tools
Clinical Specialist, Pulmonary and Critical Care Medicine, Atlanta VA Medical Center (111), 1670 Clairmont Rd, Decatur, GA 30033; tel. 404-321-6111 X2293; email cannella@atlanta.va.gov. Kathleen Cannella received her diploma from Maryland General Hospital School of Medicine in Baltimore, MD, her BS from Georgia State University, her MN in Adult Health Nursing from Emory University, her MS in Community Counseling from Georgia State University, and her PhD in Curriculum Design and Instructional Processes with emphasis in research design and statistical analysis from Georgia State University. She is a Certified Specialist in Medical Surgical Nursing and Gerontological Nursing. She has 20 years in nursing experience in a variety of clinical areas, primarily in nursing education. Stemming from her clinical and educational perspectives, her research interest in humor evolved from her long-held belief that learning as well as life should be relatively fun and enjoyable. She lives with her husband and child in the Atlanta area. She truly applies the saying, "Laughter is the best medicine."

Ditlow, Florence, RN, BS
Chapter III: The Missing Element in Health Care: Humor as a Form of Creativity
10 River Rd 3A, Roosevelt Island, NY 10044; tel. 212-888-0585
Florence Ditlow is a staff nurse at St. Vincent's Hospital, New York, NY. She discovered that the sense of humor of the nurse is an untapped miracle. Florence decided to facilitate the enjoyment of humor in health care settings and created Joke Poke, Inc. Her adventurous programs have taught nurses, patients, and health care professionals how to release their creative abilities through humor and play.

Fletcher, Doug, RN
Chapter IX: Humor Journal for Nurses
Publisher, Journal of Nursing Jocularity, P.O. Box 40416, Mesa, AZ 85274; 602-835-6165; email 73314.3032@compuserve.com
Doug Fletcher is the publisher and founder of the Journal of Nursing Jocularity, a humor magazine for nurses. He received his Associate degree in Nursing in 1987 and currently works in critical care, emergency room, and telemetry at Mesa Lutheran Hospital. He also coordinates the annual Humor Skills for the Health Professional Conference which provides CEUs for nurses on the therapeutic use of humor. He is currently single and looking for his soul mate.

Gaberson, Kathleen B., RN, PhD
Chapter XVIII: Humor in Perioperative Nursing
Duquesne University, 617 College Hall, Pittsburgh, PA 15282; tel. 412-396-6536; Internet: gaberson@duq2.duq.edu
Kathy Gaberson is an Associate Professor in the Duquesne University School of Nursing MSN and PhD programs. She has 25 years of nursing education experience. She presents continuing education programs on using humor in health care and education, and her research focuses on the use of humor as a nursing intervention. Kathy uses humor in her teaching and, even when she does not succeed in being funny, she knows she always looks funny.

Gibson, Leslie, RN, BS
Chapter VIII: Carts, Baskets, and Rooms
The Comedy Connection, Morton Plant Hospital, 323 Jeffords St, Clearwater, FL 34617-0210; tel. 813-462-7841
Leslie Gibson was one of thirteen Humor Project Grant recipients from the Saratoga Institute in New York. She created a Comedy Cart for Morton Plant Hospital which provides humor stimulation for hospitalized patients. Leslie authored "Laughter: The Universal Language," a home study course which offers 10 hours of continuing education and was published in Nursing94. She is currently a home health care nurse and coordinator for Independent Global Home Health, and speaks around the country.

Goldkuhle, Ute, RN-ANP, MS, MPH
Chapter X: Caring Through Humor: Ethical Considerations
Assistant Professor, Nursing, University of Hawaii at Manoa School of Nursing, 2538 The Mall, Webster Hall, Honolulu, HI 96822; tel. 808-533-1596; Internet email:goldkuhl@uhunix.uhecc.hawaii.edu

Ute Goldkuhle has over 20 years of nursing practice, primarily in community health nursing as home care nurse, adult nurse practitioner, administrator, and is currently Assistant Professor in Nursing at the University of Hawaii, teaching community health nursing. Her professional emphasis is on correctional health, women offenders, and nursing ethics. Ute recently developed an integrated nursing ethics curriculum which is being implemented throughout the undergraduate nursing program. She has held numerous workshops in nursing ethics at state and international conferences.

Gullickson, Colleen, RN, PhD
Chapter II: Listening Beyond the Laugher: Communicating Through the Use of Laughter
3302 Highway H, Ridgeway, WI 53582; tel. 608-924-1718
Colleen Gullickson lives with her family on a dairy farm in south central Wisconsin. She received her Master's degree from the University of Wisconsin-Madison and her doctorate in Nursing from the University of Illinois Chicago medical Center. She has worked in critical care and as a nurse educator for almost 20 years. It is from this nursing background that her interest in humor evolved. She is also a contributing editor for the Journal of Nursing Jocularity.

Herth, Kaye Ann, PhD, RN, FAAN
Chapter XVII: Humor's Role in Terminal Illness
Georgia Southern University, Landrum Box 8158, Statesboro, GA 30460-8158; tel. 912-681-5479
Kay Herth is Chair and Professor, Department of Nursing, Georgia Southern University. Dr. Herth has had extensive experience in working with terminally ill adults in several hospice programs. Her research has explored hope, humor, and grief in individuals with terminal illness and the impact on their family/significant others. She has published extensively in professional nursing journals, and has presented at numerous regional and national conferences.

LeMoine, Anne, PhD
Co-Editor; 1501 Clairmont Rd, #2008, Decatur, GA 30033-4604; tel. 404-248-0033
Anne LeMoine, Editor-Writer for Medical Sciences, holds a quadruple doctorate in linguistics and a triple doctorate in politicoeconomics (obtained in Europe, 1945-48). In 1948, she entered the French Diplomatic Corps as an International Economics Researcher (she speaks seven languages). After moving to the United States in 1970, she obtained two medical diplomas (laboratory techniques and medical terminology). In New York City (1970-79) and then in Tampa, Florida (1979-86), she was the President of American International Manuscript Services-AIMS. Her client list ranges from Time/

Life Encyclopedias (Associate Producer, 24-volume series) and the major publishers, to celebrity authors, hospitals, and universities. She now lives in the Atlanta area and works mainly with the medical community of that city. She views the basic function of editing as infinitely more than correcting grammar, syntax, or presentation: "The essence of editing is to remove the weeds and landscape the text, so that the reader is free to think beyond the written word."

Missroon, Sandra, EdD, MSN, RN
Chapter V: Humor — An Educational Strategy
2861 Players Dr, Jonesboro, GA 30236
Sandra Missroon earned her nursing diploma in the early 1960s, a BSN from Armstrong College, a Master's degree from the Medical College of Georgia, and an EdD from the University of Georgia. Her professional career in nursing spans a period of 32 years of clinical practice, of which 17 years in academia. She is currently Associate Professor of Nursing in the RN/BSN Program of Clayton State College in Morrow, GA, where she resides with her husband and children. Her professional interests are varied, ranging from being actively involved with professional organizations to providing legal consultation to attorneys in nursing malpractice cases. She characterizes herself as a true example of a lifelong learner. Her present plans include continuing her interest in humor research in education, and entering a postdoctoral Family Nurse Practitioner Program later this year.

Moses, Nancy, MSB, PhN, RN
Chapter VI: Humor in Evaluating Performance
10062 Beverly Dr, Huntington Beach, CA 92646; tel. 714-963-2619
Nancy Moses is a native of upstate New York. She received a Bachelor's degree in Nursing from Hartwick College. She received a Master's degree in Nursing Education from California State University, Los Angeles. Her nursing specialty is geriatrics. Through mid-1994, she was the nurse facilitator at the NeuroBehavioral Assessment Center at Long Beach Community Hospital. She recently retired and is consulting abroad. She is married, the mother of four children, and has recently become officially "Grandma Moses."

Opitz, Margaret P., EdD, MSN, RN
Chapter V: Humor — An Educational Strategy
Nursing Director, Joint RN BSN Program, Pembroke State University and Fayetteville State University, Pembroke, NC 28372
Margaret (Petty) Opitz received her ADN from Southeastern Community College, her

BSN from East Tennessee State University, her MSN from Medical College of Georgia, and her EdD from Virginia Polytechnic Institute and State University. Peggy has been involved in establishing nursing programs, including the first BSN program in a military college at North Georgia College. She is currently Joint Nursing Director of the RN BSN Program at Pembroke State University and Fayetteville State University in North Carolina. She is continually involved in conducting nursing research, mostly associated with nursing education. She publishes a quarterly nursing newsletter. She is involved in a number of professional and community service activities, and is a member of Sigma Theta Tau and Phi Kappa Phi honor societies.

Parfitt, Janice M., RN, MSN
Chapter XVIII: Humor in Perioperative Nursing
4789 Woodlake Dr, Allison Park, PA 15101; tel. 412-443-4516
Janice Parfitt began working in the operating room while completing her Bachelor's degree studies at Loma-Linda University in California. She has held a variety of clinical positions in critical care, obstetrical, and perioperative nursing. She has had several nurse educator jobs since obtaining her Master's degree from University of Pittsburgh, Pennsylvania. She has presented posters locally and nationally, and has published two articles in the AORN Journal. She is a member of Sigma Theta Tau and AORN. Janice believes that humor is an integral part of the "spirit of nursing."

Pasquali, Elaine Anne, RN, PhD
Chapter XIII: Humor for Long-term Mentally Ill Clients
Adelphi University, Box 516, Garden City, NY 11530
Elaine Pasquali, a nurse and cultural anthropologist, is a professor at Adelphi University. In addition to consultation, she also teaches about and uses humor as a teaching strategy with clients. Dr. Pasquali has written several textbooks about holistic health, culture and health, and/or humor and health. She has served on the nominating committee of the American Nurses' Association Council on Culture Diversity in Nursing. She is a Fellow of the American Anthropological Association and serves on the Board of Directors of Nurses' House, Nassau-Suffolk Chapter.

Riley, Julia W. Balzer, RN, MN
Chapter VII: Humor in Quality Improvement
President, Constant Source Seminars, 2216 Kensington Lane, Orange Park, FL 32073-5274 after 7/1/95: 2310 Pilgrim Mill Way, Cumming, GA 30131; tel. 800-368-7675
Julia's mission is to provide people with the skills they need to pursue joy in their personal

and professional lives. A private consultant and professional speaker for 19 years, Julia has had 13 years experience in training and development as well as management development. Publications include two home study courses on humor for health care professionals and a book, Communication for Nurses, with an emphasis on humor and spirituality (Chicago: Mosby, Fall 1995).

Ritz, Sandra E., RN, MSN, MPH
Chapter X: Caring Through Humor: Ethical Considerations, and Chapter XVI: Survivor Humor and Disaster Nursing
Lighten Up Seriously! 1532A Anuhea Place, Honolulu, HI 96816; Internet email:swritz@ uhunix.uhcc.hawaii.edu
Sandy Ritz is a legal nurse consultant and owner of MedicoLegal Research Services. A nurse practitioner and clinical nurse specialist, Sandy is pursuing a doctorate in Public Health (Dr. PH) at the University of Hawaii with a research focus on Survivor Humor in Disasters. As a frequent and humorous "edu-tainer," her presentation "Lighten Up Seriously!" incorporates her experiences as an actress and cartoonist to help others find the absurdity in adversity and lighten up seriously.

Robinson, Vera M., RN, EdD
Chapter I: Humor in Nursing: A Hysterical Perspective
Professor Emeritus, California State University Fullerton, 11286 E Baltic Place, Aurora, CO 80014
Vera Robinson is professor emeritus, California State University, Fullerton. She has publications in the area of nursing education and psychosocial nursing, but is best known for pioneering research, publications, and teaching in the area of humor and health care. Her book, Humor and the Health Professions (now in its second edition) is a classic in the field. She has been called the "Fairy Godmother of Humor."

Rosenberg, Lisa, PhD, RN
Chapter IV: Sick, Black, and Gallows Humor Among Emergency Caregivers or — Are We Having any Fun Yet? Rush University College of Nursing, 1743 W Harrison St, Rm 310 SSH, Chicago, IL 60612; tel. 708-433-5311
Lisa Rosenberg is the Associate Chairperson of Psychiatric Nursing at Rush-Presbyterian-St. Luke's Medical Center College of Nursing. She directs the four degree-granting programs offered in psychiatric nursing, including baccalaureate through doctoral levels Dr. Rosenberg presents to a wide variety of audiences on humor use as a strategy for coping with stress. She has published and been interviewed locally and nationally on the benefits of humor use for stress reduction.

Strickland, Donna, MS, RN, CS
Chapter XV: Humor and Recovery for Substance Abusers
P.O. Box 18423, Denver, CO 80218; tel. 303-777-7997
Donna Strickland is a frequent keynote speaker with special interests in humor and healing. She is president of the Denver, Colorado based management consulting firm, The People Connection. She speaks nationally on humor and healing. Her special interests include humor as a component of the "caring moment." Donna is a faculty associate at the University of Colorado Center for Human Caring. Currently, she is traipsing around the world learning, celebrating, and feeling grateful.

Wooten, Patty, BSN, RN
Chapter XI: Humor in the Ha-Ha Hospital
Jest for the Health of It, P.O. Box 4040, Davis, CA 95617; tel. 916-758-3826; email: jestpatty@ mother.com
Patty Wooten is a nurse humorist, clown, professional speaker, and recognized leader in the field of humor and health. She combines over 25 years of clinical experience with her humorous perspective on life and helps nurses, health professionals, patients, and pedestrians understand the importance of humor and laughter. Patty is vice president of the American Association of Therapeutic Humor, an editor and featured columnist for the Journal of Nursing Jocularity, and author of Heart, Humor, and Healing.

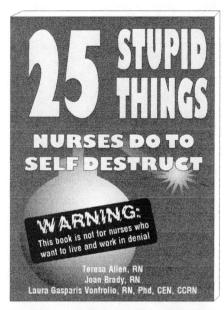

Nursing Perspectives on Humor

Addendum

Table 3. (continued)*

Title and Author(s)	Administration	Reliability** TR,IC,PF,IR	Validity*** CNT,CRI,CNS	Used as Data Collection Tool in Studies
Situational Humor Response Questionnaire, Martin & Lefcourt	paper and pencil	TR: .70s range IC: .70-.85	CRI: .37 CNS: .16-.53	1983, Martin & Lefcourt 1984, Martin & Lefcourt 1986, Lefcourt & Martin 1987, Porterfield 1988, Martin & Dobbin 1988, Nezu, Nezu, &Blissett 1988, Rim 1989, Lefcourt, Davidson-Katz, & Kueneman 1990, Yovetich, Dale, & Hudak 1991, Thorson & Powell 1992, Deckers & Ruch 1992, Hampes 1993, Deaner & McConatha 1994, Kohler 1994, O'Quin
Structurally Matched Neutral, Taboo, & Salient Jokes, Kuhlman	paper and pencil	NR	CNT: theme of each joke was categorized by 5 judges, themes matched those of authors in 128/130 comparisons	1985, Kuhlman
Antioch Sense of Humor Inventory, Mindess, Miller, Turek, Bender, & Corbin	paper and pencil	NR	NR	1985, Mindess, Miller, Turek, Bender, & Corbin
untitled, Gavanski	paper and pencil	NR	NR	1986, Gavanski
untitled, Powell	paper and pencil	NR	NR	1986, Powell
Humor in Teaching Research, Opitz	paper and pencil	IC: .91	NR	1993, Cannella, Opitz, & Missroon
Your Humor Quotient, Paulson	paper and pencil	NR	NR	1989, Paulson
Laughter Self-Ratings, Labott, Martin, & Eason	paper and pencil	NR	CRI: r = .42 with total laugh duration	1987, Labott, Martin, & Eason 1990, Labott, Ahleman, Wolever, & Martin
Total Laugh Durations, Labott, Ahleman, Wolever, & Martin	observation, stopwatch	IR: r=.99	NR	1990, Labott, Ahleman, Wolever, & Martin

Note: *NR = not reported.
          **TR=test-retest, IC=internal consistency, PF=parallel forms, IR=interrater reliability.
          ***CNT=content, CRI=criterion, CNS=construct.

Table 3. (continued)*

Title and Author(s)	Administration	Reliability** TR,IC,PF,IR	Validity*** CNT,CRI,CNS	Use Tor
Sumners Attitude Toward Humor Semantic Differential, Sumners	paper and pencil	IC: prof.practice setting = .85 personal life setting = .78	CNS: supported by factor analysis	19
Humor Questionnaire, Crawford & Gressley	paper and pencil	NR	NR	
O'Quin's Multidimensional Sense of Humor Scale, O'Quin	paper and pencil	NR	NR	
Humor Appreciation Scale, Overholser	paper and pencil	TR: .60	NR	
Humor Creativity Ratings, Overholser	paper and pencil	NR	NR	
Multidimensional Sense of Humor Scale, Thorson & Powell	paper and pencil	IC: .89-.91	CNS: r= -.17 with depression (CES-D) r = -.41 with serious r = -.47 with bad mo r = .68 with cheerfu	
untitled, Derks, Staley, & Haselton	paper and pencil	IC: .858-.983 per dimension	NR	

Note: *NR = not reported.
          **TR=test-retest, IC=internal consistency, PF=parallel forms, IR=interr
          ***CNT=content, CRI=criterion, CNS=construct.